A note from the author

On a cold, overcast morning in June, 1993, as I sailed towards Juneau on an old Alaska State ferry, I saw my first whale. It was just a blow in the distance, barely more than a small puff on the horizon, but for me this has always been my Alaskan moment. The sight of the whale brought the great wildness of Alaska to life. It wasn't just the whale, it was what the whale said about the world around: this was a place that was wild enough for a whale.

The time was just after 4 am and I was on the outside decks of the ferry, where most penny-wise backpackers sleep under the stars. Surprisingly, my fellow passengers were a little less enthusiastic about this sighting than I had expected. So I watched by myself, as the whale blew and then dove, down deep into the cool waters of the fjord.

Since that day, I've been lucky enough to spend much of my life in the company of whales. I conduct research on humpback whales in the waters of Alaska and Hawaii and teach under-graduate students about whales and the natural world around them. And to this day, my first sight of a whale in Alaska stays with me, as a moment of hope and motivation that the world will always include places that are wild enough for whales.

My hope in writing this book is that you will find your Alaskan moment on your cruise through Alaska. Whether it comes to you as you watch a glacier calve, or as you spot a whale or a bear from the decks of the ship, or maybe just as you look out at the unending Alaskan wilderness, these are the moments that let us know wild places still exist today. It will likely take the care and commitment of all of us to protect and maintain these places. But we protect the things that we care about and we care for the things we know. Hopefully, this book will help you get to know Alaska for yourself and you'll join the ranks of those of us who are committed to the care of this wild place.

So, here's to your Alaskan moment and your Alaskan vacation.
Have a great trip, pack your raingear, and remember to keep the binoculars handy!

Sincerely,
Rachel.
Ship's Naturalist, Princess cruises; 1998-2005.

This book is dedicated to Alaska's Naturalists
and all those who work to protect our wild places.

The Alaska Cruise Companion

A Naturalist's Guide to Alaska's Inside Passage

CONTENTS

Where to find the wildlife
Wildlife in focus

The awesome orca
page 68

The black bear
page 100

The bald eagle
page 106

The humpback
whale page 158

The moose
page 194

The brown bear
page 218

The sea otter
page 222

The harbor seal
page 226

The mountain
goat page 230

The Steller sea lion
page 234

Field Guides

Hiking

Alaska's Wilderness Bays

Where to see the wildlife!

Wildlife in Alaska is abundant however each different species has different favored hotspots throughout the region. Look for these wildlife logos on your Alaska Cruise Companion map and on the maps included in this book, and you'll know where and when to find each different character in Alaska's wildlife show!

Wildlife Key

Humpback Whales

Puffins

Killer Whales

Shorebirds

Dolphins and Porpoise

Mountain Goats

Harbor Seals

Moose

Steller Sea lions

Black Bears

Sea Otters

Brown Bears

Wildlife sightings optimistically forecast, but not guaranteed

Find your route

- Select your sailaway (departure) port.

- Next look for your first port of call and the scenic cruise that is included in your itinerary.

- For each different cruise itinerary, you'll then find the day-by-day details of your route through Alaska.

On the page numbers listed, you'll find fascinating stories and full details on the local history, scenic highlights and wildlife hotspots in each region.
Happy cruising!

Vancouver's Canada Place

Sailaway port: Whittier
• First port of call Skagway
• Scenic cruising – Yakutat Bay and Glacier Bay

The view across Cook Inlet, Anchorage

Sailaway port: Seattle
• First port of call Juneau
• Scenic cruising – Glacier Bay

Day 7 – Arrive Seattle

Seattle's famous Space Needle

Sailaway port: Seattle
- First port of call Juneau
- Scenic cruising – Tracy Arm

A young humpback whales breaches in the waters around Juneau.

Sailaway port: Seattle
- First port of call Ketchikan
- Scenic cruising – Tracy Arm

Day 7 – Arrive Seattle

Sailaway port: San Francisco
- **First port of call Ketchikan**
- **Scenic cruising – Tracy Arm**

Cruises departing from San Francisco bound for Juneau as their first port of call follow the Seattle - Juneau routes.

Chapter 1
Alaska, the Greatland

Alaska, the Greatland

Maybe it's the moment you see your first wild whale, hear the clap of white thunder as a glacier calves, or touch a 200 year-old piece of ice; there's a moment on every Alaskan vacation when you know for sure that you are in Alaska, the Greatland.

The name "Alaska" comes from the Aleut word, Alyeska, which means "the great one." And as you look up at the heights of Mount McKinley or gaze across the endless, untamed wilderness of Southeast Alaska's icy bays, the name rings true. When the U.S. purchased Alaska from the Russians in 1867 it was called "Seward's Folly," the "Great Ice Box" or "Walrussia", largely seen as a place of endless ice and the longest, darkest nights imaginable. But the riches Alaska had to offer were soon revealed. Its waters teemed with life, from sea otters and whales to salmon and halibut. The first fortune-seekers to head for the region were fur-traders, they were followed closely by whalers and fishermen and with the discovery of gold in 1896, prospectors from across the U.S. joined the trek north to Alaska.

Tales of pristine wilderness, natural beauty and adventure made for a winning combination, and steamboat routes catering solely for sight-seeing were soon established. Boats set sail from Seattle and San Francisco and offered cruises through Alaska's protected passageways to Juneau and beyond, where travelers could experience firsthand "the untamed lands of Alaska."

Today, Alaska retains its reputation for beauty and adventure. It remains our last great wilderness, a place where we can still view nature at its best and see wildlife roaming wild and free. Wallace Stegner describes wilderness as part of the "geography of hope," evoking our need to stand at its edge and look out at its vastness. On a cruise through Alaska, you'll travel through the heart of a last, vast, untouched wilderness. At the end of such a trip, there can be no doubt; Alaska is indeed a great land.

"Have you been to Alaska? Have you climbed a glacier? And if you have not, why not?
The Alaskan trip today has taken its place among the world wonders, among the things that the well-informed must enjoy."

Pacific Coast Steamship
Company brochure, 1905

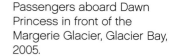

Passengers aboard Dawn Princess in front of the Margerie Glacier, Glacier Bay, 2005.

Mt McKinley, Denali

Alaska's mightiest peaks

Alaska is home to 17 of the 20 tallest mountains in the US.
Here are the top ten in Alaska and BC:

1.	Mount McKinley	20,320 ft	Alaska Range
2.	Mount Logan	19,541 ft	Saint Elias Range
3.	Mount St. Elias	18,008 ft	Saint Elias Range
4.	Mount Foraker	17,400 ft	Alaska Range
5.	Mount Lucania	17,257 ft	Saint Elias Range
6.	King Peak	16,972 ft	Saint Elias Range
7.	Mount Bona	16,550 ft	Saint Elias Range
8.	Mount Steel	16,470 ft	Saint Elias Range
9.	Mount Blackburn	16,390 ft	Wrangell Mountains
10.	Mount Sanford	16,237 ft	Wrangell Mountains

Other notable peaks:

Mount Fairweather	15,325 ft	Saint Elias Range
Mount Hubbard	14,950 ft	Saint Elias Range
Mount Rainier	14,471 ft	Cascade Range

Alaska...by the Numbers

With an area of 571,951 miles, Alaska is the largest state in the U.S. and more than twice the size of Texas, its closest rival. In comparison to all the other states in the U.S., it is sparsely populated, with a total population of 686,293, translating to roughly 1.2 people per square mile. Compare this with the rest of the U.S., which has on average 76 people per square mile and Manhattan, which has 70,000 people per square mile; even Canada has 9.2 people per square mile! At the very tip of the Aleutian Island chain, you're only 220 miles from Asia and you've gone so far west that you're actually in the Eastern hemisphere. And if you stand on the westernmost point of the Seward Peninsula and look out across the Bering Sea, Russia is only 55 miles away; can you see it? Maybe...

Anchorage is Alaska's largest city, with a population of 284,994—almost half the state's population. Juneau and Fairbanks vie for second place, the most recent population counts being 30,427 and 30,367 respectively. But while Alaska may be small in population, it surely makes up for this in other arenas. Along with 17 of the 20 tallest mountains in the U.S., Alaska has over 70 potentially active volcanoes. The Alaskan coastline stretches 6,600 miles and including all the islands, the total shorelines of Alaska stretch 34,000 miles. There are 3,000 rivers and more than three million lakes over 20 acres in size. Over 50% of the world's glaciers are located in Alaska; they number over 100,000, and most remain unnamed and unmapped. The largest protected wilderness area in the US, the Wrangell St. Elias National Park and Preserve, also lies in Alaska. Some 30% of Alaska is within the Arctic Circle and just less than 20% of this area comprises the Arctic National Wildlife Refuge.

The coastline of Alaska's Inside Passage stretches over 15,000 miles.

Alaska by Season

"To the attentive eye, each moment of
the year holds its own beauty."

Ralph Waldo Emerson

There is a saying in Alaska "if you don't like the weather then wait ten minutes, it's sure to change by then". Once you've been in Alaska just a day or two, you'll see that this is true. But Emerson's more profound observation also holds true. As Alaska emerges from its long winter, the seasons change almost while you watch and each has its own highlight.

In early May, it's springtime in Alaska. The scenery in Alaska is spectacular; snow often still stretches down to the waterline and glaciers are at their most active, propelled by millions of gallons of fresh melt-water. Waterfalls spring from every overhang, while rivers and streams are full to bursting. Bears are often easy to spot in springtime; newly emerged from hibernation, they head for high ground, up above the tree line where they'll graze on roots and tubers. Or you'll see them right down on the beach front feasting on mussels and clams along the shoreline.

As June arrives, spring gives way to summer. The days lengthen and by the summer solstice nights last a scant three hours in Southeast Alaska, while twilight gives way straight to dawn in the Far North. This is the time for wildflowers. Lupines, chocolate lilies and indian paintbrush bloom across sub-alpine meadows. In the wilderness bays, harbor seals and sea otters and their new young occupy the ice-floes in front of the glaciers, Steller sea lion haulouts are full to overflowing and humpback whale numbers start to rise; regions such as Snow Passage and Sumner Straits are early season humpback whale hotspots.

July brings in the salmon and by mid–month most of the active streams are bursting with silvery life. Wildlife emerges from every corner to feast on the salmon. Eagles, bears, even wolves and of course whales will make the most of this free and easy lunch. For locals, July 4th is often seen as the last big celebration of the summer. Although the light persists for many months, temperatures slowly start to fall. Rain becomes more frequent, but wildlife sightings peak. By mid-July, silver salmon runs in the waters of Johnstone Strait, British Columbia, draw in killer whales. Meanwhile, hungry humpback whales fan out across the bays and fjords of the Inside Passage, making the most of blooming krill and huge schools of herring.

By August, fireweed is in full bloom and the berries are ready to pick. No dog days of summer here; for many Alaskans, this is the busiest time of year. They fish, hunt, pick berries, can and smoke their surplus and generally get ready for the winter ahead. By mid-month, the very first snow dusts the highest peaks – it's called termination dust and truly signals the end of another Alaskan summer. In Interior Alaska the tundra turns to a burnished coppery red, while in the waters of Southeast Alaska, Steller sea lions head out to sea and harbor seals wean their pups. But bears, eagles and other wildlife remain clustered around the salmon streams and killer whales in BC waters persist through August too.

As September arrives, birch, aspen and cottonwood trees turn to gold. This is the peak time for whale numbers; good regions for sightings include Frederick Sound and Chatham Straits. This is also the time of the rut, the mating season for caribou and moose. Across the tundra in Denali, males display their racks and look for romance. Cool, clear, crisp fall days are also perfect conditions for northern lights too, so if you're in Alaska at this time of year, be sure to take a look outside before you call it a day.

Meet the Locals

Alaska is very lightly populated; towns are small, typically isolated and along the Inside Passage, many are reachable only by air or by sea. Perhaps as a result of this isolation, you'll see that no two towns in Alaska are alike; each town has its own unique charm and sense of identity and each offers its own version of Alaskan life. Ketchikan is lively and cheerful, and life is based around fishing and salmon, Juneau has all the respectability you would expect from a state capital and Skagway celebrates the glory days of the Gold Rush. Interior towns such as Fairbanks and Talkeetna are different again. These towns sit in the midst of vast wilderness, and local people have a resilient, pioneer vibe. But wherever you are in the state, you will find that Alaskans are storytellers and meeting the locals is part of the fun. Be sure to take time to chat with the shopkeepers and the tour guides you meet along your way. As long as you have time for a story, they will have one to tell. One thing you'll soon notice is that many die-hard, true-to-the bone Alaskans were actually born elsewhere. Currently, around 30% of Alaskans were born in the state, but to quote a newly-arrived Juneau fisherman, "Alaska isn't a place, it's more a state of mind". Spend some time around Alaskans and you'll soon see this.

How do you know you're an Alaskan?

Many locals will tell you that you're officially a local once you buy your first pair of rubber boots. Known as Alaskan tennis shoes, the unofficial state footwear doesn't come in a rainbow of colors; most Alaskans will select a standard, sensible brown boot. The most popular ones, with a traditional cork base and soles from Goodyear, are made by Xtratuf. At around $60 a pair, they aren't cheap, but they are ubiquitous in Alaska. Try a pair on and you'll see why – they're warm and waterproof, and they last forever. What more could you want from a pair of boots?

An alternative use for Alaskan Rubber Boots.

Alaskan Bachelors

A not-so-rare species – the Alaskan Bachelor

Looking for love? At least for the ladies, Alaska may be the place. It used to be said that men outnumbered women ten to one and that may have been true in times gone by. Today the ratio is more like two to one, but this still varies between regions. Most of the female population is in Anchorage, while the out-lying areas and small towns, especially fishing ports, are still predominantly male. This isolation and off-the-grid lifestyle led to a frequently repeated but uncharitable quote about Alaska's men; "the odds may be good, but the goods may be odd." But again, times are changing, and there are plenty of very eligible bachelors in the state. Check out the Alaskan Men website at www.alaskamen.com. This site was originally set up by the mothers of single Alaskan men and provides profiles and pictures of eligible Alaskan bachelors. A monthly magazine accompanies the site and you can even leave a note for your potential Alaskan soul mate.

The Alaska Permanent Fund

Living year round in Alaska is not for the faint hearted, but it does come with rewards. In October each year, full-time Alaskan residents receive a check from the Alaska Permanent Fund. All residents including children receive a check, and the day the checks are issued is a recognized school holiday, "Dividend Day." The checks come from The Alaska Permanent Fund, a fund established in 1980 by then-Governor Jay Hammond. Basically, the fund is comprised of oil revenue, with one quarter of all mineral lease royalties directed into it. The state invests the money and the fund pays out from the interest and dividends on these investments. Currently, the fund stands at four billion dollars and is self-supporting. Check amounts vary; they hit an all time high of $2,069 in 2008 and in 2011, the payout was $1,174 for every resident. Typically, the total payout is around one billion dollars. A large portion of the funds are spent on air tickets, as many residents typically take a trip to the sunshine before the long winter sets in. The payout also helps offset the incredibly high cost of living in Alaska. Before you leave, walk around a local grocery store and you'll see how high food prices are. A gallon of milk may cost as much as six dollars, and fresh fruits and vegetables are especially expensive.

Alaska's Native Culture

The first people arrived in Alaska over 15,000 years ago. An ice-age persisted at this time, so sea levels were lower and a 900 mile land bridge connected Siberia and North America. It's thought that nomadic people followed the migration of large animals across this bridge into the region. The first true settlers arrived between 14,000 and 12,000 years ago, also coming overland from Asia into the Northern regions of Alaska. The Athabascans headed into interior Alaska while the Tlingit and Haida headed south along the broad shorelines of that time into Southeast Alaska and British Columbia. The remaining native groups, the Inupiat, the Yupik and the Aleut, arrived by sea some 6,000 years later, settling in the Far North along the western coastline and in the Aleutian Islands. Each of these groups had to adapt to the climates of their chosen regions. For the Tlingit and Haida people, the cool, moist climate of Southeast Alaska offered abundant resources and a sophisticated culture quickly developed. In colder, more northern regions, conditions were more challenging. Nevertheless, these native groups persisted and within each cultural group innovations evolved that were specific to the challenges of each distinct region.

Today, the region's native cultural landscape is a rich mosaic reflecting these individual groups. Like many indigenous cultures around the world, the current trend of urban migration is reducing the numbers of young people adopting traditional lifestyles. However, each group has a unique language, and as these languages are recognized as the key artifacts of each culture, teaching the language to the next generation has become a priority in preserving each unique way of life. Some groups have set up immersion programs aimed at pre-schoolers while other groups are taking a new, modern-day approach; Inupiaq, the language of the Inupiat people, is the latest addition to Rosetta Stone's list of language courses.

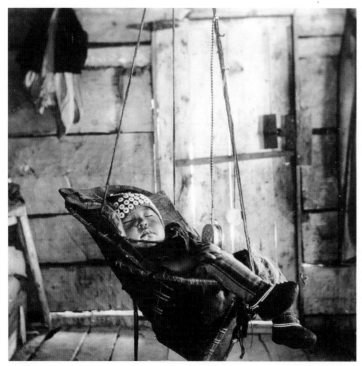

Sleeping baby, circa late 1800's. Baby wearing a Tlingit beaded hat sleeps in an Athabascan-style sling.

Source: Alaska State Library, Winter & Pond Photograph Collection, Identifier: P87-0180

Young native girls from Alaska's Interior. Taken between 1919-1939.

Source: Alaska State Library, Dr. Daniel S. Neuman Photograph Collection, Identifier: P307-0033

The indigenous people of Alaska's Northern and Western regions, the Inupiat Inuit and Yupik, are collectively known as the Inuit. This term replaces the term Eskimo, which is generally considered an out-dated and somewhat derogatory term. The Inuit people succeeded in an otherwise unmatched human accomplishment, settling and thriving in arctic regions.

Arts and crafts have always been a mainstay of Alaskan culture and commerce. Here, Tlingit women offer moccasins for sale to some of Alaska's very first cruisers.
Source: Alaska State Library, Clarence Leroy Andrews Photograph Collection, Identifier: P45-1283

Alaska's Ecology – A Quick Primer

Southeast Alaska: A land of fjords and forest

Alaska's Inside Passage winds its way through Southeast Alaska, a region which in turn comprises a narrow strip of the mainland between the shoreline of the Pacific and the peaks of the Coast Mountain Range. There are over 1000 offshore islands within the region, collectively known as the Alexander Archipelago, and the ecology of this region has been shaped by two key factors. First of all, this region is wet–yearly rainfall totals are frequently record-breaking in many places, winter sees heavy snowfall and even in summer, mist and fog frequently cloak the shorelines. Secondly, this is a wild region. While the intricate channels of the Inside Passage may have confounded early navigators, today this interlacing network of blind-ended fjords and hidden, protected bays is a haven for wildlife. Within this myriad of waterways, places still remain where remnant stands of virgin forest surround deep fjords and the ecosystem that comprises the unique ecology of Southeast Alaska is intact and functioning.

The copious amounts of rain that fall throughout the year in Southeast Alaska are a consequence of the geographic location and topography of the region. Clouds roll in from across the Pacific on the prevailing weather patterns. The Coast Mountains push the moisture-heavy clouds up and the rain falls. During the summer months, early morning clouds may quickly dissipate and give way to quite beautiful sunny days. But there will be occasional days even in summer when a gentle curtain of mist remains draped across the mountain sides for most of the day. In spring and fall, rain is consistent and heavy across most of the region and in the winter, the rain falls as snow and accumulates high in the mountain ranges. Over the years, subsequent layers of snow lead to compression and the formation of glacial ice. Where sufficient ice accumulates it eventually overflows, pouring out from the high mountain range as a river of ice. These huge, heavy rivers of ice carve their own paths down into the mountain side. With sufficient fuel from the ice-field, glaciers may advance and eventually flow right down to the ocean. If climate changes or rainfall slows, the glacier retreats back into the huge U-shaped channel it has created. Saltwater flows in as the glacier retreats and a fjord is created.

A retreating glacier reveals the U-shaped channel created as the glacier advanced.

Fjords in Southeast Alaska are known by a variety of names. Canals, passages, inlets, straits, arms and even some bays are all in fact fjords that formed in this way. These fjords permeate Southeast Alaska, providing mile upon mile of marine habitat that is protected from the wild weather of the open Pacific Ocean. Marine life takes full advantage and the region brims with wildlife. As glaciers calve and meltwater flows down into the fjords, ground up bedrock produced by the glacier, often called glacial silt, enters the fjord and provides essential nutrients for phytoplankton, the microscopic photosynthesizers that form the base of the marine food chain. The abundance of phytoplankton leads to blooms of krill, tiny shrimplike creatures, known as amphipods, that feed on the phytoplankton. Everything from large whales to small fish feed on the krill and the food chain blossoms. As the summer progresses the salmon arrive, returning from the open waters of the Pacific. Salmon school in the fjords, then migrate into the freshwater system, providing a bounty of food and a flood of nutrients into the forests as they disperse throughout the rivers and streams of the region.

Along the shorelines of the fjords, the cool, damp climate of Southeast Alaska is perfect for **temperate rainforest**. This is one of the rarest ecosystems on earth and in the oldest of these forests, individual trees may be four or five hundred years old. True old growth forest must be undisturbed by logging or fire for more than 250 years. This allows mosses to develop and cover the forest floor, protecting the forest from floods and drought. Southeast Alaska is typically too wet for lightning or forest fires, but winter storms fell individual trees and this opens up the canopy, allowing a mosaic of small shrubs and berry bushes to move in. During the summer months, wildlife such as deer and black bears find food across many regions of the Southeast Alaskan landscape. But old growth forests are the safety net of the ecosystem and in the challenging months of winter, wildlife retreats to the forests and these old-soul stands of evergreen trees provide essential food and shelter for deer, bears and other wildlife.

Temperate forest lines the shoreline of the fjord.

Old growth forests are characteristically found from sea level up to 2500 feet, but slope and altitude bring changes. At around 1500 feet above sea level, mountain hemlock starts to replace western hemlock and by 2500 feet trees peter out. In these areas the summer time temperatures are not warm enough to support reproduction in trees, and winter accumulations of snow crush woody plants. This is the tree-line, and from here to the alpine regions a margin of herbs and annually flowering plants springs up. These are the **subalpine meadows of Southeast Alaska**. It might be quite a hike to reach these regions, but the rewards are well worth it. Here among the wildflowers, the views are spectacular and in the summertime the meadows become home for a wide variety of wildlife. Black-tailed deer and brown bears move up into these regions in summer and Dall's sheep and mountain goats are lured down from higher ground by the abundance of food. Ground mammals such as the hoary marmot, are especially at home in these flower meadows—for them, just about everything looks like lunch. Keep a look-out around rocky outcrops in the flower meadows and you'll spot them.

On poorly drained soils, at the marshy interface between forest and freshwater, another marginal community emerges, known as **muskeg**. Here, a mosaic of alder and cottonwood, skunk cabbage and sphagnum moss reflects each undulation of the substrate. Small, isolated ponds, known as kettle ponds, formed when large remnant icebergs cast off by a retreating glacier grounded and compacted the ground below, dot these areas. Some ponds may still be filled with water, but others may be just a hollow in the substrate, like a giant, persistent glacial footprint. Ridges and high outcrops also mark the path of retreating glaciers, indicating spots where an ancient glacier paused in its retreat, just long enough to deposit a ridge of poorly draining silt in an area. Poor soil drainage means that trees growing in this area will be small and stunted but other plants flourish, taking full advantage of the fresh supply of minerals in the silty substrate. Berry bearing plants such as elderberry and salmonberry occupy open areas, while wetter regions on the periphery of the forest are the domain of the skunk cabbage. One of the most overlooked but otherwise impressive plants of the Southeast Alaskan ecosystem, the large yellow-green leaves of the skunk cabbage may be four or five feet long. Individual plants produce 30 or more giant leaves over the course of a single season and can live to 70 years old. The leaves were used by indigenous people for wrapping salmon and to line berry baskets and steaming pits.

A view from the sub-alpine meadows looking down over Juneau.

Skunk Cabbage is found in the muskeg and may grow to heights of 3-4 feet.

The Intertidal Zone

Southeast Alaska includes some 15,000 miles of marine shoreline. Conditions vary dramatically, from wild and exposed open ocean shorelines to protected fjords where freshwater flows mix with saltwater. With the high to low tide difference typically ranging from 12 to 20 feet, low tide exposes a wide swath of beach. These are food-rich regions and as the local saying goes "When the tide is out, the table is set."

Available food ranges from seaweed to clams and mussels and just about all forms of life in Alaska, including locals, will wander down to the beach in search of lunch. The upper reaches of the beaches that are only inundated at high tide are the home of limpets and barnacles. In the mid-tide zone you'll find chitons, mussels and clams on the beaches, and sea anemones in remnant tide-pools amongst the bladder kelp, while the lower intertidal zone is home to sea stars, shrimp, crab and even octopus. The tide-pools of Southeast Alaska are a well kept secret. If you're on the beach, spend some time exploring this area and if you're on the water, be sure to keep an eye out, as the shoreline is premium wildlife habitat. At low tide, the beach is always a good area to look out for bears, especially in the early season.

Alaska's shorebirds include some 38 different species, ranging from the charismatic puffin to the uncelebrated but prolific scoters. Some over-winter in Alaska but for the majority, Alaskan shorelines comprise critical summertime habitat. Shorebirds journey from all points of the globe to feed, reproduce and raise their young along Southeast Alaska's shorelines. Many travel as mated pairs that stay together for life.

A pair of black-legged oystercatchers forage among the kelp.

Interior Alaska – From taiga to tundra

To travel from taiga to tundra in Southeast Alaska you need to climb a mountain. You could start right at sea-level in the coastal forest, but you would have to climb to a breathless height of around four or five thousand feet to reach true tundra. Alternatively, you could take a trip through Interior Alaska; you'll see the same changes as you head north, and with changing latitude you'll travel from taiga to tundra. It's a fascinating trip and definitely one of the truly unique aspects of exploring Interior Alaska.

The term **"Taiga"** comes from the Russian word for forest. In biological terms, taiga refers to the boreal or coniferous forests that encircle the globe at latitudes from 50 to 60°N. This is the largest single biome, or life zone, and accounts for 29% of the world's forests. In Alaska though, the term taiga is used to refer specifically to the northern most reaches of these evergreen forests. On these margins, soils are shallow and poorly draining due to the presence of a layer called **permafrost**, a frozen layer within the soil that is impervious to water. The depth at which the permafrost occurs varies with slope and aspect, but typically it starts somewhere from 10 to 50 feet down. It is discontinuous or patchy in occurrence, but widespread across Interior Alaska. Water can't drain through this layer, so the soil above the permafrost frequently becomes very water-logged. Consequently, evergreen trees may grow as seedlings in these areas, but their growth is stunted and they never reach full height. Individual trees may be 50 to 100 years old, but only 4 or 5 feet tall. As trees reach the maximum height that the depth of water-logged soil can support, they start to lean and slowly

Interior Alaska's drunken taiga forest.

topple over. These slowly toppling trees are often called **drunken forests** and you'll see them throughout Interior Alaska. While soggy areas may be challenging for full size evergreen trees, this is prime habitat for smaller shrubs and wetland plants. Moose find the best of both worlds in these areas as browse is good and cover is still available. In slightly drier, more elevated areas, such as the Copper River region, evergreen forests give way to broadleaf forests of quaking aspen and silver birch. If you're traveling from the south, the rustle of their papery leaves is a surprise after the quiet of Southeast Alaska's evergreen forests.

Tundra comes from the Russian word for treeless, and the transition to tundra is marked by the complete disappearance of trees, leaving a vast, open landscape. In alpine tundra, the region is limited to the upper reaches of mountain chains, but in Alaska's Interior you're north of the treeline and the tundra rolls to the horizon like a huge ocean. The first time you look out across the tundra is memorable; it's quite breath-taking to gaze across the limitless landscape. Tundra typically has two key seasons; winter and summer. The cold, harsh winter dictates which plants survive here, and plants must also grow speedily and reproduce quickly in the short, warm summer. Low lying berry bushes are abundant across the tundra and the berries draw in bears. Though typically smaller, the grizzly bears of Interior Alaska are the same species as the brown bears of the Inside Passage. And grizzlies favorite graze? Berries – elderberries, blueberries and cranberries to name just a few. As summer draws to a close, berries ripen across the tundra and grizzly bears feast. Biologists studying bear scat estimate a typical bear may consume 200,000 cranberries a day. Other summertime wildlife of the tundra include caribou, wolves, Dall's sheep and a myriad of migratory birds. A visit to this region adds a whole new perspective to your view of Alaska. This is wilderness, truly wild and untamed.

Endless tundra, with Mount McKinley in the background.

Alaska's wildlife

Alaska's Inside Passage and its Interior offer some of the last untouched places in the U.S. to see wildlife. The numbers are impressive; Alaska boasts some 30,000 brown bears in total, with islands such as Kuiu Island and Admiralty Island home to the world's densest populations of black and brown bears. Four hundred different species of birds migrate through the State and Alaska is home to over 90% of the world's bald eagles. In interior Alaska, the Porcupine herd of caribou that migrates across the Brooks Range numbers 150, 000 and the state as a whole has more caribou than people. However, as you stand on the deck of the ship and look out, many a passenger has been left wondering—where is all this wildlife?

The reality is that Alaska is a big place and even despite these amazing statistics, it can still take some patience as you wait—and wait—to catch a glimpse of one of Alaska's wildlife stars. Still, there are some suggestions that can really help. Firstly, nearly all animals in Alaska are in these regions to find food. Think of it as looking for a teenager on the ship—you would be well-advised to first check the pizza bar. For wildlife it's just the same. In Alaska's short summer, food is always a priority and luckily for us, many favored feeding spots are predictable. Generations upon generations of wildlife have used these specific areas at specific times of year, as each generation teaches the next about their favored fishing spots and haul-outs. These areas offer the best chances to see wildlife from the ship. On the map that accompanies this book, these hotspots are marked as waypoints; these are the places when you'll want to head to the open decks and in many of these areas, your onboard naturalist will be on the bridge ready to make announcements and point out wildlife as you sail by.

Wildlife hotspots – the best of the best: Where to find Alaska's top ten

Killer whales – Johnstone Strait, BC, July onwards. The waters around Victoria, B.C.

Humpback whales – Snow Passage, Frederick Sound, waters around Juneau.

Black bears – Steep Creek, Mendenhall Glacier, Mud Flats in Tracy Arm.

Brown bears – Shorelines of Glacier Bay, Denali National Park.

Moose – Shorelines around Haines, Kenai Peninsula, Denali National Park.

Wolves – Denali National Park, occasional sightings around Juneau.

Sea otters – Entrance to Glacier Bay, and Point Packenham, Prince William Sound.

Harbor seals – Ice floes in front of the glaciers in any of the wilderness bays.

Steller sea lions – Waters around Juneau, Icy Straits outside Glacier Bay.

Puffins – Entrance waters of the Glacier Bay and Yakutat Bay.

Secondly, the most useful tip for seeing wildlife in Alaska: be sure to bring binoculars. As this is an entirely wild environment, wildlife chooses to come—and go—on their own schedule. Using binoculars brings distant animals in close and allows you to watch their behavior as they move across your field of view. Scan across your horizon and watch for movement. As you cruise through the wilderness bays, look above the tree-line for bears, sheep and mountain goats. The shiny color of the coat can help. When you're looking for marine life, look along the shore-line. This is where most marine life feeds and the contrast along the shore-line makes them easier to spot too. In icy areas, look on the ice-floes; these are favorite haul-outs for seals and sea otters. Finally watch out for the famous bush bear and his cousin the rock whale—they catch us all out once in a while.

Princess Cruises is committed to operating sustainably in sensitive wildlife regions.

Black bears forage along the high tide line.

Your Alaskan Cruise

Don't leave home without…

Warm clothes
Cool clothes
Everything in the between!

Packing for Alaska is a challenge. Over the summer, temperatures may range from the low 50's on a cool day in Juneau to the mid 80's on a sunny day in Fairbanks. Keep in mind too, that as you change altitude temperatures will change too. The trick in Alaska is to dress in layers and bring a little of everything. And of course, you can always do a little holiday shopping, if you do leave something behind.

Good, comfortable footwear is a must for Alaska. Unless you're a serious hiker, waterproof boots aren't necessary, but a good pair of light boots or sturdy tennis shoes is highly recommended, so you can strike out confidently for the trails. Also, a hat is a necessity, both for hot and cool weather and as you'll see in Alaska, hats are quite the fashion statement too.

Other essentials: sunscreen, sunglasses and raingear, a small backpack and water bottle, camera, binoculars and last but by no means least; your sense of adventure!

Choosing binoculars:

Binoculars are pretty much essential for watching wildlife in Alaska. Even though wildlife is abundant, this is still a huge region and the wildlife is free to roam as it chooses. Binoculars will bring sightings into view. You'll be able to watch behavior and see details of the wildlife that otherwise are easy to miss.

When choosing binoculars, you'll see two numbers displayed; the first refers to magnification and the second to the field of view. Moderate magnification is most appropriate, as this is more forgiving on a (slightly) mobile platform, such as a ship and you'll want to go for wide angle binoculars, as these improve your chances of spotting wildlife: 7 x 50 is just about right.

Passengers ready to cruise:
dressed in layers,
binoculars at the ready.

The Alaskan Naturalist Program

As part of the Princess Cruises Enrichment Program, Princess Cruises invites an expert naturalist to join the crew of each Alaska-bound ship for the cruising season. The naturalists come from wide-ranging backgrounds and all have a wealth of personal experience in Alaska. Over the course of your cruise, they provide a full program of onboard presentations specifically designed to enhance your Alaskan experience. The presentations are lively and entertaining and provide rich insights into the culture, history and wildlife of the region. Full details of times and locations are posted daily in the Princess Patter.

Princess naturalists also provide narration from the bridge as the ship cruises through scenic regions and in areas where wildlife can be sighted easily from the ship. The map that accompanies this book shows places along your route where you will want to be out on deck. Or you can always ask your ship's naturalist; they know these regions well and will be able to provide up-to-the minute advice on where and when to head outside.

If your itinerary includes Glacier Bay a team of park rangers will join the ship for your day in the park. Their onboard program includes a presentation, you'll see the rangers out and about on the decks and they provide the narration from the bridge during your time in the park. A junior ranger also joins the youth staff and hosts a special children's activity program which is very popular with our youngest cruisers.

John Muir – The Original Alaskan Naturalist

"Climb the mountains and get their good tidings. Nature's peace will flow into you as sunshine flows into trees. The winds will blow their own freshness into you, and the storms their energy, while cares will fall off like autumn leaves"

This is just one of the many well known and unforgettable quotes taken from the writings of John Muir, Alaska's original naturalist.

Born in Scotland in 1838, Muir immigrated to America with his family at the age of 11. The family originally settled in Marquette County, Wisconsin, John's early life led him through a wide variety of jobs, and at the age of 30, he made a conscious choice to dedicate his life to the study of nature. He headed for the mountains of California, exploring the length and breadth of Sierras, before setting out to Alaska for the first time in 1879. Accompanied by an alluring cast of characters that included Chief Toyatte, a local native Tlingit chief, Sitka Charley, a colorful hunting guide, S. Hall Young, a young, evangelical minister and Young's dog, Stickeen, Muir and his companions explored the Inside Passage onboard a range of vessels, from comfortable steamboats to open canoes. The glaciers of the region were his key focus; Muir held a then fairly unpopular view that glaciers shaped landscapes. In traveling to Alaska he hoped to find support for this theory, and along his way he kept detailed journals in which he recounted his travels. Following this first exploration of Alaska, John Muir repeatedly returned to the region. His writings were published in newspapers and magazines and it was only after his death in 1914, that the volume "Travels to Alaska" was actually published as a complete novel.

John Muir painted a picture of the natural world with words not photographs. His words helped inspire then-President Theodore Roosevelt to put in place innovative conservation programs, establishing the first National Monuments and Yosemite National Park. In 1892, Muir and other supporters formed the Sierra Club "to make the mountains glad." John Muir's last great battle was to save Hetch Hetchy Valley, the second Yosemite. In this he failed. The valley was flooded to provide a hydro-electric system to power San Francisco. But President Roosevelt, inspired by his time spent with John Muir, went on to set up the National Park Service shortly after Muir's passing and the Sierra Club continues to be at the forefront of the environmental movement of today.

Sailing through the pristine waters and glittering, glacial bays of Alaska's Inside Passage, there is no better place than this to appreciate the legacies left by John Muir. Through his tireless work and inspiring writings, attitudes towards to Alaska were irrevocably changed, from a cold, frozen wasteland useful only for its resources, to an icy and wonderful wilderness, a place that should be set aside, preserved and enjoyed by all. When you stand on the decks of your ship and look out to see a whale sound or a glacier calve, here's hoping you can spare a moment, to remember and to thank Alaska's original naturalist, John Muir.

Hiking in Alaska

Hiking may be an acquired taste. Novelist John McPhee, author of the classic and most highly acclaimed modern account of Alaska "Coming into the County", said of hiking "Given a choice between hiking and peeling potatoes, I would choose peeling potatoes". Even John Muir was known to agree – he recalls "Hiking - I don't like either the word or the thing. People ought to saunter in the mountains - not hike!

And therein perhaps lies the key to enjoying hiking in Alaska; choose your own pace and set your own goals. In this book you'll find details for both short and longer hikes in each port of call. Some are just short strolls to local viewpoints, while others require advance planning and will occupy your entire day. Choose the one that suits you. The real appeal of hiking in Alaska is the payback. Just a short way off the beaten path, you'll find cascading waterfalls, leaping salmon and stunning scenery. And you'll often find a peace and quiet like nowhere else. Walk to the shores of Mendenhall Lake, and you'll find it's quiet enough to hear the ice melt. Take the cable-car up Mount Roberts and walk for 30 minutes and you'll get an eagles view of Gastineau Channel. Whichever path you take, hiking in Alaska is well worth the effort.

Hiking in Alaska:
Just a few precautions to keep in mind

Hike with a buddy.

If you're headed to the trails, be sure someone knows where you are going and when you intend to be back.

Be prepared for changing weather. Always carry raingear.

Wear reasonable footwear; many trails are muddy and can be steep.

Take water with you, even when the weather is cool.

In remote areas, add a bearbell to your pack, keep a conversation going or sing as you hike so that wildlife will hear you coming.
Startled wildlife may be dangerous.

Vancouver for a Day

Vancouver, British Columbia, offers plenty of ways to spend a day before you join your cruise ship. The two cruise ship terminals where Princess ships dock are within easy reach of all the main attractions; Canada Place is a five minute walk from the heart of the city and the Ballantyne dock is a ten minute taxi ride into town.

Vancouver's Stanley Park

Vancouver's signature attraction, **Stanley Park**, is located at the west end of downtown, the entrance just a short cab ride or a 30-minute stroll along the waterfront from Canada Place. You can pick up a map of the park at the information booth inside the Georgia Street entrance. The park's attractions are as diverse as the city itself, ranging from a First Nation totem pole park to an English rose garden. During the summer months, a hop-on hop-off shuttle service around the park makes it easy to get around and see the major attractions. On a sunny day, one of the best ways to take in the park is by bicycle. Bikes are available for rent at numerous bike shops located on the periphery of the park, and the favorite route for amateur cyclists is the six mile perimeter drive along the shoreline. Prospect Point is a great place to linger and check out the views across the Bay. Or you can leave the majority of park visitors behind and indulge your inner Euell Gibbons as you explore the miles of trails that meander through the old growth forest comprising the heart of the park.

Connecting Vancouver's West End with the heart of downtown is world-renowned **Robson Street**, Canada's home to high-end shops and designer outlets. It's easy to while away an entire afternoon on Robson Street. The Vancouver Art Museum is on Hornby, just off Robson Street, in the midst of the main shopping area. The museum houses contemporary art and is best known for its native and nature-inspired works. There are also plenty of restaurants to choose from in this area, and the number of coffee shops rivals Vancouver's sister city, Seattle.

Granville Island, to the south side of the city, was developed in the early twentieth century as an industrial site and was first named Industrial Island. Fast forward a hundred years and you'll find the island transformed into a bastion of hip culture and trendy restaurants. A testament to 70's urban development, Granville Island features artists and art galleries, street performers, a first-class farmer's market, live theatre and waterfront restaurants. Cab fare from Canada Place should be between $10 and $12; allow a good 20 to 30 minutes each way.

To the east side of the city is **Gastown**. This region was named for Gassy Jack, who opened the first saloon here in the 1860's. His nickname, by all accounts well deserved, referenced his

Granville Island.

chatty personality. Slowly the city built up around these early roots, and at one time Gastown was Canada's third largest city. Today, many of the original Victorian-era buildings have been restored and Gastown is resurging as the hippest region of this already very hip city. Renovated heritage buildings located on cobbled streets and in historic squares house eclectic art galleries and New Age restaurants. This area of town comes alive at night, when many of the bars carry live jazz and some of Vancouver's trendiest night spots open their doors.

The Gastown Steam Clock

The steam driven clock in Gastown was constructed in 1977 over a major steam vent that was part of Vancouver's original underground steam heating system. The original purpose of the clock was to prevent people from sleeping on top of the vent. Today, it is Gastown's most famous landmark. It has been renovated but is still steam powered and you'll hear it whistle, rather than chime, to signal the time.

And speaking of clocks—a quick reminder: be sure to check your cruise ship schedule and allow plenty of time to make your way back to the dock. All passengers need to be onboard at least one hour before departure.

Seattle for a Day

If Seattle is your departure port and you're a first time visitor to the region, plan to spend some time in the city before you sail. Seattle, the Emerald City, is a dazzling blend of natural beauty and interesting local culture. Its high-tech roots pervade the city, and the downtown area is appealing and well-organized. In summertime, cloudy Seattle skies give way to clear, beautiful summer weather. The main cruise terminal is right in town and a second terminal used by Princess Cruises, Smith Terminal, is just a short cab ride away. You can pick up maps at all the main entry points to the city, the major attractions are well signed and a very easy-to-use monorail system makes locations around town easily accessible. In addition, a small army of District Downtown Ambassadors in bright yellow T-shirts are on hand to provide directions.

Seattle's bodacious **Pike Place Market** is probably the best known of Seattle's attractions. The oldest continually operating outdoor market in the United States, it is the original farmer's market. Overlooking Elliott Bay Waterfront, the atmosphere here epitomizes the Pacific Northwest. Stands of fresh seafood are interspersed with flower stalls, with a liberal sprinkling of street musicians and arts and crafts. The market is a must-see if you have time in town. The famous fish toss is something of a photo call, but otherwise the area has a very authentic feel as locals and tourists mingle. Before leaving Pike Place Market, be sure to enjoy a fresh brewed coffee; this is the home of the original Starbucks coffee shop.

A trip to the top of Seattle's **Space Needle** will be on many people's one-day bucket list for Seattle. Ride the elevator up 500 feet in 41 seconds to the observation deck, where, when the weather cooperates, you will have stunning views of Mount Rainier, Puget Sound and the Seattle skyline. The easiest way to reach the Space Needle is on the monorail. The Needle is

Pike's Place Fish Market.

Contemporary art at the Downtown Art Museum, Seattle.

Art lovers will thoroughly enjoy **The Seattle Art Museum**. The museum comprises three separate venues; the downtown Seattle Art Museum, Olympic Sculpture Park, and the Seattle Asian Art Museum. Between these three facilities, the museum houses displays ranging from ancient Egyptian art treasures to contemporary American nature photography. The downtown museum houses an excellent installation showcasing the native culture of the region. And if you don't make it to Olympic Park before boarding your cruise ship, you'll be able to see the outdoor sculptures as your ship leaves port.

Pioneer Square, Seattle.

part of Seattle Center, an area replete with family attractions born of the remnants of the 1962 Seattle World's Fair. Family-friendly features include the Pacific Science Center, where you'll find impressive interactive science exhibits; the Experience Music Project, another interactive museum celebrating rock and roll, and a third museum covering the history of Sci-fi. All the exhibits are suitably high-tech, as befits the region. In fact, Paul Allen, co-founder of Microsoft, underwrote the cost of these unique venues.

A final area you might wish to include on your tour of Seattle is **Pioneer Square**, especially if your trip to Alaska is inspired by stories of the Klondike Gold Rush. From its small beginnings on the site of Pioneer Square, Seattle flourished when gold was discovered in the Klondike and the city became the jumping-off point for prospectors searching for gold and adventure. Several of the buildings in and around Pioneer Square are included in the Klondike Gold Rush National Historical Park, which also includes most of the town of Skagway, Alaska, plus key portions of the famous Chilkoot Trail and Dawson City, the ultimate destination of the gold rushers. This conglomerate of buildings, towns and trails now preserves one of the most exciting tales of America's more recent history.

San Francisco for a Day

The Golden Gate bridge and downtown San Francisco.

San Francisco, the storied city by the bay, has provided inspiration for a century of songwriters and poets. While Tony Bennett famously left his heart in San Francisco, Rudyard Kipling found only one drawback; "tis hard to leave." Perhaps George Sterling described the city most lyrically as "the cool, grey city of love", but Mark Twain's observation on the weather is probably most well-known; "the coldest winter I ever saw was the summer I spent in San Francisco."

Even if you don't catch the city on a sunny day, you won't be short of things to do: from the Golden Gate Bridge, Alcatraz Island, Fisherman's Wharf and the largest Chinatown in North America, to the eclectic assemblies of shops and cafés found in the Mission District, North Beach and along Haight Ashbury, there's more than enough to fill a day or even a weekend before you join your ship.

The main Visitor Information Center is located on the lower level of Hallidie Plaza, 900 Market Street. This is centrally located, so here you can pick up maps, organize your day and strike out in any direction.

The most visited section of San Francisco is **Fisherman's Wharf** and **Pier 39**.

Alcatraz, San Francisco Bay.

Named for the fishermen who have docked their boats here for generations, the wharf and surrounding area are home to a unique assemblage of shops, street performers, restaurants, and attractions. Dungeness crab is the local delicacy and street vendors sell clam chowder and other ocean fresh seafood all along the wharf.

The ferry to Alcatraz leaves from Pier 33 and offers a pleasant afternoon out in the bay. Nicknamed "The Rock" and formerly a notorious federal prison, Alcatraz is now a national park and home to rare flowers, plants, marine wildlife and thousands of nesting seabirds. But it's the tales of its days as a penitentiary that remain the highlight of island tours. It's typically rated as the number one attraction in San Francisco and if you are in town overnight, there is a nighttime tour that is especially recommended, so long as you don't scare easily. For tours at any time of day though, it's as well to book in advance if this is on your must-see list; go to www.alcatrazcruises.com.

Of course, the iconic attractions of downtown San Francisco are the **cable cars** and the famous **Lombard Street**, one of the steepest and most crooked streets in the U.S. You can use one (the cable cars) to reach the other (Lombard St). Just board the Hyde St cable car at Fisherman's Wharf and you can get off right at the top of Lombard Street. Overall, the cable cars are a great way to tour the city. You can board the cable cars at any stop marked with the distinctive brown and white cable car sign and purchase your ticket from the conductor onboard. All day passes can be purchased ($13.00 at the time of writing and you need cash to buy tickets onboard). There are three different routes through the city that will take you to all the main attractions. For details, visit their official website. The site is definitely entertaining, there's even an interactive trolley you can take for spin (www.sfcablecar.com)

For a more unusual destination, try the **Palace of Fine Arts** for an afternoon. Designed by Bernard Maybeck, this is considered by many as a must-see for first time visitors to San Francisco. Be warned however; this is neither a palace nor an art museum. Built for the 1915 Panama-Pacific Exposition, the picturesque grounds may look familiar as they have been the background for numerous television and motion picture shoots like the Streets of San Francisco and The Karate Kid. You can tour the grounds and located inside the Palace is the Exploratorium, an intriguing interactive museum designed to let you explore, discover and play. With over 600 exhibits, this is a family friendly destination guaranteed to provide something to amuse all ages. The Palace lies just to the west of town, so any of the transit buses headed for the Golden Gate Bridge will pass close by. From Fisherman's Wharf, you'll want the #30 Stockton bus, or you can hop a cab.

Chapter 2
Cruising the waters of British Columbia

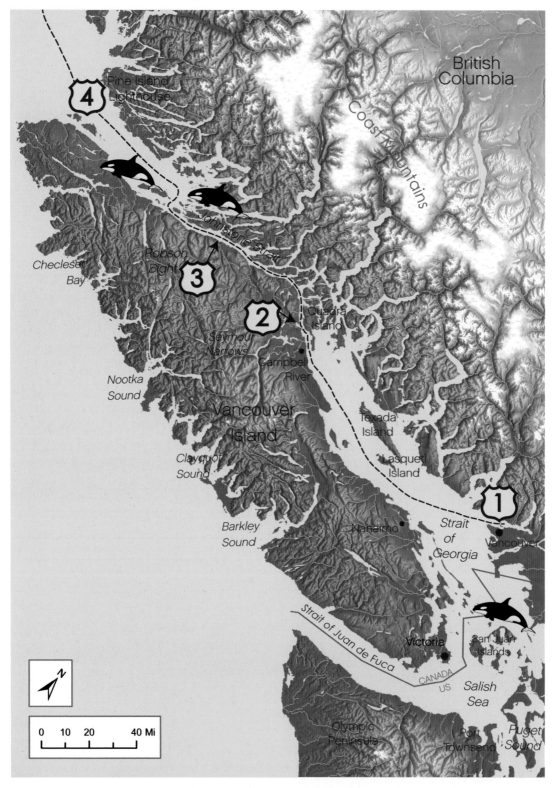

British
Columbia

Coast Mountains

④ Pine Island
Lighthouse

Johnstone Strait

Checleset
Bay

Robson
Bight

③

②

Quadra
Island

Seymour
Narrows

Campbell
River

Nootka
Sound

Vancouver
Island

Texada
Island

Clayquot
Sound

Lasqueti
Island

①

Barkley
Sound

Nanaimo

Strait
of
Georgia

Vancouver

Strait of Juan de Fuca

Victoria

San Juan
Islands

CANADA
US

Salish
Sea

Olympic
Peninsula

Port
Townsend

Puget
Sound

N

0 10 20   40 Mi

Cruising highlights
Vancouver Cruises

Waypoint 1: Point Atkinson Lighthouse
Marks the ship's entrance into the Strait of Georgia. Your ship makes a sharp turn to starboard at this point and heads north to Alaska.

Waypoint 2: Seymour Narrows
Narrowest point of the cruise. Site of the former Ripple Rock and the world's largest non nuclear explosion—to remove Ripple Rock.

Waypoint 3: Robson Bight
Home of the famous "rubbing rocks" beaches used by the region's killer whales. Good chance of killer whale sightings between here and Waypoint 4 from mid-July onwards.

Waypoint 4: Pine Island Lighthouse
Located at the Northern end of Queen Charlotte Strait. The open waters of Queen Charlotte Sound lie ahead.

Vancouver Sailaway

The city of Vancouver, British Columbia, lives up to its reputation: dynamic, vibrant and naturally beautiful. The sailaway from Vancouver ranks as one of the world's most scenic, so as your ship gets ready to sail, be sure to head to the outside decks and allow at least an hour to enjoy the highlights.

Set within the dramatic peaks of the Coast Mountain Range, Vancouver is one of the busiest ports on the Western Seaboard and remains firmly anchored to its maritime past. Even the cruise terminal, Canada Place, blends the city's bright, urban vibe and its sea-faring roots; the iconic white roof was designed to resemble the sails of an old Spanish Galleon. Today it's one of the most widely recognized features of the city's skyline.

From the dock at Canada Place, your ship will head out into the waters of Burrard Inlet. The newly completed Vancouver Convention Center sits beside Canada Place and sleek high-rise apartment buildings, plazas and outdoor cafes line the shoreline on the port side, making it easy to see that Vancouver deserves its reputation as one of the world's most livable cities. To the starboard side, the very southern extent of the Coast Mountain Range is in view. This range of mountains runs along the entire length of the mainland British Columbia coastline and stretches the length of Alaska's Inside Passage.

Several prominent buildings in downtown Vancouver were built for the World's Fair Expo in 1986, an event that coincided with the city's centennial birthday celebrations. These include the cruise ship terminal, Canada Place, the golf ball-shaped polyhedral, which now houses an interactive science museum and the B.C. sports stadium, the building with the billowing white rooftop just to the left of Canada Place.

This appealing region has been a popular home site for centuries. Archeological remains reveal that the shorelines of Burrard Inlet were first occupied as long ago as 10,000 years, when the Coast Salish people arrived in the region from Asia. The abundant salmon and pleasant climate provided for a rich West Coast lifestyle even then, and the early Salish First Nation camps quickly became permanent settlements along these shorelines.

Europeans arrived much later, in the late 1700's, propelled by their search for the elusive Northwest Passage. Captain Cook, officially the first European in the region, made landfall on Vancouver Island in 1778. In 1791 the Spanish Mariner Narváez sailed into Burrard Inlet for the first time, and in 1792 Captain Vancouver followed in his footsteps and was the first to map the region.

As you sail through Burrard Inlet, Stanley Park lies on your port side and several of the park's main attractions are visible from the ship. The small island to the left of the park is Deadman's Island. It was originally used as a native cemetery and later it became a jail for overly-exuberant sailors. The main portion of the park lies just ahead, ringed by a seawall five miles long. The seawall is one of the park's most popular and most-used features and an eclectic mix of art and antiquities lines the wall. Keep your binoculars handy, as you can spot some of these attractions from the ship as you sail by.

Art and antiquities along the shoreline of Stanley Park

The nine o'clock gun
This cannon sits just to the right of Deadman's Island along the shoreline of the park. It was donated by the British and installed in the park in 1894. It was originally installed to allow the authorities to communicate to fishermen, and remind them of the 6 o'clock closing of fishing on Sundays. However on it's installation, it was more consistently used by sea-faring vessels to set the ships' chronometers while in the harbor. So the timing of firing was reset to a daily schedule and it was, and still is, fired at nine o'clock each evening.

Girl in a wetsuit
This very pretty statue sits slightly offshore of the seawall and may well look familiar; the statue was designed as a modern interpretation of the Little Mermaid statue that sits at the entrance to Copenhagen Harbor, Denmark. *Girl in a Wetsuit* is now the unofficial mascot of the city. She made local headlines in the spring of 2011, when some generous and puckish benefactors added a Canucks shirt to her outfit during the Stanley Cup ice hockey finals.

SS Empress of Japan
Back along the seawall to the right of the statue, you'll see the masthead of the *SS Empress of Japan*, one of the first ships to sail regularly between Vancouver and the east coast of Asia. Between 1891 and 1922, the ship made over 300 crossings of the Pacific. The original figurehead was rescued during salvage and installed in the park in 1927 to serve as a reminder of the strong East-West ties that have always characterized the region.

The next landmark along your route is Lion's Gate Bridge. The bridge spans the inlet, and for Alaska-bound cruisers it has always been the gateway between the city and the open waters and adventure ahead. The bridge is named for two peaks, the East and West Lion, which look down on the port from the Coast Mountain Range on the northern side of the bay. It was built by the Guinness Distilleries in 1936 to connect the British-held properties on the west side of the city with downtown Vancouver.

Just beyond the bridge on the port side is Prospect Point, a popular viewpoint within Stanley Park. Originally this lighthouse had a resident keeper, whose principal task was to roust the local longshoremen from the bars of Gastown as ships headed into port. Today it's a popular café where locals frequently gather at sunset to wave a friendly bon voyage to the ships passing by.

Waypoint 1: Point Atkinson Lighthouse

This picturesque lighthouse sits at the mouth of Burrard Inlet. Though it's only seven miles from downtown Vancouver, Point Atkinson seems far removed from the city. This point, like nearly all the prominent nautical features in the region, was named by Captain Vancouver; Atkinson was one of his favorite crew. The original lighthouse was first built in 1874 and was replaced by the current lighthouse in 1912. Though many of the lighthouses in British Columbia are still manned by lighthouse keepers, this one is fully automated. It serves as a welcome sight to mariners at the end of a long sea voyage, as it marks the approach to Burrard Inlet and Vancouver.

After passing the lighthouse your ship will make a definite right turn, sailing out into the waters of the Strait of Georgia. As you head north, Vancouver Island lies to the west along the ship's port side and the mainland and offshore islands of British Columbia lie to the east, along the starboard side. At this point you're in the waters of the Inside Passage. These protected waterways stretch over 1,000 miles north, providing an (almost!) continuous, protected route to Alaska. Following the route first charted by Captain Cook and made famous by the naturalist John Muir, you are on your way to your Alaskan adventures.

Sunset on the waters of the Inside Passage.

Waypoint 2: Seymour Narrows

Whether you're traveling north or south, you may notice quite a dramatic change in speed as your ship approaches Waypoint 2. The timing for this part of the cruise is scheduled around the ship's passage through the notorious Seymour Narrows, and depending on the tides, your vessel may speed up or slow down as passage through the Narrows has to be carefully timed. Take a look at your Princess Patter to see what time your ship is aiming to transit the passage. If it's during daylight hours, it's well worth heading to the open decks to watch.

Seymour Narrows is the very narrowest portion of the entire route; the Narrows measure just 41 meters (that's only 135 feet!) across. And if seeing the ship pass through such a narrow passage isn't excitement enough, at high and low tides currents running through the Narrows may reach 15 knots. For this reason, ships—and even the local wildlife, for that matter—will wait for slack tide to make the passage. These days, thanks to the removal of Ripple Rock, the passage is easily accomplished.

Image 1245 courtesy of the Museum at Campbell River

"Old Rip" was the surprisingly affectionate name given to a wash rock that used to sit right in the middle of Seymour Narrows, adding to the adventure of passing through the narrow channel. At low tide the rock was just nine feet below the surface, which made a perilous transit through the narrows for many mariners. Between 1875 and 1958, over 120 vessels and 117 lives were lost as ships hit the rock and capsized or got caught in strong currents.

Attempts to remove the rock began in 1943. In the first attempt, a drilling barge was anchored in place over the rock, the plan being to drill down into the rock, load it with explosives and detonate them. Six anchors weighing almost 200 tons each were used, but the drill barge constantly broke free in the strong currents. In a second attempt in 1945, huge steel cables running from the shoreline were attached to the barge, but they too were insufficient against the strong currents of the Narrows. It wasn't until 1958, on a third attempt, that the removal project was successful. Engineers drilled down from the shoreline and up into the rock and then loaded in over 1,000 metric tons of Nitromex. At 9.30 a.m. on April 5th, 1958, in a huge explosion that was broadcast on live TV, the top of Old Rip was removed and ships could finally find safe passage through the treacherous Narrows.

Northbound from Seymour Narrows, the waters of the Inside Passage beckon with few if any further signs of life along the shorelines. If you're southbound, your route to Vancouver continues through the Strait of Georgia. The lights of small towns such as Nanaimo and Campbell River along the coast of Vancouver Island can be seen on the starboard side, and the inlets and bays along the port side soon give way to the twinkling lights of Vancouver, welcoming you back from your adventures.

Waypoint 3: Robson Bight, Johnstone Strait

If you've ever watched an Animal Planet or Discovery Channel special on killer whales, chances are that at least some if not all of it was filmed in the waters of Johnstone Strait. Killer whales, or orca as they are also known, are notoriously unpredictable and typically hard to find. However, they are more reliably sighted in these waters than anywhere else in the world. So if killer whales are on your wildlife checklist, be sure to head outside and spend some time on the open decks as you cruise through this area.

It's the availability of salmon, and particularly silver salmon, the killer whale's prey of choice, that attracts the whales to these waters. As a result, peak sightings coincide with the mid-summer salmon runs, starting in early to mid-July and lasting through mid-September each year. Most frequent sightings are between Waypoints 3 (Robson Bight) and 4 (Pine Island Lighthouse). If you're northbound, you'll most likely pass through here quite early on your first sea day. For southbound cruisers, timings through this region are dictated by the tides at Seymour Narrows (see previous page). You'll probably be in the area sometime after noon on your last day at sea and your best bet will be to check in with your onboard naturalist for more precise and updated timing for your cruise.

Midway along the western shoreline of Johnstone Strait is a world-renowned spot for killer whale sightings. Robson Bight is just a small bay along the shoreline of the Strait, however on the beaches of the Bight, smooth, round, perfectly sized rocks pile up at just the right angle for killer whales to come in and rub on these rocks. Rubbing on the rocks removes parasites and barnacles from the whale's skin and apparently, for killer whales, it feels good! Scientists studying killer whales in the area have noted that the same local family groups of whales visit the Bight together each year. Each group even arrives at around the same time each year, and it's now seen as a predictable summertime tradition for these families.

In large family groups such as this it's easy to tell males from females. Mature males have high-standing dorsal fins while females have smaller, more curved dorsal fins.

Between Waypoints 3 and 4: Blackfish Sound and Alert Bay

At the right time of year, between mid-July and mid-September, this region comprises prime killer whale habitat. Between Waypoints 3 and 4, your ship will take one of two routes depending on the time of day, the tide and the number of local fishing boats in the region. One route takes a sharp turn through Blackney Passage into Blackfish Sound, and from there follows a scenic route through the offshore islands of mainland B.C. towards Pine Island (Waypoint 4). The other route continues along the shoreline of Vancouver Island through the waters of Queen Charlotte Strait, passing by Alert Bay and the small island community at Sointula. Your ship's captain and local B.C. pilot will pick the best route based on tides and levels of local traffic, especially fishing vessels. Both routes are extremely scenic and you might see those elusive killer whales anywhere along either of these routes.

If your ship does cruise by Alert Bay, be sure to head to the outside decks and take your binoculars. Located on Cormorant Island just across the Strait from Vancouver Island, Alert Bay has a unique claim to fame—it is home to the world's tallest totem pole. The Sun Pole reaches to 176 feet. It was originally built for the World's Fair in Vancouver in 1986 and tells the story of the creation of the Kwakwaka'wakw people of the First Nation, who were the original settlers of this region.

Originally the Sun Pole stood at 171 feet, but when a rival pole erected in Seattle stole the "tallest" title, a five foot extension was added to place the Sun Pole back in the record books. The distinctive Sun at the top of the pole makes it easy to spot as you sail by. Other story, commemorative and family crest poles can be seen throughout the village and today the village is well-established as the cultural hearth of the modern-day Kwakwaka'wakw people.

Photo: ©Kraig Anderson/www.lighthousefriends.com

V

Waypoint 4: Pine Island Lighthouse

The lighthouse at Pine Island is an authentic, working lighthouse, staffed and operated by the Canadian Coast Guard. Its location at the southern extent of Queen Charlotte Sound makes it an important navigational landmark. Traveling north, you'll see it on the port side of the ship and if you're southbound, it will be on the starboard side. The large gray helicopter pad marks the spot of the original lighthouse that stood here until it was literally washed away by a rogue wave during a violent storm in the winter of 1967. The new lighthouse was built on the foundations of the original house, with the new tower was located at the top of the cliff, hopefully beyond the reach of even the most exciting winter waves.

This stormy history is a good reminder, too; if you're northbound, from this point your ship will be heading into the open waters of Queen Charlotte Sound, the most unprotected stretch of ocean along your route. On calm days, the Sound is known for long fetches and deep, rolling swells as waves roll across the Pacific unchecked. On windy days it may be a little rougher, so you might wish to prepare for the "motion of the ocean." For southbound cruisers, the light-house marks your entrance into protected waterways, so from here it's smooth sailing ahead.

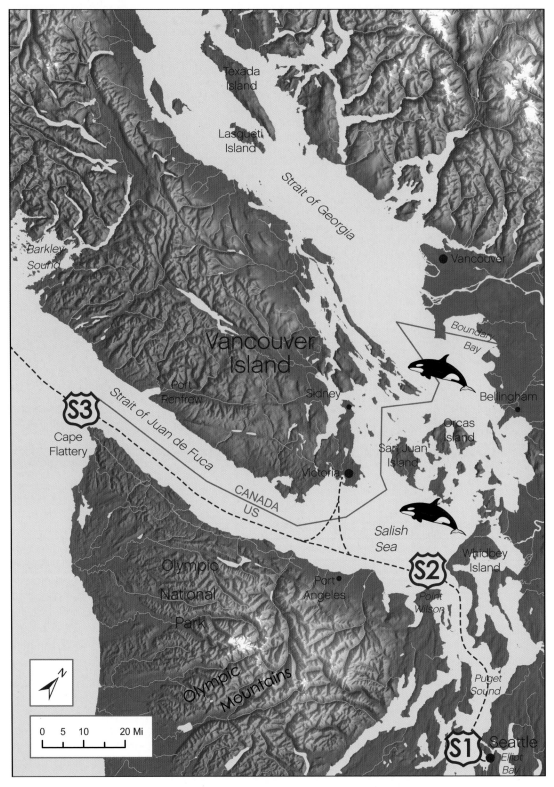

Texada Island

Lasqueti Island

Strait of Georgia

Barkley Sound

Vancouver

Boundary Bay

Vancouver Island

Port Renfrew

Sidney

Bellingham

S3

Strait of Juan de Fuca

Cape Flattery

CANADA
US

Victoria

Orcas Island

San Juan Island

Salish Sea

Olympic National Park

Port Angeles

Whidbey Island

S2

Point Wilson

Olympic Mountains

Puget Sound

N

0 5 10   20 Mi

S1 Seattle

Elliot Bay

Cruising highlights
Seattle Cruises

Waypoint S1: Elliot Bay
This is the starting point for the cruise from Seattle. Seattle's Space Needle and spectacular skyline are in view from the ship. Look for Seattle's famous sports stadiums too; these are visible from the port side as you sail through the Bay.

Waypoint S2: Point Wilson
Key navigational point, marked by Point Wilson Lighthouse. Marks the point where Puget Sound opens into the Strait of Juan de Fuca.

Waypoint S3: Cape Flattery
This lies to the port side of the ship on northbound cruises. It's the northernmost point in the contiguous United States and was named by Captain Cook in 1778. The mountains of the Olympic Peninsula are in view on the portside.

Waypoint S4: Cape Scott
Northernmost point of Vancouver Island. A rugged and remote region of windswept coastline accessible only by boat.

Seattle Sailaway

Seattle's favorite nickname may be the Emerald City, but if you're setting sail from Seattle Harbor on a clear day, it's the snow capped mountains—especially the amazing views of Mount Rainier—that will grab your attention. The soaring peaks of the Cascade Mountain Range sit to the east and southeast of Seattle. The mountains of the Olympic Peninsula beckon to the west and cast a rain shadow across the downtown region, so despite the city's reputation, sunny skies in summer are not too rare a sight.

Setting sail from Terminal 91, you'll have sweeping views of downtown Seattle and a chance to get some waterline snapshots of Seattle's iconic landmarks. The Space Needle, slightly to the west of the city, rises to 520 feet and defines the city's skyline. Columbia Center, with its Sky View observation deck, lies closer to downtown and is the tallest building in the city, rising to 1,040 feet. The other prominent feature of the Seattle skyline is Smith Tower. This was the first of the city's high rise buildings. Built in 1914, it reaches 522 feet and when completed, it was the fourth tallest building in the world at that time. Today, its claim to fame is the 300 year old Wishing Chair on the top floor, guaranteed to provide husbands within a year for single women who take a seat there.

Just to the east of the city you'll see the city's well known sports stadiums. The home of Seattle's NFL team, the Seahawks, is easy to spot by the distinctive metal arches of its roof. The field was recently renamed the CenturyLink Field and loyal Seahawks fans have already chosen a nickname; it's to be known as the Clink, which is also the name of a notorious jail in the U.K. Next door to the Clink is Safeco Field, home of Seattle's baseball team, the Mariners.

Numerous cranes along the shoreline provide evidence of Seattle's continuing prominence as a seaport. The blue and white ferries crossing the bay are part of the Washington State ferry system. These ferries link the outlying islands with downtown Seattle and are very much a mainstay of the local transport system for tourists and commuters alike.

Mount Rainier looks out over Seattle from the Southeast. Located 50 miles from downtown, the mountain rises to 14,411 feet and ranks as the third highest peak in the U.S. It is a stratovolcano with two crater lakes at its peak. It also has three distinct summits, all visible from the water on a clear, sunny day.

Waypoint S1: Elliot Bay

Elliot Bay is the starting point for your cruise and officially the most southerly portion of the Inside Passage. As you leave downtown Seattle behind, you'll cruise through Puget Sound, weaving between Whidbey Island on the starboard side and the Olympic Peninsula on the port side.

Though the ice-sheets have long since retreated, like most of Alaska's Inside Passage these channels and bays were originally sculpted by glaciers. Today, the Sound consists of four main bays, linked by deepwater channels and shallow water sills mark the original extent of the glaciers. The snowcapped mountain peaks of the Cascade Mountain Range to the east and the Olympic Mountains to the west provide a very scenic backdrop for the Sound, and serve as reminders of the region's icy origins. And if skies are clear and the mountain is "out", Mount Rainier will be in view to the South.

Race Rocks Lighthouse, built in 1860, marks the southernmost point on Canada's west coast.

Waypoint S2: Point Wilson

Point Wilson marks the point where Puget Sound flows into the Strait of Juan de Fuca. Just beyond this point you may notice a small boat approaching the ship. This coastguard vessel comes alongside the cruise ships to pick up the local B.C. pilots, an operation that involves a sprightly dash down a ladder from the ship's lower decks onto the (moving!) pilot boat.

After passing Point Wilson, the southern tip of Vancouver Island will be in view to the starboard side. This is the southernmost point on the Pacific Coast of Canada and a well-known lighthouse, Race Rocks, marks the spot. The name of the lighthouse—and the rocks—refers to the racing currents in this area. An eight knot current is not uncommon here, and huge tidal flows can add to the excitement for navigators. The lighthouse itself is quite the landmark, too. It was constructed in 1860 by the British Admiralty to ensure safe passage for ships entering and leaving Victoria, using granite mined in Scotland and shipped out piece by piece.

From Race Rocks, your route continues west through the waters of the Strait of Juan de Fuca. The snowcapped mountain peaks of the Olympic Peninsula remain in view and the protected waters of the Strait make for a comfortable cruise for your first evening at sea.

Lighthouses of British Columbia

In 1860, the construction of the two sister lighthouses, Race Rocks and Fisgard, marked the start of a nautical and cultural tradition of lighthouses and lighthouse keepers along Canada's coastlines. Today, 40 lighthouses illuminate the rugged and treacherous coastlines of British Columbia and they remain a defining feature of the region.

Most are in remote regions accessible only by boat and you might expect that with the march of modern technology, "lighthouse keeper" would be another occupation winding its way into distant memory. But that isn't happening here in B.C. While lighthouses around the world have become automated, Canada is holding strong to its tradition of manned lighthouses and resident lighthouse keepers. It's not a profession for the weak of heart; with wicked winter storms renowned in the region, at times it's truly a risky occupation. Still, when the Canadian Coast Guard recently announced plans to phase out lighthouse keepers as a cost-cutting measure, the public outcry was heard all the way to the Federal government. Government fact-finding committees were formed, reports were written, and in March 2011 the Canadian parliament officially "advised" the coast guard to halt its de-staffing plans.

Today, some 27 lighthouses in British Columbia remain staffed, and lighthouse keepers' roles have expanded to include weather reporting, scientific data collection and wildlife monitoring. Race Rocks Lighthouse and Fisgard Lighthouse are now both automated, but there are eight manned lighthouses on the remote outer coast of Vancouver Island.

For a wealth of information on B.C. lighthouses, visit http://www.fogwhistle.ca/bclights. This site has full details of all the lighthouses in British Columbia and even gives email contact information for many of the lighthouse keepers.

Fisgard Lighthouse, the sister lighthouse to Race Rocks, sits on the southeastern shoreline of Vancouver Island. Built in 1860, this is the oldest lighthouse on the west coast of Canada. It pre-dates Race Rocks Lighthouse by just over a month, having been first operated on November 16, 1860. Like most B.C. lighthouses, it is still in operation and serves an important role, guiding ships safely through this rocky region.

Waypoint S3: Cape Flattery

As the ship passes Cape Flattery at the entrance to the Strait of Juan de Fuca, the open waters of the Pacific and Queen Charlotte Sound lie ahead. (Sea conditions can be a little rough once the ship clears this point, so you might want to prepare for "Neptune's pulse.") Cape Flattery is on the U.S. side of this inlet and marked by a prominent lighthouse that predates the B.C. houses by some six years.

The Cape was named by Captain Cook, as the story goes that the inlet had flattered him into thinking he had found the elusive Northwest Passage. This exhaustive search dominated maritime exploration of the area at that time. For more information on this era, take a look at the "History in Focus" section on page 66.

Sailing north from Cape Flattery, the remote west coast of Vancouver Island lies to starboard and during daytime cruising the snowcapped peaks of the ruggedly beautiful Strathcona Mountain Range on Vancouver Island may be in view. The west coast of Vancouver Island is sparsely populated. It's best known for its long, windswept beaches and fabulous sunsets, and is also enjoying newly found popularity as a winter storm-watching location.

West Coast of Vancouver Island and the Strathcona Mountain Range.

Nootka Sound is a truly remote location on the West Coast of Vancouver Island. It's accesible only by boat or floatplane and you'll probably pass by it overnight, but it is a place that resonates with history and therefore maybe warrants a note. It was in the waters of Nootka Sound that Captain Cook became the first European to come into contact with the First Nation people of this region—an event that changed the cultural landscape of the region forever. The cove is now called Friendly Cove, and by all accounts the interaction was positive. Captain Cook and his crew on the Resolution traded biscuits for sea otter pelts; these would soon become the fashion of the day in Europe. Cook's visit profoundly marked the end of the isolation of the First Nation people and the beginning of European exploration of the region, most of which initially centered around the quest for valuable sea otter pelts. Officially, the region's first "gold rush" began here and sea otter pelts were the sought-after prize.

Waypoint S4: Cape Scott

Cape Scott marks the northernmost point on Vancouver Island. If you're traveling north, you'll pass through much of this area overnight, but if you're southbound, this first sight of Vancouver Island marks your progress to Victoria, your final point of call. It's worth keeping a look out for whales along this coastline. Humpback whale numbers in the region are rising and they are more likely seen offshore. Look for a tall, standing blow and you'll also glimpse a dorsal fin as the whale dives. Gray whales are also common on the west coast of Vancouver Island. Though most grays head north to the Bering Sea for summer feeding, some linger and feed in the bays along the coastline. Look for a smaller, rounded blow and no sign of a dorsal fin.

Vancouver Island is famous for its spectacular sunsets.

History In Focus – The Search for the Elusive Northwest Passage

Captain George Vancouver, often considered the hero of modern navigation. Captain Vancouver didn't find the fabled passage, but made a tremendous contribution to the charting of Alaskan and Canadian waters.

The history of this region was irrevocably shaped by the early explorations of mariners from across the globe. Traders came in search of sea otter pelts, but the earliest mariners had a single goal—to find the elusive Northwest Passage.

The search for the Northwest Passage dates back to the days of Columbus. Just five years after Columbus reported the existence of the American continents, the British began the search for an all-water route across the continent of America in the hope of gaining access to the lucrative trade routes of Asia.

Ships were equipped and mariners were sent out from across Europe with the explicit mandate of discovering a new route. The first stories of success came in 1592, from Juan de Fuca, a Greek navigator sailing through the region under a Spanish flag (and with an assumed Spanish name). Though the exact details are vague, essentially Juan de Fuca sailed north, following the coast from Acapulco to the Pacific Northwest. When he found the entrance to the wide open channel that is now named the Strait of Juan de Fuca, he presumed it would connect across the continent and exuberantly claimed that he had found the elusive Northwest Passage. Unfortunately, he didn't actually check the extent of this new route to make sure his assumption was true. Russian, British, Spanish and Portuguese sailing fleets followed, and soon revealed that the Strait of Juan de Fuca came to an abrupt end in Puget Sound.

In 1778, Captain Cook sailed into the region for the first time and onboard his ship was a young officer named George Vancouver, age 14. During that voyage Vancouver studied with Cook, learning the latest navigation skills and charting new regions under Cook's watchful eye. In 1792 he returned to the region as a captain in his own right in charge of two ships, the Discovery and the Chatham. He was charged with the same mission as Cook—the discovery of the Northwest Passage.

As Vancouver charted the coastline in detail, he added names to prominent features and so local landmarks became a Who's Who of his favorite friends and shipmates. Peter Puget, Zachary Mudge, Joseph Baker and Joseph Whidbey were all officers on the Discovery, while William Broughton, James Hanson and James Johnstone were officers onboard the Chatham. Check the current nautical maps for this region and you'll spot all these names.

Fur traders and other explorers would soon be headed to these waters from all points of Europe, and the detailed and precise charts compiled by Vancouver and his officers would save many a life in these treacherous waters. However, Vancouver's precisely crafted charts also put to rest the fabled existence of the Northwest Passage. No such route existed, and until the opening of the Panama Canal in 1914, ships traveling between Europe and America would continue to make the long trip around Cape Horn.

However, the story of the search for the Northwest Passage continues to unfold. In the early 17th century, the infamous early explorations of Captain Henry Hudson to find an alternate northwest route across the northern-most reaches of the North American Continent and through the Arctic Sea had ended in mutiny and loss of life. On August 27, 1905, Captain Roald Amundsen and his crew actually completed this passage, starting out in the Atlantic and ending in the Pacific Ocean, but their route held little commercial potential; it took the crew two years to navigate their way through a maze of ice-choked channels across the northern reaches of Canada.

In recent years, a surprising final chapter to this story is taking shape. Global climate change has meant that Arctic regions are warming up and in late summer each year, as the extent of the Arctic Ice Cap retreats a little further, a Northwest Passage across the Arctic Sea, skirting the northern shoreline of Canada and Alaska, opens up. During a six to eight week window each summer, cargo ships may now sail from the Pacific to the Atlantic Ocean without detouring around Cape Horn or passing through the Panama Canal. You can even take a cruise through this northern passage, though it's not one of Princess Cruise's itineraries...yet!

A note on marine artist John Norton:

Widely recognized as a pre-eminent marine artist of today, John Horton's work is renowned for its historical accuracy and attention to detail. See more of John's stunning images at www.johnhorton.ca.

An American trading ship cruises the waters of the Pacific Northwest. Ships such as these relied on the accurate charts created by Captain George Vancouver.
Artist: John Hogan, www.johnhorton.ca

Wildlife Profile: The Awesome Orca

Fast Facts:

Common name: Killer whale, or orca.

Scientific name: *Orcinus Orca*

Best areas for sightings: Johnstone Strait, B.C. Occasionally seen in Glacier Bay, the waters around Juneau, Prince William Sound.

ID: Distinct black and white coloration and tall, black dorsal fins (males: up to six feet; females: two to three feet and curved).

Size: Males up to 30 feet in length, females up to 25 feet.

Lifespan: Males up to 30 years, females typically up to 50 years; some may live to 80 years old.

Mating and reproduction: Mating is frequent and random, but not seen between whales of the same clan; females reach maturity around age 15, males don't breed till age 20. Females produce single calves every three to four years.

Typical group size: Residents seen in family groups of four to twelve; transients typically seen alone or in small groups of two to four.

Diet: Variable. Resident killer whales eat fish and silver salmon comprise 95% of their diet. Transients feed on other marine mammals, from seals to large whales. Offshore killer whales feed on shark and other large fish.

Recommended websites: For daily updates on killer whales sightings in Johnstone Strait, visit www.orca-live.net, or orcasound.net where you can also listen to a live underwater audio stream from the region.

Wildlife in focus - The awesome orca

If ever a whale got a reputation it didn't deserve, the killer whale would be that whale.

The name and reputation of the killer whale as a "killer whale" dates back to whaling days, when whalers witnessed killer whales hunting and devouring their marine mammal prey. Most killer whales, however, are predominantly sociable whales; they live in long term family groups, feed on fish and really don't view other marine mammals as lunch. The confusion arises because there are several different races—or ecotypes—of killer whales. The killer whales most frequently seen in coastal regions are known as residents; these whales feed on fish and don't attack marine mammals. Another distinct group known as transients routinely feed primarily on other marine mammals such as seals, sea lions, sea otters, dolphins and even large whales. There's also a third group, the offshore killer whales, found only in offshore waters where they feed on large fish, including shark. The three groups don't mix or interbreed. Typically, as transient killer whales enter an area, resident killer whales leave. Still, all killer whales belong to the same species, *Orcinus orca*. Biologically, they are classed as odontocetes (whales with teeth) and they are the largest members of the dolphin family.

Individual killer whales are identified and recognized by the saddlepatch markings just behind the dorsal fin, so researchers have been able to compile detailed life histories on individual whales dating as far back as the 1950's for some Johnstone Strait residents. Of the three ecotypes, residents are the best known and most closely studied. These whales are highly social. Family ties are strong, they stay together for life and family groups (called pods) are led by the matriarchal female. Their prey of choice is silver salmon, they hunt and feed as a group and mature females are commonly seen sharing their catch with younger members of their pod. Typically, they are very vocal. Each family pod has a distinct repertoire of around a dozen specific calls that are used in specific contexts, such as feeding and socializing, and each separate family can be recognized by their distinctive calls, almost like regional accents. Several different family groups may have quite similar dialects, suggesting that they are descended from the same maternal line. These closely related groups comprise a "clan."

As the name implies, resident groups tend to stay within distinct regions. There's a Southern Resident population numbering around 88 animals that stays principally in the waters around the San Juan Islands and southern B.C. This group includes only 88 animals in three key pods and is currently listed as endangered. The Northern Resident population comprises around 220 known individuals. This population includes 16 different pods and ranges between Northern B. C. and Southeast Alaskan waters. Typically, cruising groups range in size from four to twelve direct family members, but occasionally multiple clans meet to socialize and form "super pods." Mating most likely takes place during these periods and as these super-pods are highly vocal, scientists suspected that whales use the different dialects to select unrelated mates. DNA analysis confirmed this, indicating that whales choose mates from different clans, effectively reducing any issues of inbreeding in the otherwise small groups. Super pods may stay together for a few hours to a few days. Their locations and movements are usually tracked online and they make for some spectacular whale-watching.

Transient killer whales are socially very different to residents. They live more solitary lives; maternal females may be accompanied by their offspring for a year or two after they give birth, otherwise groups form for the sole purpose of feeding and then disperse. While typical prey for transient killer whales range from seal pups to large whales, generally it's the juveniles in any of these prey groups that are most at risk. Transients cruise the oceans in search of favored prey, and the same individuals seen in Glacier Bay in the summer have been spotted preying on gray whale calves off California the following winter.

When hunting, transient killer whales may reach speeds of up to 45 mph and use some quite sophisticated hunting techniques. On the Peninsula Valdes in Argentina, killer whales make dramatic high speed lunges, and even beach themselves, to catch South American sea lions that stray close to the shoreline. In the Antarctic, groups of transient killer whales work together to create waves that wash their favorite prey, Weddell seals, off of icebergs and into the water where their accomplices wait to catch them. This behavior was also recently witnessed in Alaska, in Tracy Arm, where pairs of killer whales were seen working together to "wash" harbor seals off the ice and into the clutches of waiting whales. After a successful hunt, transient killer whales may be very active at the surface. They feed on their prey together, and then slow down and rest in a tight, almost silent group for two to three hours at a time. It's easy to see how this group got the name "Wolves of the Sea."

A single male killer whales cruises the waters of the Inside Passage. A single male such as this is most likely a transient killer whale.

Killer whales are frequently active at the surface and scientists believe their surface behaviors serve as a means of communication. A whale using its huge swimming muscles to slap its tail flukes down on the surface of the water is likely displaying aggression.

For all killer whales, breeding in females starts at around age 15, however most males don't breed until they are well into their twenties. Female killer whales produce a calf every three to four years until about age 40 and then after reproduction, they remain in their family group as high ranking members, an extremely rare situation in animal societies. (Elephants are the other well-documented exception). Killer whales calves typically have a yellowish tint to their white patches that usually lasts till about age two. The calves within any family group quickly become the focus of the group. Calves nurse till they are two to three years old, and females other than the mother help with calf-sitting duties. Still, calf survival is low; only about 60% survive, and researchers have yet to understand why this might be.

For the most part, killer whale populations worldwide are holding strong. Researchers are concerned that as top predators, some populations in Arctic waters now have high levels of toxins in their blubber, but as yet no side effects are apparent. Within British Columbia, numbers of transient killer whales have been increasing slightly in recent years, but numbers within both the resident northern BC and the southern BC groups have been more of a concern. These groups originally supplied many of the killer whales to amusement parks and aquaria around the world. A total of 48 whales were live-captured from this region between 1963 and 1974, and another 12 died in the

A whale may leap entirely out of the water, an action referred to as a breach. It takes plenty of energy, so scientists would expect it has a function. It may be communicative or it may help in hunting, but as yet there is no firm explanation.

process. In such small populations this can have a tangible impact. Live captures were halted in the 1970's and numbers then started to climb. Today they are protected, the Northern Resident population is growing very slowly, but recent drops in numbers have been notable for the Southern BC group (from 98 in the 1970's to 78 in the late 90's). The current group numbers 88 individuals and is listed as an endangered population. Primary challenges are thought to be competition with the fishing industry for fishing resources, pollution of their favored fishing habitat, and unfortunately, overly attentive whale watching vessels which may reduce their access to food resources. On a brighter note, the plight of this group is now well documented and every effort is being made to ensure the future health of these and other killer whales around the world. Springer's story, on the next page, reminds us of our deep connections with these iconic whales.

Springer's Story

Springer in the waters of Johnstone Strait.

As killer whale populations continue to face challenges in the waters of Seattle and Southern B.C., the story of one whale casts a ray of hope...

It was a typically cold Seattle day in January, 2002, when a young female killer whale was spotted, alone amid the busy harbor traffic of Puget Sound. Breaching alongside incoming ferries and playing in the wakes of huge tankers, Seattle's newest resident seemed in good health and lively spirits and quickly made the local evening news.

But days became weeks and as the young whale stayed put, concerns began to mount. It seemed just a matter of time before she would be hit or injured by vessel traffic or well meaning on-lookers. By early February she was showing signs of ill health. She had developed a rash across large swaths of skin, she was looking thin and her breath had a heavy acetone smell, a clear indication that the young whale was not feeding. Biologists from NOAA, along with experts from SeaWorld and Vancouver aquarium, gathered shoreside and a plan began to take shape.

Comparing her markings to known catalogues, the biologists had already identified the young whale as Springer, a two year old female whose mother, Sutlej, had disappeared the year before. The biologists also knew that as well as being alone and orphaned, the young whale was far from home. Springer belonged to the Northern Resident population, a group whose typical range includes the Northern British Columbia coastline and the inter-island waterways around the northern reaches of Vancouver Island. The waters of Johnstone Strait comprise the most southerly portion of their range and from Seattle, this region was more than 300 miles away.

While several aquariums quickly offered to provide a new home for Springer, government officials and the public alike all agreed that this young female whale should stay in the wild if at all possible. And so they embarked on an inspiring rescue mission involving researchers, government officials, local boat operators and volunteers. Their aim; to reunite Springer with her family.

Springer's vocalizations were easily recognized as belonging to a well-known sub-family or clan that passes through the waters of Johnstone Strait each summer between June and August. For Springer, this period was the window of opportunity and there was no time to waste. On June 13, 2002, Springer was herded into a small pen in Seattle Harbor. Once there, she was well fed, treated for her skin condition and checked for communicable diseases in preparation for her journey north. A local boat operator donated a high speed catamaran. The boat was rigged with a huge holding tank and on July 12, 2002, Springer began her journey home.

First she was loaded into a crane and moved from her pen in the harbor to the tank on the boat. Throughout the operation, her handlers were astonished by her cooperation, even raising her fins to allow the sling to be fitted and waiting calmly as she was lowered into the tank. The boat then set out at full speed north, arriving five hours later in Johnstone Strait and delivering Springer to a small, sheltered bay on Hansen Island, which lies right at the northern tip of the strait. An area of the bay had been netted off and First Nation locals had stocked the netted area with 75 local silver salmon, a favorite treat for killer whales.

Within a day of arriving at her island home, researchers picked up the underwater sounds of her family group swimming into the area. As the sounds reached Springer's enclosure, she breached repeatedly and dove deep to the bottom of the inlet. On July 13 at 3.30 p.m., less than a day after arriving in the bay, members of Springer's clan swam by the enclosure. Researchers opened the net and held their breath...and Springer swam out to rejoin her family.

There were a few false starts and a few more anxious days as Springer appeared to vacillate between joining her old family and staying with her new caregivers. But over a period of a few weeks, she assimilated successfully back into the clan, first associating with other young whales and finally being adopted by a 16-year-old female named Nodales who had recently lost a calf.

Like any good story, a book (Saving Springer) and even a movie deal (well, a NOAA documentary) followed. But the real happy ending is still to be seen today; Springer has a new companion, Sunny, and the pair are seen yearly, cruising the wild, salmon-rich waters of B.C. Springer is quite easy to spot. She's a small female so she has a small, curved dorsal fin, she has a misty colored saddlepatch around the base of the dorsal fin, she's frequently seen breaching and perhaps in recognition of her past adventures, she regularly approaches passing vessels.

Sadly, not all stories of killer whales that come into contact with people end as well as Springer's story. The most famous killer whale in recent history, Keiko, passed away before ever being successfully released into the wild and the tale of Luna, another young, orphaned killer whales that chose Nootka Harbor on the west coast of Vancouver Island as a haven also ended badly. But with each successful outcome, scientists learn more about whales in the wild and so become better equipped to ensure the health and well-being of killer whales in the waters of B.C. and Alaska.

Queen Charlotte Sound

Between Waypoints 4 to 5

All routes

Whether you're traveling from Vancouver or Seattle, and headed for Ketchikan or for Juneau as your first port of call, once clear of the northern reaches of Vancouver Island, all ships must now head out into the open waters of Queen Charlotte Sound.

Queen Charlotte Sound was named in 1778 by James Strange in honor of Queen Charlotte, the wife of King George III. Strange was one of a flood of fur traders who headed to the region in search of sea otters, or more specifically sea otter pelts. For mariners today, crossing the Sound is perhaps the biggest challenge of any Alaska bound cruise, as it is the largest body of open water along an otherwise entirely protected route. The Sound extends from the northern tip of Vancouver Island to the southern tip of the Haida Gwaii archipelago, an island chain previously known as the Queen Charlotte Islands. If your first port of call is Ketchikan your ship will now sail to the east of the islands, in the slightly more protected waters of the Hecate Strait. If your first port of call is Juneau, then you'll sail to the west of the islands and the open waters of the Pacific will stretch to the horizon on your portside.

Marine life abounds in these open waters. Look out for the rooster-tail splash left by the fast-moving Dall's porpoise. These days, humpback whales may be frequently spotted crossing the Sound too and even killer whales will make the crossing. Look for their high standing dorsal fins as they cruise by.

A pod of killer whales cruises the waters of Queen Charlotte Sound.

Haida Gwaii: The Galapagos Islands of the North Pacific

If you're cruising through this area during daylight hours, you'll see the Haida Gwaii Islands in the distance; a faint and somewhat mysterious line of high peaks on a distant horizon. In the 1700's, prior to European contact, as many as 10,000 Haida lived on the islands. Sadly, after their arrival, many Haida succumbed to European diseases, particularly smallpox. By the early 1900's, only 350 Haida survived and travelers would see very few signs of life in these remote locations. Currently though, the islands and the Haida people are resurging. Today, some 4,000 people live on the islands of Haida Gwaii, and along with the islands' new name comes an invigorated sense of identity and stewardship for this unique archipelago.

The islands are referred to as the Galapagos of the North in recognition of the unique assemblages of plants and animals found here. The southern tip of the island chain, the Gwaii Haanas National Park Reserve and Haida Heritage Site, is especially rich in wildlife and home to over 750,000 nesting seabirds in any one season. This is the one place in Canada where horned puffins nest and the reserve also boasts the highest density of breeding Peregrine falcons anywhere in the world. This profusion of life is due to upwellings along the islands' outer shoreline that provide abundant food and in addition, the isolation of the islands reduces nest predation. The abundance of food also attracts marine mammals. The reserve boasts the largest colony of Steller sea lions on the west coast of B.C. or Alaska and was recently ranked by National Geographic as one of their top 50 destinations worldwide.

Waypoint 5 - Triple Island Lighthouse
Vancouver and Seattle Cruises

Triple Island Lighthouse marks the southern reaches of the Dixon Entrance, a small body of open water that connects the Hecate Strait in British Columbia, Canada with Alaska's Clarence Strait in the U.S. So, you might ask, where does the actual border between the U.S. and Canada lie?

Interestingly, this is a point of contention dating back to the 1903 Alaska Border Treaty. Officially, Canada marks the border at what is referred to as the A-B line, which lies at 54° 40' north and runs between the tips of the adjacent islands. But not all parties agree. At stake are the fishing and sea floor mineral rights of the region, and the dispute continues. Nonetheless, be assured that somewhere very close to latitude 54° 40' north, you will officially enter—or leave—the waters of Alaska's Inside Passage.

If you're sailing south, a pleasant day's cruise through the waters of British Columbia lies ahead. If you're northbound, welcome to Alaska! You're now in the calm, protected waters of Alaska's Inside Passage. The route you take from here depends on your first port of call. To reach Ketchikan, you'll cruise through the waters of Revillagigedo Channel, passing by the entrance to Misty Fjords National Monument on the starboard side to reach Revillagigedo Island, where the town of Ketchikan is located. Most ships arrive in Ketchikan in the very early morning, so you'll probably pass through this region during the night.

Waypoints S5 and S6
Seattle Cruises - First port of call Juneau.

If you sailed from Seattle or San Francisco and your first Alaskan port of call is Juneau, your ship will head slightly west and follow the western shoreline of the Haida Gwaii Islands and then Prince of Wales Island. You can read more about the Haida Gwaii Islands on the previous page. As for Prince of Wales Island, this is one of the largest islands in the region, and though remote and sparsely populated it does have a claim to fame; its a hot spot for Bigfoot sightings. Waypoint S6 lies along this outer coastline of the island and you'll pass through this area overnight.

Waypoint 7 at Cape Decision marks your entrance into the more protected waters of Chatham Strait and from there you'll sail to Juneau via Frederick Sound. The waters of the Sound are especially favored by humpback whales - you can read more about this area on page 127.

A humpback whale prepares to dive
in the waters of Frederick Sound.

Chapter 3

Welcome to Ketchikan

Ketchikan

Ketchikan goes by many names. As the first port of call for cruise ships heading north, it's known as Alaska's First City or The Gateway City. It also claims to be the Salmon Capitol of the World. More infamously, it holds the title of Rainfall Capital of the U.S., receiving on average 162 inches of rain a year. But all the rain has its blessings: the area surrounding Ketchikan boasts some of the world's most impressive stands of old growth temperate rainforest. Abundant, well fed freshwater rivers and streams are bursting with salmon each summer and as a result, the region is teeming with wildlife.

Ketchikan is also a hearth for the native culture of the Southeast Alaska. Around 20% of the population of Ketchikan can trace its heritage to the three predominant regional tribes, the Tlingit, the Haida and the Tsimshian. Even the city's name, Ketchikan, reflects these strong roots; in the Tlingit language, Ketchikan means Eagle Wing River and stems from a word describing the swish of eagle wings in flight.

When the first people passed through this region over 12,000 years ago, the cool climate and easy availability of food, from fish in the streams to berries in the forests, drew some to settle here year round. European settlers arrived much later, during the gold rush days of the late 19th century, when prospectors too late to strike it rich in the gold fields of the Yukon saw the profusion of salmon in the local streams. Fish processing plants were established and the town quickly grew. Today, fishing is still the number one industry in Ketchikan and the town boasts more boats than cars, but tourism runs a close second.

Creek Street, Ketchikan.

Dolly's, a museum with a twist on Creek Street. It's said that both the salmon and the fishermen came to Creek Street to spawn. Interestingly, the road leading here from town is called Married Man's Way!

Creek Street is undoubtedly the heart of Ketchikan. It's constructed over boardwalks that run along the banks of Ketchikan Creek, and from late June onwards each year, the waters of the creek are brimming with five different species of wild salmon and trout. The fish return from the open ocean and migrate back to their birthplace to spawn. There are several good viewing spots along the boardwalk on Creek St. By mid-summer, the sheer numbers of fish are amazing and you'll see locals fishing for lunch right from the bridge.

Further along the boardwalk you'll find local art galleries and an eclectic mix of book shops, popular local bars and old bordellos that recall Ketchikan's boisterous past. Dolly's, now maintained as a museum, is the best known of these. It still has its own madam, Rosie, who has plenty of tales to tell.

Like Rosie, Ketchikan today is a town that doesn't take itself too seriously. Neighbors are close and residents light hearted. The favorite local landmark is Deer Mountain, which sits right behind town and acts as the local weather forecaster. Locals will tell you if you can't see the top of Deer Mountain it must be raining, and if you can see the top of Deer Mountain it's going to rain soon. Whatever the weather, Ketchikan is a great introduction to Alaska. The town is easily explored on foot; excellent hiking trails close to town take you into stunning old growth rainforest and the surrounding region offers great wildlife viewing opportunities. So, head out early, have fun, and don't forget your raingear.

Ketchikan - Naturalist's highlights

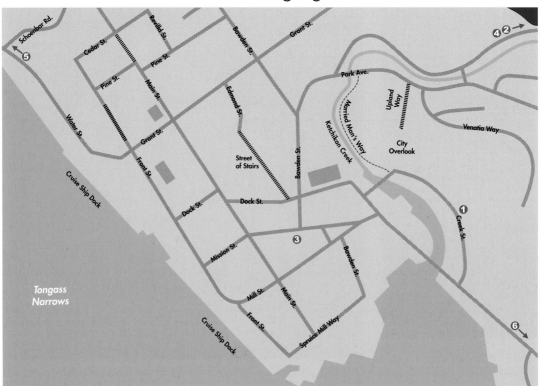

In Ketchikan:

PPI 1. Creek Street: shopping and salmon viewing from late June onwards.

PPI 2. Deer Mountain Hike: stroll through old growth rainforest.

PPI 3. South East Alaska Discovery Center: provides town and trail maps, interpretive displays and a great overview of the region.

PPI 4. Totem Heritage Center: the oldest selection of authentic totem poles gathered from across Southeast Alaska.

Around Ketchikan:

PPI 5. Totem Bight State Park: extensive collection of totem poles set against a backdrop of old growth forest.

PPI 6. Saxman Native Village: a working Tlingit community with totem poles on display and a working carver-in-residence.

PPI 7. Misty Fjords: over two million acres of true wilderness featuring granite cliffs, waterfalls and excellent opportunities to spot wildlife.

PPI *See your Port Guide: Princess Points of Interest for more details.*

In Ketchikan

Like many Southeast Alaskan towns, Ketchikan sits on its own island, Revillagigedo Island. Named after Spanish soldier Revilla Gigedo, who later became the Viceroy of Mexico, the island is the fifth largest in the archipelago, measuring 55 miles long and 33 miles wide. Most of the island comprises a steep, craggy wilderness, and its well deserved nickname is the Rock. The town sits along the edge of the island and spills out over the water in the downtown area. Most of the shoreline streets, including the cruise ship docks, are in fact built over a complex array of trestles and boardwalks.

Allow at least an hour to explore the town on foot, a little more if you like to browse. A good first stop is the **Southeast Alaska Discovery Center**, where you can pick up a walking map of the town. From there, follow the road along the shoreline as it curves to the right and you'll reach the entrance to **Creek Street**. The red bridge crossing the creek is a popular fishing spot with locals; take a moment to look down and you'll see salmon teeming in the water below.

The boardwalk on the south side of the street meanders through the attractions of Creek Street. Follow this route to a second, smaller bridge, another good viewing spot, and then return to the boardwalk and continue along Creek Street. A short quarter mile walk takes you up to a small waterfall, where you can see the salmon taking their first leap up the creek to their spawning grounds. From here, you can either retrace your steps along the boardwalk or take a left turn at the end of the boardwalk and follow the street back into town.

One of many prime spots for salmon viewing along Creek Street.

Returning to town by either route, you can't help but notice the totem poles scattered through town, many of which are accompanied by interpretive signs that briefly detail the story each pole tells. To learn more about the history of totem poles in the region, take a right at the end of the Creek Street boardwalk and follow the signs to the **Totem Heritage Center**. The center is world renowned and houses an extensive collection of original totem poles. The poles were collected from Tlingit and Haida settlements that were abandoned during the challenging days of the late 1930's. Many of the poles date back to the 19th century, and while some have been restored or replicated, other original poles are slowly decaying, giving a real sense of the intended ephemeral nature of these cultural storyboards.

Just over the river and connected by a short footpath, you'll find the **Deer Mountain Tribal Hatchery and Eagle Center**. The center provides tours and fascinating insights into the science behind salmon management in this region. Two rescued eagles are also on display.

Around Ketchikan

The most popular attractions around Ketchikan are the totem pole parks. **Saxman Native Village** lies three miles to the south of town; it's a working Tlingit community, including an artisan carver-in-residence you may see practicing his craft. **Totem Bight State Park** lies 12 miles north of town in a very scenic setting, right on the shoreline with the poles set against the backdrop of the forest. Both parks include reconstructed longhouses and offer fully guided tours. Including one of these destinations on your itinerary will give you a chance to see the rich native culture of the region up close and hear fascinating first-hand accounts of the stories the poles have to tell.

Totem Bight State Park houses an impressive collection of authentically reconstructed totem poles.

Misty Fjords

Often referred to as the "Yosemite of the North," Misty Fjords is a heart-stopping, jaw-dropping region of natural beauty. Covering over two million acres of the Tongass National Forest, the monument's trademark views comprise steep granite cliffs that plunge over 3,000 feet to valley floors where streams and rivers meander through emerald green forests. You can access the area only by air or sea. "Flight-seeing" trips provide spectacular aerial views, boat trips offer a greater opportunity to observe the wildlife in the region and combination fly-in sail-out trips cover the best of both options. Typical wildlife sightings include mountain goats, black and brown bears and an array of birdlife. A network of fjords permeates the region, and all five species of Pacific salmon use its streams and rivers, so marine sightings include seals, sea lions and even killer whales.

Before the National Monument was fully established, the area was slated for mining as vast deposits of molybdenum, a very valuable rare metal, were found in the region. Environmental protection organizations joined forces with local fishermen concerned for the pristine salmon streams in the region, and mining activities were hampered by protests. In 1980 the area was signed into full protection as a designated wilderness region, however the corridor to the mine and the proposed mining region were exempted. Local pressure to ensure full environmental protection continued, and eventually, in 1991, the mining company, Borax, suspended its plans indefinitely. Today Misty Fjords remains an untouched and spectacular highlight along Alaska's Inside Passage, a testament to the power of "a few concerned citizens."

New Eddystone Rock, Misty Fjords

New Eddystone Rock is a distinctive basalt tower that stands at the entrance to Rudyerd Bay, one of the most scenic waterways in the Misty Fjords area. As a prominent landmark, the rock is referenced in many of the early explorations of this region, including those of Captain Vancouver and his crew as they carried out their exhaustive searches through the network of winding fjords in search of the Northwest Passage.

The rock is composed of basalt, and rises over 280 feet above the island surrounding it. On seeing the rock, Captain Vancouver was reminded of the Eddystone lighthouse off Plymouth on England's south coast, so the rock was named New Eddystone Rock.

On one particular morning while Vancouver was exploring this region, a group of natives approached Vancouver's vessel and extended an invitation for breakfast. Vancouver declined, as there had been recent reports of unrest in the region. During their time in the fjords a crew member sketched the area and the painting below, by John Horton, is based on that sketch.

See more of John's work at www.johnhorton.ca

Meeting at the New Eddystone Rock East Behm Canal, Alaska.

Take a hike

Deer Mountain Trailhead

Level: Moderate to Difficult

Elevation: 3,000 feet to summit

Attractions: Old growth forest, incredible views

Tip: Take a taxi to the trailhead

Deer Mountain Trail

Deer Mountain Trail is a well marked trail through old growth rainforest and offers splendid views of the surrounding area. The best way to reach the trailhead is by taxi. This will be $10 well spent, as it's a very steep half mile climb along paved streets to the trailhead otherwise. All the local taxi drivers know the trail and will be happy to come and pick you up again later. If you do choose to hike to the trailhead, the route is well posted from the far end of Creek Street. Once on the trail, allow three to four hours to reach the first lookout and six hours for the summit.

The first few hundred yards of the trail cross through a section of muskeg. As you enter the forest, an interpretive sign provides a map of the trails and updates on any recent wildlife sightings. It's a good idea to take a look at the sign to orient yourself. The trail is easily passable and well-maintained, though frequently muddy. It includes extensive sections of boardwalks, small bridges and wooden staircases. The first overlook is just over a mile from the start of the trail, at 1500 feet; if you have only half a day, this is a good turn-around point.

A second overlook another mile along, at 2500 feet, is a more arduous climb. The summit of Deer Mountain lies half a mile (up!) from the second viewpoint, at an elevation of 3,001 feet. If you make it this far, the view over Tongass Narrows and the surrounding area is incredible. Alternatively, follow the signs just above the second overlook to Blue Lake. The lake is too far to make in a day, but a half mile hike along this (flat!) trail takes you into a beautiful subalpine meadow replete with wildflowers, waterfalls and granite outcrops. Be aware that you will need a full day in port to reach these areas, and always be prepared for changes in the weather.

Deer Mountain trail.

View from the first overlook.

Deer Mountain Trail Map

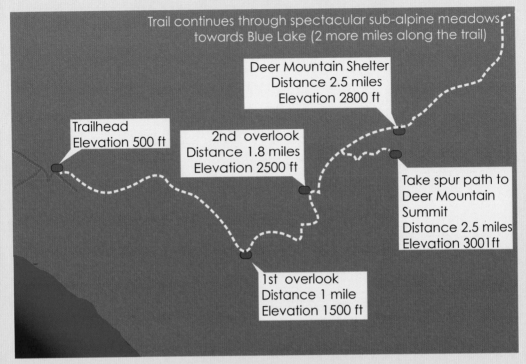

Trail continues through spectacular sub-alpine meadows towards Blue Lake (2 more miles along the trail)

Deer Mountain Shelter
Distance 2.5 miles
Elevation 2800 ft

Trailhead
Elevation 500 ft

2nd overlook
Distance 1.8 miles
Elevation 2500 ft

Take spur path to Deer Mountain Summit
Distance 2.5 miles
Elevation 3001ft

1st overlook
Distance 1 mile
Elevation 1500 ft

To the trailhead:
Time required: 30 minutes on foot,
     less than 10 minutes in a taxi!

Directions:
Follow Front St into town then take Mission St, turning towards town. Follow Mission St and go left on Bawden St, then stay to the right as this becomes Park Ave. Stay on Park Ave through town and this leads via Fair St into Ketchikan Lakes Rd. The next 500 yards is a steep climb through a housing area. When you reach the top of the hill, go through the gravel parking lot to the trailhead. Alternatively, a quick taxi-ride saves both time and energy for the trail. Typical fare is $10; you can grab a cab on Front St and most cab drivers will be happy to come back to the trailhead and pick you up at the end of your hike.

Take a hike through an old growth forest.

Forest Bathing

While mountain air and fresh ocean breezes have long been recognized for their inherent health benefits, newly emerging research suggests that forests should also be added to our list of nature's best cure-alls. Forest-Bathing, or Shinrin-yoku, the practice of retreating to a forest to escape the stresses of urban life, has long been a tradition in Japan. Typically, city residents may spend one weekend a month in a forest retreat to reap the full benefits and now recently published scientific studies are adding some solid support for this evergreen therapy.

The active ingredients are phytoncides, or wood essential oils; naturally occurring anti-microbial compounds that trees produce to fend off fungus. As the oils are volatile, they evaporate into the air of the forest giving the forest its characteristic scent. The health benefits come from inhaling these vapors, working in much the same way as aromatherapy. Benefits range from increased immune response and lower cortisol levels to lower blood pressure and heart rate and even improved sleep regimes. In studies conducted in Japan, participants saw these benefits after just two hours spent walking in a forest on two consecutive days. So, be sure to spend an hour or two exploring Alaska's beautiful evergreen forests; turns out its good for the heart as well as the soul.

For answers to the questions of the universe, take a walk in a forest.

John Muir.

The Tongass National Forest

The Tongass National Forest is often referred to as America's Forest. Designated as a national forest by Teddy Roosevelt in 1907, the forest represents over 75% of the land in Southeast Alaska and includes more than 1,000 islands, 14,000 miles of shoreline and 17 million acres of forest. This makes the Tongass America's largest national forest; it's bigger than each of the nine smallest states and rivals the size of Switzerland. As a national forest, this is public land and officially set aside for recreation, the protection of natural resources and wilderness preservation.

The steep slopes and evergreen forests along any route through Alaska's Inside Passage fall almost entirely within the Tongass National Forest. Along these coastlines and especially in areas of steep terrain, rain is plentiful throughout the year. Fog and mist are also commonplace; as a result, forest fires are rare. These conditions, combined with cool summers and cold winters, provide the perfect environment for one of the rarest ecosystems on the planet, the coastal temperate rainforest. Currently, this unique ecosystem covers less than 1/1000th of the earth's surface.

Forests that have been left to grow undisturbed for over 250 years officially earn the label "old growth forest," and in most parts of the world such forests are long gone. Today, one-third of all the old growth coastal temperate rainforest left on the planet is found within the Tongass National Forest. These old growth forests are incredibly diverse and very special places. They are the linchpins, connecting the fish, the forest and the wildlife, essential to the success of the region's ecosystem.

Trees of the Tongass National Forest

Western hemlocks have soft needles, small cones and a draped appearance. Younger trees may have a single, slightly droopy crown and older trees an open, spiral crown.

Hemlock needles are small and lay flat to the branch.

Sitka spruce are the typical Christmas tree. They have rigid, prickly needles, large cones and a triangle-shaped crown.

Sitka spruce needles are prickly and spiral around the branch.

When a tree falls in the forest...

The defining characteristic of old growth forest is the preservation of the natural mosaic of the forest floor. In old forests fire is rare, but winter storms and the very occasional lightning strike can fell trees, creating a patchwork of small openings within the forest canopy where light can penetrate to the forest floor. Within these small, sunlit glades, plants that need light can gain a foothold, and soon each spot where sunlight seeps through becomes part of a flourishing mat of shrubs and small plants.

Moss, fungi and lichen move in. It may take as long as 50 years for a full carpet of moss to develop, but once established, this mossy layer acts as a huge sponge, absorbing vast amounts of water during rainy periods and supplying it to the forest during dry spells. The forest floor becomes an all-you-can eat buffet as deer, bear and myriad small ground mammals move in to feed on the berries and foliage of the understory. As fallen trees slowly decompose, their rotting trunks become nurseries for young tree saplings and havens for wildlife, offering nesting space for birds and nourishment for insects that then become food themselves. Finally, the tree returns its nutrients to the very soil that nourished it.

Around streams and rivers, fallen trees play another vital role within the forest ecosystem. They create small pools and eddies in otherwise fast flowing waterways, providing perfect egg-laying habitat for salmon. Once the eggs hatch, the young fry and juveniles will stay in these pools, where the fallen branches and trees provide protection from larger predators and reduce the risk of being washed out to sea in spring floods. The fry persist until they are ready for the open ocean. Once they migrate, they'll spend between two and five years at sea. Then, as though returning a favor, they will come back to the very stream where they originally began their lives, bringing vital nutrients back to the forest that nurtured them through their earliest days.

Salmon in the Trees

In her recently published book Salmon in the Trees, author Amy Gullick explores the exquisite relationship between fish and forests. With engaging stories and great photography, Gullick relays a story first uncovered by scientists more than a decade ago. The book is an excellent addition to any vacation reading list. In the meantime, here's the story in a nutshell.

Forests such as the Tongass National Forest remain our key sources for wood and timber products and consequently resource managers continually face the challenge of meeting the demands for timber while ensuring the effective protection and conservation of these national gems. The best strategy, from both a conservation and management perspective, is to replant previously logged areas with young saplings that grow quickly and therefore produce good timber yields, allowing old growth stands to be set aside and preserved. However, successive replanting can quickly deplete the meager resources of the thin soils that characterize many Alaskan pine forests

In south-east Alaska, forest managers had long been aware that young Sitka spruce along the shorelines of streams with healthy salmon runs grew around three times faster than their counterparts around waterways without active salmon runs. With the ever-mounting pressure to increase yield from previously logged areas, forest managers were keen to find out why. Initial testing showed differences in the soil in these regions and on closer inspection, soil scientists found high levels of nitrogen, a key plant food, in the soil along the shorelines of the streams which hosted healthy salmon migrations each year. Following the trail of isotope signatures in the soil also revealed the source of the extra nitrogen; it was marine derived nitrogen and it was being brought into the forest by the salmon in the streams.

Essentially, young salmon spend their first winter or two nestled within the pools and eddies of the forest streams, before heading out to the open ocean. They feed in the marine system for 2 to 5 years and then begin their epic migration back to the exact location where they originally hatched out. A lucky few may get to spawn, but with the exception of king salmon, this will be their final journey, ending in demise. Vast numbers of returning salmon will be caught in commercial fisheries that target the salmon schooling within fjords and at the mouths of favored streams and rivers. These schools also attract natural predators; eagles, orca, sea lions and even basking shark make the most of this easy prey. Those salmon that make it to the freshwater system, then run the gauntlet through more fishermen, black and brown bears and yet more eagles. They forge their way through currents and leap up waterfalls using the very last of their energy stores to reach the site where they hatched out, and there they lay their eggs. King salmon may then return to the ocean, but all other salmon die after spawning.

As the dead and dying salmon break down, they suffuse the system with marine nitrogen. The nitrogen permeates into the soils surrounding the streams. It's transported through the mossy sponges that cover the forest floor and from there, its absorbed by the trees, shrubs and plants of the forest. So the salmon become a part of the forest, and in closing this entire cycle, the healthy forest then nurtures the developing eggs left by the salmon and protects their young fry once they hatch.

Still, for scientists, a mystery remained. The reach of marine nitrogen into the forest went far beyond the banks of the streams and peaked in unusual, erratic spots in the mossy banks. Close observation soon revealed the cause of these peaks; the bears. When salmon were caught by bears, some bears would eat their salmon right there in the stream, but most bears, and especially black bears, naturally seek cover and head back into the forest with their catch. On average, a typical black bear may transport as many as 40 fish a day into the forest. By late season, fat and fussy bears frequently feed only on the energy-rich eggs of the salmon, so the rest of the salmon gets left to decompose within the forest, where it releases its crucial package of nitrogen into the soil. Even the fish that the bear eats eventually return to the forest as readily available nutrients, as bears do what they are known to do in the woods. As the forest understory flourishes, deer stroll in and a myriad of birds feed on seeds and insects. And so marine nitrogen, donated by the ever-generous salmon, seeps like life-blood through the flourishing forest

Meanwhile, healthy, thriving forest along the shoreline of salmon streams keeps the waters cool, clean and clear. Trees provide shade and fallen branches provide pools that are perfect for the next generation of salmon that will migrate to open ocean, and then return to fill the nets of region's local fishermen, feed the region's wildlife and ultimately nourish the surrounding evergreen forest.

Some of Ketchikan's 200-strong commercial fishing fleet at the dock in Ketchikan, with Deer Mountain in the background. The fertile fishing grounds around Ketchikan and flourishing old growth forests of the region are intimately linked.

Field Guide to Alaska's Salmon

Five species of Pacific salmon may be found in Alaskan waters and all are anadromous, which means they move between saltwater and fresh water environments. The oceans provide bountiful food resources and the cool, clear, healthy freshwater systems of Alaska ensure breeding success. Chinook, sockeye and chum spend 2-5 years at sea, pink and coho return within 1-2 years. They return to the exact site where they hatched out and most will spawn within 10-20 feet of their original hatching site. After spawning, only chinooks return to the ocean, all other species die. Steelhead, Dolly Varden and cut-throat trout (not shown here) are closely related. They follow a similar life-cycle and may also be found in Alaska's streams and rivers.

Chinook (king) salmon

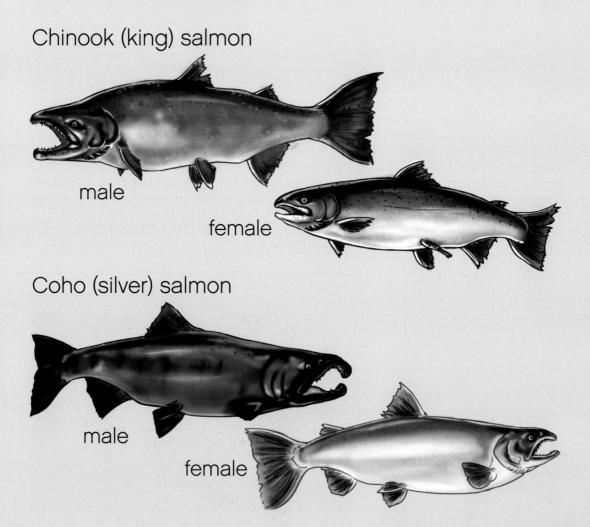

male

female

Coho (silver) salmon

male

female

Sockeye (red) salmon

male

female

Pink salmon

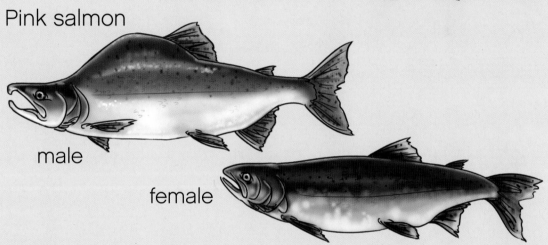

male

female

Chum (dog) salmon

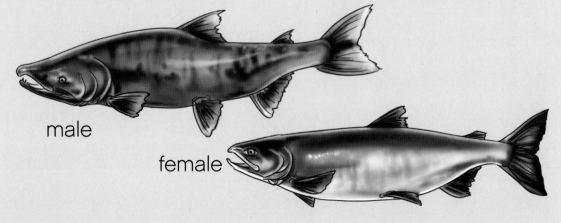

male

female

Wildlife Profile: The Black Bear

Fast Facts:

Common name: Black bear

Scientific name: *Ursus americanus*

Best areas for sightings: Bear-watching trips from Ketchikan, Mendenhall Glacier, Haines (near Skagway), the shoreline and alpine meadows of College Fjord.

ID: Color varies from cinnamon blond to black, claws short and curved, snout straight along the top edge and a small hump between shoulder blades.

Size: Males stand 30 inches to the shoulder, up to 5 ft in length from snout to tail; typical adult weight 180-200 pounds and males larger than females.

Lifespan: Up to 25 years for both genders.

Mating and reproduction: Usually takes place in June and July; females breed every two to three years; typical litter size two to three cubs, born during hibernation and weighing about one pound each. Cubs emerge from hibernation at about three to four months weighing five pounds.

Typical group size: Cubs accompany their mother for one to two years. Otherwise, adults entirely solitary apart from mating activities.

Diet: Varies through the season. Includes roots, tubers, salmon and berries.

Recommended websites: http://www.bear.org; check out the live webcam links.

Wildlife in Focus: The Black Bear

Black bears are the bears of the forest. From an evolutionary standpoint, bears have the same ancestors as wolves and large cats, but over the course of millennia they've lost many typically carnivore traits. Watch them attempting to catch salmon and you'll quickly see that this is true. In fact, for bears in Southeast Alaska, fish and other animal protein makes up about 20% of their diet and they augment this with plant bulbs and berries rather than by catching and killing animal prey.

A closer look at black bears further reveals their connection with the forest. Black bears have short, curved claws suited for climbing trees and grasping branches. Their smaller size makes them agile enough to escape into the nearest tree rather than take on would-be opponents. Black bears also typically hibernate within the forest, bedding down in a moss-covered gully or rocky overhang for the cold winter months.

To distinguish black bears from brown bears, look for the following traits: black bears have short claws, a straight snout and are smaller in size than brown bears, but even veteran hunters can mistake a large black for a small brown bear. Color is variable, especially in black bears. In Southeast Alaska, cinnamon colored black bears are quite common. Other rare but well-known groups of bears, such as the creamy-white Kermode or "spirit bear" of the coastal forests of British Columbia and the bluish-gray glacier bear of Yakutat Bay, are in fact black bears with different colored coats.

Sightings of black bears have been recorded in forty-nine states, excluding only Hawaii. At last count, the black bear population across Southeast Alaska was estimated at 17,000. Black bears tend be more adaptable and more tolerant of human presence than brown bears, though this can be a double-edged sword. While black bears are not as easily displaced as brown bears, they are more likely to be tagged as nuisance bears. Towards the end of the feeding season, as bears prepare for hibernation, black bears are frequently sighted in downtown Juneau and Sitka. These semi-urban bears can be hazardous; like any wild animal, they will become aggressive and potentially very dangerous when cornered or hungry, and females will fiercely defend their cubs.

Remember – bears are wild animals. Never approach a bear in the wild, don't ever attempt to feed a bear and always be "bear aware" while hiking.

Bear bins such as these are used throughout Southeast Alaska. The bins have a hidden handle on the underside of the lid, which so far has kept the bears out. However in downtown locations, there have been quite a few misplaced postcards!

The Biogeography of Bears in Southeast Alaska

While it is sometimes a challenge to tell large black bears and small brown bears apart, apparently this is not the case for the bears themselves. In the few mainland sites where brown and black bears mix, brown bears quickly chase black bears out of premium fishing spots and away from prime berry bushes. In Southeast Alaska, the only places where black and brown bears do meet are sites along the coast of the mainland. The islands of the Inside Passage are all home to either black or brown bears, but not both. Admiralty, Baranof and Chichagof Islands are home to brown bears, while Kuiu, Kupreanof and Prince of Wales Islands are home to black bears.

Scientists have yet to fully understand why this is. Certainly there is a difference in home range, with brown bears exploiting more open habitat while black bears remain principally in wooded areas. Of the two, black bears are far more adaptable and tolerant of human activity, while development tends to easily displace brown bears. Notwithstanding, both of these species are flourishing in Alaska. Admiralty Island has the world's densest population of brown bears, at one to each square mile, and neighboring Kuiu Island has the world's densest black bear population, with four for each square mile. Generally, the healthy salmon runs on these islands support the high numbers, and as you cruise through these areas you will likely spot bears along the islands' beaches.

A black bear browses along the tide-line.

Tall Tales from the North

Perhaps it's the long, dark nights of winter, perhaps the many hours Alaskans spend around summer campfires. Whatever the reason, Alaskans are inveterate storytellers. While most if not all of their stories carry at least a grain of truth, many have become modern folk tales, told, retold and embellished along the way. Here's one such tale, along with its own kernel of truth.

Nimrod's Teeth

Nimrod was a woodsman living far off the beaten track deep in the Alaskan bush. His poor diet each winter and lack of oral hygiene had led to the loss of all his teeth. No longer able to eat meat, Nimrod was staring starvation in the face. So he took his gun and headed for the forest. There he spotted a young bear in the fullness of health. The woodsman took aim and shot the bear, being careful not to hit its handsome head. Along with securing the meat from the bear, the woodsman took out all its teeth. Back at camp, he fashioned them into a new set of dentures and enjoyed his first solid meal in weeks, tucking into the delicious bear steak, which he chewed with his new bear teeth....

Certainly this sounds like a tall tale. Author Ernie Pyle, the predecessor of Charles Kuralt (of Travels with Charlie), was sent to Alaska by the Washington Daily News in 1935 to find tales and stories from the Last Frontier. Ernie heard the tale of Nimrod and set out to find the truth.

Ernie actually located Nimrod, who was alive and well and living in his cabin just outside Eagle, a small town on the Canadian side of the Alaska-Yukon border. Nimrod's real name was Ervin Robertson and he was originally from New England. A jeweler by trade, he had come to Alaska in 1898 in search of gold. During the winter of 1905, while he was working a small gold claim, wolves got into his camp and ate all his supplies, leaving him only with canned food for the winter. Nimrod got scurvy and over the course of the winter lost all his teeth.

Far removed from any dentist, the skilled craftsman decided to fashion himself new teeth. He built a plate of aluminum and drilled out holes for the teeth. He used mountain goat teeth for the front of his dental device, added four caribou teeth on each side and used bear teeth for the molars, one on each side. He wore the teeth for twenty five years before selling them to a visiting dentist from Seattle, who in return sent him a more conventional set of dentures.

Nimrod ate a lot of meat from a lot of bears, but you'll be pleased to hear, he didn't eat the bear that donated its teeth.

For more stories from Ernie Pyle's Alaska, add The Reader's Companion to Alaska, edited by Alan Ryan, to your vacation reading list.

Wildlife Profile: The Bald Eagle

Fast Facts:

Common name: Bald eagle

Scientific name: *Haliaeetus leucocephalus*

Best areas for sightings: Along shorelines throughout Southeast Alaska, especially in regions with good salmon runs.

ID: White head, golden beak and talons, dark brown body; immature eagles lack golden beaks and talons and plumage is dappled brown and white.

Size: Wing span ranges up to seven feet, weight up to 14 pounds; females larger than males.

Lifespan: Up to 30 years in the wild, much longer in captivity.

Mating and reproduction: Pairs typically mate for life; cooperatively raise one or two offspring per year.

Typical group size: Pairs commonly seen. Large congregations typically associated with rich food resources.

Diet: Principally fish feeders—salmon, herring, flounder and pollock.

Recommended websites: For background information and details of the Annual Eagle Festival in Haines, Alaska, visit www.baldeagles.org.

Wildlife in Focus: The Bald Eagle

America's iconic symbol, the bald eagle, is an integral part of the Alaskan landscape. While these birds are facing tough times in many of the lower 48 U.S. states, here in Southeast Alaska they continue to thrive. In times gone by, fishermen mistakenly surmised that eagles were taking their salmon, and the birds were so plentiful that the state placed a bounty on them, awarding up to two dollars for each pair of talons it received. The bounty was finally removed in 1953, and when Alaska became a state in 1959, the bald eagle was fully protected under the Bald Eagle Protection Act of 1940.

In actual fact, eagles rarely take live salmon. They are predominantly fish feeders, but prefer to steal their prey from other birds or feed on dead salmon. They only take to the air to catch their own food as a last resort. This reluctance to fish is related to the energy costs entailed. The eagle's wingspan measures up to 7 feet, and even though the bones are hollow, a full size adult can weigh as much as 12 pounds, so it takes a lot of energy to get—and stay—airborne. Adult eagles spend 98% of their time perched, but once they do take flight, they are well equipped hunters.

If you see an eagle flying at height, watch for a few moments and you'll see that these birds are master gliders. They are also known for their heart stopping aerial acrobatics. As part of their courtship ritual, a mating pair will clasp talons mid-flight and spiral down through the air. In a real live game of chicken, they split apart just before impact. This seems to be a precursor to mating, as pairs disappear into the woods following these breathtaking displays.

Once the deal is sealed, many eagles stay paired for life. But others trade partners if mating doesn't go well; one known female in Haines is on her fourth partner. Pairs may separate for the winter and then reunite each spring at favored nesting sites. Typically, the pair will nest within 200 meters of the shoreline, preferably in an old growth tree that has stood 400 years or more. The initial nest is constructed quickly, it may reach five feet across and two feet in depth and the expectant parents carefully add a lining of feathers and small twigs to the inside of the nest.

The eagle's primary sense is its vision. An eagle's eyes take up most of the space in its head, and its vision is about eight times better than ours. Depending on the size of their prey, eagles may spot a food source as far away as two miles. Typically, they perch above favored feeding sites, then drop like a rock to grab their prey. The talons are designed for grasping and lock in place once the prey has been seized. The prey can only be released once the eagle alights, which explains why sometimes you'll see eagles with very large prey in tow. There are reports of eagles drowning from the weight of their prey and other stories of eagles swimming to shore if the salmon they choose are too large to fly with.

Alaskan Eagles in the Golden State

While bald eagles have been recorded in every U.S. state except Hawaii, they haven't fared well in many of those places. In California, bald eagles in coastal regions were entirely wiped out when DDT that had entered the marine food chain through illegal dumping magnified up the food chain and led to a thinning of the eagles' eggshells. Fledging success was effectively reduced to zero; by the mid 90's the coastal bald eagle population of California's Channel Islands was gone and golden eagles had moved into their niche.

Over the last seven years, however, a huge effort to re-instate bald eagles in California has been undertaken. A limited number of juveniles were gathered from nests around Juneau and translocated to California. On site in California, the Alaskan eagles mingled with captive bred animals with the hope that their wild behavior would transfer to their urban cousins.

The program has been widely successful, and bald eagles are now re-established throughout California's Channel Islands, from Catalina to Santa Cruz. The new nests are monitored very carefully and you can watch them for yourself through live webcam feeds. Check out the live feeds at: http://www.iws.org/2011design/interactive__nestchat.html.

If the site works out, the eagle pair will return to the same nest each year, simply refurbishing it before mating. The female lays three to four cream-colored eggs and the male and female share incubation duties. Incubation lasts about a month. When the chicks hatch, they are small, helpless and blind. Offspring grow quickly, however. The firstborn hatchling will soon gain a size advantage, and what follows can only be described as one of the most dramatic examples of sibling rivalry in nature. As other chicks hatch, the firstborn will steal their food and attack them when the adults aren't looking. It's not unusual for late-born chicks to be thrown out of the nest by feisty siblings. Generally, two chicks in each nest will survive to fledging. (Overall survival to fledging is low, around 30%.) The youngsters grow quickly, and with flight feathers longer than those of adult birds, by the end of the season can actually seem larger than their parents. Their dappled brown and white coloring, a pattern that persists until age five, sets them apart from adult eagles.

Juvenile bald eagles quickly grow to adult size but remain dappled until around age 5.

Culture In Focus: The Tlingit, First Nation of the Inside Passage

Stretching south to Cape Fox and north as far as Yakutat Bay, Alaska's Inside Passage is the homeland of the Tlingit. Their history in the region spans further than most modern groups and can be traced as far back as 10-12,000 B.C.

As the last ice age came to an end, polar ice caps were still extensive and sea levels were lower than today. Consequently, land passage from Siberia to Alaska was possible, and it is generally believed that the first people on the North American continent arrived from Siberia via this route. Roughly 20% more coastline was exposed at this time and beaches were broad and wide, so Alaska's first inhabitants were able to move easily down the coast into what is now Southeast Alaska.

These early residents of the region are generally recognized as one of the first societies to transition from a nomadic to a settled, resident lifestyle. The abundance of food, from salmon in the streams to berries in the forests, meant that people could stay in the area year round and live off the land without the need for agriculture. As a result, a rich, vibrant society characterized by a sophisticated political structure emerged.

Then, as now, long, dark winter nights were part of the Alaskan climate, and this climate molded a unique lifestyle. Summertime was spent fishing, hunting and gathering berries and fruits from the forests. Food was set aside for winter, when the clans would gather in community homes. There, through the dark nights, stories were told, innovative, intricately designed tools and works of art were crafted and a rich culture thrived.

And still today, Alaskans follow the same schedule as the earliest Tlingit settlers. Through the summer months they are extremely active and energetic, up with the early dawn and often out till dusk, busy making a living during the short summer season. Then, during the long winter, they are ready to retire to the peace and solitude of their homes. Families draw close, stories are told, and much of the beautiful artwork you'll see in Alaska is produced. Also, you'll notice that most babies born here arrive in late summer...

A replica clan house and totem poles at Saxman Native Village—one of several places around Ketchikan where you can explore the native culture of the region firsthand.

Tuxekan Native Village, Alaska. Source: Alaska State Library, Case & Draper Photograph Collection, Identifier: P39-0686.

Tlingit Society

Tlingit society was and remains structured and complex. Essentially, each community is divided into two groups, or moieties, the Eagles and the Ravens. These two principal groups are further divided into clans identified by animal monikers, such as the wolf, the bear, the whale and the salmon. Traditional custom required that marriages were of mixed moieties, i.e., between Eagles and Ravens. Descent is matrilineal, so children take the moiety and the clan of the mother. Each clan also has specific traditions and stories, and these were also matrilineal. The totem poles next to each house, like those in the picture above, often identify the lineage of the occupants.

Ties within families were further cemented when children reached puberty, and their care would be handed over to the uncle on the mother's side, so that the traditions of the clan could be taught and perpetuated. Handing over the care of teenagers to close family members was also seen as a way to ensure that parents didn't spoil or over-indulge their children. It also played a fundamental role in maintaining social connections within the clans.

In modern Tlingit society today, many of these traditions persist. The rules of marriage have been relaxed, but asking questions about a potential partner's moiety is still likely in early dating. And while children now stay with their own parents to adulthood, uncles and aunts remain closely connected to the family.

11 woven baskets and a water bottle circa 1894. Source: Alaska State Library, Lantern Slides of Alaska Photograph Collection, Identifier: P208-146.

Tlingit Crafts

Tlingit craftwork is both beautiful and functional. Baskets such as those in the photo were originally constructed from spruce roots, grasses and twisted cedar bark. They were watertight and used for carrying and storing water. They were also used in cooking; heated rocks were dropped into water held in the baskets until the water boiled and the food was cooked. The best baskets were made from split spruce roots, and five different twining methods were used. Local grasses and stalks of fern were dyed and woven into the baskets to add color and function. These artistic embellishments became more common after contact with Europeans, who sought baskets in trading negotiations.

Native woman and child sit on a fur rug, the woman working on a basket, circa 1906. Source: Alaska State Library, Case & Draper Photograph Collection, Identifier: P39-0062.

The Potlatch

Potlatches remain a fundamental and distinctive feature of Tlingit society. The potlatch originally worked as a mechanism to ensure that the wealth and prosperity of a particular clan or house was fairly and equally distributed across all the groups' members. Typically a clan chief, leader or affluent neighbor would host the potlatch. The celebration would last for days and would include dancing, festivities and the best food and drinks. Awards would be given to the guest who ate the most, and all attendees would be showered with gifts, thereby redistributing the wealth across the group.

In giving away all his worldly goods, the generous host traded material wealth for social standing. Especially affluent hosts would even destroy their own property at these events. The potlatch tradition was based on the principle of reciprocity, and etiquette required that those attending the potlatch and receiving gifts would host their own event within two years.

Potlatch Etiquette

The most lavish potlatches were recorded on totem poles—as were potlatch faux pas. One totem pole you can find in Saxman Native Village in Ketchikan tells the story of the visit of then Secretary of State William H. Seward to the region in the late 1800's. The local community held a large potlatch in the visiting statesman's honor and showered him with gifts. Unfortunately, the statesman had not been briefed on this tradition. He came empty handed, and he never hosted a potlatch in return. As a result, the pole recording the potlatch is topped with a carving of the Secretary of State wearing his gifted potlatch hat, but the rest of the pole, which would normally show all the gifts he offered in return, is bare.

The Centennial Potlatch

The three chiefs in the picture opposite held one of the largest potlatches on record, in Sitka in 1904. The Tlingit at the time were being encouraged to abandon their heritage and adopt western culture, so the event was billed as the last great potlatch and funded by then-governor of Alaska at the time, John Brady. Tlingit from across the region attended and the potlatch lasted for a month. But far from marking the end of the potlatch culture, the meeting of so many Tlingit clans from across the region served to reinforce their beliefs and culture. The Tlinglit people left the potlatch with a renewed sense of identity and commitment to their cultural practices, including the potlatch. The tradition survived, and thrives today. Potlatches continue to be held regularly, typically to celebrate births, marriages and graduations or to commemorate the passing of a family member.

Chiefs of the Kaagwaantaan (Wolf) clan who gave the Sitka Potlatch 1904.
Source: Alaska State Library, Warren Merrill Photograph Collection, Identifier: P57-022

Field Guide to totem poles

There is no more iconic image of the Tlingit culture than the totem pole. Far from having religious significance, the poles tell family and cultural stories and pass on information. They are carved from western red cedar and were traditionally colored using salmon eggs, red pumice pebbles and charcoal to provide a distinctive blue-green, red and black color palette. Today, the craft of carving totem poles is evolving as young artisans take up their tools, telling new stories and using bright, modern colors.

Still, many totem poles retain a very natural look, and once constructed and installed are purposely left untouched to age naturally and blend back into the forest from whence they came.

Types of Poles

House front poles display the lineage of the home owner, typically describing the matrilineal clan.

House posts located inside the house tell the story of the family crest.

Heraldic poles tell stories; myths and legends are especially important in the Tlingit culture and are even considered to be the property of specific clans.

Mortuary poles are commemorative. They celebrate the life of a loved one who has passed on, and many include a specially carved compartment where the ashes of the departed are kept.

Ridicule poles are constructed to record a moment of shame or ridicule. The blunder or social mistake is recorded for all to see as story on the pole. The most famous of these, recording the famous potlatch faux pas of Secretary of State Seward is at Saxman Native Village.

Story pole telling the tale of Raven entering human form, Totem Bight State Park.

Lincoln pole, Saxman Native Village.

Eagle Insignia, Totem Heritage Museum.

Memorial pole, Saxman Native Village.

Clan house, Totem Bight State Park.

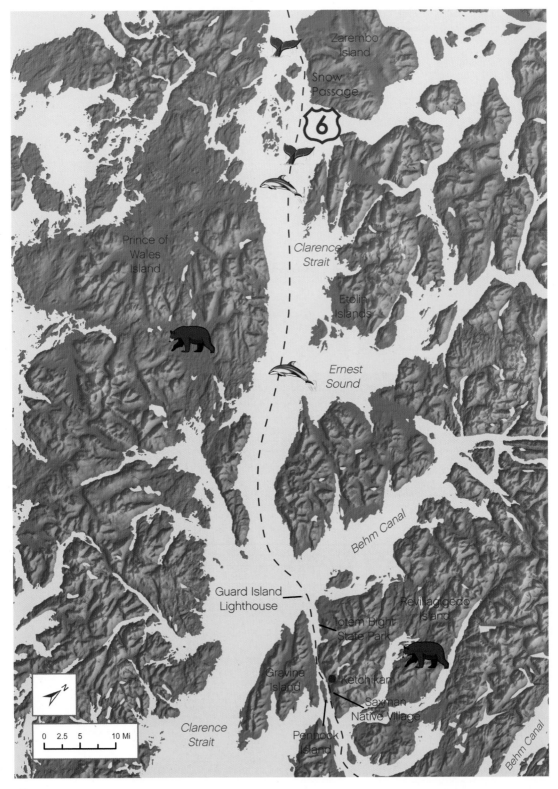

Zarembo Island

Snow Passage

6

Prince of Wales Island

Clarence Strait

Etolin Islands

Ernest Sound

Behm Canal

Guard Island Lighthouse

Revillagigedo Island

Totem Bight State Park

Gravina Island

Ketchikan

Saxman Native Village

Clarence Strait

Pennock Island

Behm Canal

N

0   2.5   5   10 Mi

Cruising highlights

Ketchikan Sailaway (Northbound)
Nice views of town to starboard and Gravina Island lies to port. Watch for the eagles' nests along either shoreline. Totem Bight State Park is visible to starboard roughly 30 minutes after departure.

Waypoint 6: Snow Passage
Your ship will approach Snow Passage approximately four hours after departure from Ketchikan. Very good chance of spotting humpback whales in this area.

Ketchikan Sailaway (Southbound)
Nice views of Deer Mountain at sailaway. Saxman Native Village comes into view about 15 minutes after departure on the port side of the ship.

From here the ship sails south through the picturesque scenery of the Revillagigedo Channel and passes by the entrance to Misty Fjords National Monument.

Float planes at the dock in Ketchikan.

Ketchikan sailaway

Whether north- or southbound, most ships sail from Ketchikan during the afternoon or early evening, so it's an ideal time to enjoy the sailaway. Leaving the dock and heading out into the waters of the Tongass Narrows is equivalent to pulling out onto a major interstate anywhere in the Lower 48. The principal channels of the Inside Passage are in fact marine highways, and as you'll see if you're on deck, the Tongass Narrows is one of the busiest. The Alaska State Marine ferries, locally known as the Blue Canoes, are the buses of this system, providing public transport along these marine highways. They run year round and in pretty much any weather, and for many small towns of the region, they are their main connection to the outside world, transporting everything from fuel to family members between these isolated communities.

The Tongass Narrows is also a runway. Alongside the ferries, private boats and cruise ships, you'll also see numerous floatplanes coming and going. The town also has a land-based international airport, but because land on the main island of Ketchikan is in short supply, the airport is located on the opposite side of the narrows from the city, making this the only airport in the country where air passengers arrive by ferry boat. You can see the airport from the port side of the ship if you're sailing north. The infamous "Bridge to Nowhere" that was a talking point for pundits on both sides in the 2008 presidential election was to have spanned this channel and replaced the ferry. In the midst of the ensuing controversy the $223 million project was cancelled, so if you ever fly out of Ketchikan you'll still have to take a ferry to get to your flight.

Whichever direction you're sailing, the main wildlife attraction in this area are the eagles. Look on the opposite side of the channel to the main town along the shorelines of the adjacent islands; that's Gravina Island to the north and Pennock Island to the south. You'll see what look like golf balls high in the trees along the shoreline. Take a look with your binoculars and you'll see that those "golf balls" are actually bald eagles. In prime habitat such as this, there will typically be an eagles' nest for every mile of shoreline, and several are quite easy to spot from the ship.

If you didn't get to see the totem pole parks in port, you'll get a chance to see the poles from the water. Totem Bight State Park comes into view about 30 minutes to the north of town and Saxman Native Village is easy to spot if you are headed south. Both parks have interesting stories behind their names. Totem Bight, constructed by the Civilian Conservation Corps (CCC), was first named Mud Bight; once the area was opened for tourism, the city decided to change the name to something more inherently appealing. Saxman Native Village was named for local Presbyterian minister and schoolteacher Samuel Saxman, who drowned while searching for a new home-site for the displaced Tlingit of the town of Fort Tongass. When the new site was chosen, it was named in Saxman's honor.

Whichever direction you're headed, the surrounding scenery of this region is charming, marked by small rocky outcrops, the rounded profiles of low lying islands and protected waterways. Be sure to spend some time on the outside decks in this scenic region, and as always, don't forget the binoculars.

Look for the eagles nest just to the left of the green channel marker.

A pod of humpback whales cruises the waters of Alaska's Inside Passage.

Waypoint 6: Snow Passage (Northbound Cruisers)

If you're headed north from Ketchikan, at the end of the Tongass Narrows you'll pass Guard Island and continue into Clarence Strait. Open areas like this are favored by the region's resident dolphins and porpoise. The larger groups leaping above the water with a pretty, swirling coloration are Pacific white sided dolphin, while the symmetrically colored, fast moving dolphins that leave a rooster tail splash as they dive are Dall's porpoise. See the Field Guide for Marine Mammals on page 124 for further tips on identifying marine mammals in the wild.

Between four and five hours after leaving Ketchikan, you'll head for a narrow passage known as Snow Passage. Currents can be very swift through here, especially at low and high tides. These currents bring nutrients into surface waters, firing up the regional food chain and making the area a favored spot for humpback whales. You may see whales from either side of the ship, and your ship's naturalist, along with the bridge crew, will also be keeping a good lookout for you. Your best bet is to choose a spot where you can easily move from one side of the ship to the other. You'll need your binoculars, and of course your camera, to record your first sightings of whales in the wild.

The whales you'll see here are humpback whales, the gentle giants of Alaska's Inside Passage. Up to 45 or 50 feet in length, they weigh upwards of a ton per foot yet subsist on phytoplankton and small schooling fish. They are the fifth largest of the baleen whales, they're the most surface active, easily the most charismatic and certainly an exciting whale to watch.

Seeing a whale in the wild is one of the true treasures of visiting Alaska. John Muir described these great whales as "the heartbeat of the ocean." Watch for a high-standing blow as the whale exhales. Generally, humpback whales exhale several times in a row. Wait a few seconds after the first blows and you'll see the whale's small dorsal fin. Then the whale will arch and finally throw its 15-foot-wide fluke high in the air. As it dives, you'll have a chance to get that memorable shot of a whale's tail in the wide open wilderness of Alaska.

Once through Snow Passage, look for two small islands off the port side. These are known as Bushy and Shrubby Islands. If you have your binoculars handy, you'll see large harbor seal colonies on the shorelines of these islets. Steller sea lions are quite common in this area too. Typically they congregate around the buoys and channel markers, but you may see some in the open water as well. Diving birds such as surf scoters and white scoters, otherwise known as the poor man's puffin, are also common, along with large flocks of smaller migratory birds such as plovers and Pacific loons are known to nest throughout the region. You can often hear their calls on a still night's cruise through this area.

From here, your ship will pass through Sumner Strait, another open body of water. If you're watching for the sunset, be aware: Sumner Strait takes the ship in a westerly direction but heads south for a while, placing the setting sun on the starboard side of the vessel.

Field Guide to Alaska's marine mammals

Ranging in size from the gentle, but giant leviathan the humpback whale, down to the feisty but diminutive sea otter, Alaska's marine mammals are as exciting as they are diverse. Interestingly, each feeds on a slightly different food source, reducing direct competition and leading to this rich community of marine mammals. There are multiple places to see marine mammals along Alaska's Inside Passage. These are all highlighted in the map that accompanies this book.

Humpback whale

Gray whale

Minke whale

Resident killer whale;
male and female

Dall's porpoise

Pacific white-sided dolphin

Harbor Seal

Steller sea lion;
male and female

Sea Otter

Bushy and Shrubby Islands, Clarence Strait.

Waypoint 7: Cape Decision

For the ship's navigators, Cape Decision is always a key point along the cruise route. At this point the ship heads into Chatham Strait on its way to Juneau. If you're sailing from Ketchikan, you'll notice that the setting sun is now back on the port side of the ship, confirming that you're heading north. If you're sailing from Seattle and Juneau is your first port of call, you'll pass by Waypoint S6, on the outer coastline of the Inside Passage overnight, and Waypoint 7 marks your re-entry back into the protected waters of the Inside Passage, so it's smooth sailing ahead.

Cape Decision was named by Captain Cook at the end of his explorations of the region in the summer of 1793. At this point in his cruise, Captain Cook officially abandoned his search for the Northwest Passage and set his sails for warmer waters. As the exact date was September 20 and the weather was turning cold, the decision was probably a popular one.

Cape Decision marks the entry point into Chatham Strait, the most open and navigable of the waterways that comprise the Inside Passage in this area. Chatham Strait runs between two of the largest islands of the region, Baranof Island to the west and Admiralty Island to the east. The Lynn Canal, which leads to Skagway, is roughly a straight shot to the north, but most ships will bear right and pass from Chatham Strait into Frederick Sound to head for Juneau.

Waypoint 8: Frederick Sound

Frederick Sound was named by Captain Vancouver in honor of Prince Frederick, the Duke of York and Albany at the time. Ships headed north to Juneau from Ketchikan may cruise through Frederick Sound overnight. If you're sailing from Seattle or if you're on the southbound cruise, however, you'll likely pass through here during daylight hours—a treat for sure, as this again is prime humpback whale territory. Any time you're on deck, make sure to keep your binoculars handy.

Overall, the population of humpbacks across Alaska's Inside Passage is estimated to be around 1500. For humpback whales in Alaska, this is feeding time, and as they only feed for around six months each year, it really is all about the food. They may feed on small fish such as herring or pollock or on small shrimplike crustaceans known as krill. Frederick Sound is favored by krill feeders, and their presence in the region is in sync with the blooming of the krill. The same whales return here each year to feed, often forming groups to feed more effectively. The most recent research indicates that they even fish sustainably, taking only mature krill that have had the chance to breed.

Heading north through Frederick Sound, you'll see a small group of islands on the port side of the ship. A favored haul-out used by one of the largest groups of Steller sea lions lies in these islands, and if your ship passes close enough you will hear them. From the starboard side of the ship you'll see Five Fingers Lighthouse, a well known landmark in the region and a favorite with local artists, as the backdrop could not be more Alaskan.

A humpback whale dives in the waters of Frederick Sound. For more on the natural history of humpback whales, see the Wildlife in Focus section on page 158.

Waypoint 9: The Entrance to Tracy Arm

Towards the northern end of Frederick Sound, lies the almost hidden entrance to Tracy Arm, a beautifully scenic fjord. In fact, two adjacent fjords, Endicott Arm and Tracy Arm lead off Holkham Bay, which is on the eastern shoreline of the Sound.

Known as "little Yosemite", Tracy Arm is renowned for its tall, granite cliffs and tumbling waterfalls. It stretches some 21 miles back to terminate at the South Sawyer Glacier. This steep glacier produces large, deep-blue icebergs that often float out into the Sound. If you're cruising through here in daylight, look out for these trademark bergs of Tracy Arm.

Wildlife abounds in the region too. Bears are frequently seen along the shoreline, mountain goats scale the rocky peaks and the icy bergs in front of the glaciers are a favorite haul-out for harbor seals. Several Princess Cruise Itineraries include a detour here to cruise the waters of Tracy Arm. A special section covers this cruise, in Chapter 6. Otherwise, you can also see the area on day trips from Juneau.

Heading for Juneau

Continuing north across Frederick Sound, the island to port is Admiralty Island, fortress of the bear. As mentioned earlier, Admiralty Island hosts the world's densest population of brown bears. Many of the boat-based wildlife tours from Juneau will cruise along portions of the shoreline of Admiralty Island, as there is always a good chance of spotting a brownie cruising the beach. From here, the route to Juneau takes you through Stephen's Passage, the Gastineau Channel and on to Juneau, Alaska's state capital.

A peaceful start to a day exploring Tracy Arm.

Chapter 4

Juneau, Alaska's State Capital

View from Mount Roberts.

Juneau

From the moment you arrive in Juneau, you know without a doubt you're in the heart of Southeast Alaska. Looking out from the ship, you'll see that you're surrounded by snow capped mountains that rise above soaring, pine-covered slopes. On a sunny day, you can see clear to the skyline in all directions. During the early hours of a rainy day, ribbons of ethereal mist cloak the mountain-sides, then slowly rise to reveal the stunning scenery as the day progresses. To the east lie the Coast Mountains, to the north and west the Chilkat Mountain Range and to the south the mountains of Admiralty Island may be in view. Gulls and bald eagles dot the shoreline, salmon leap in the waters of Gastineau Channel alongside the ship, and seals, sea lions, even the occasional whale cruise the shorelines. Truly, you're surrounded by Alaska.

Although it's hard to tell, Juneau sits on the shoreline of the mainland. The border with Canada is nearby but despite the proximity, there is no road connection and this state capital, like so many towns in Southeast Alaska, is accessible only by air or by sea. The streets of downtown Juneau where the ships dock are broad and wide, but look down and you'll see that much of the shorefront real estate sits over the water. As you continue into town the streets become narrow and winding, and eventually give way to a complex maze of stairways that hug the mountainside. These are the streets of old Juneau. Originally designed for horses rather than buses and cars, the city has grown organically from its early roots, and today you'll find state government buildings, museums and native corporations in the midst of residential neighborhoods.

As Alaska's third largest city and its state capital, Juneau is a working city. While Ketchikan, to the south, thrives on its wealth of salmon, and Skagway, to the north, celebrates the excitement of the gold rush, Juneau was founded on the hard work of mining. The city is named for the infamous Joe Juneau, who is credited with Alaska's first major gold strike. The first gold was found in the creeks and streams of the area, but the real wealth was buried deep in the mountains. Mines ran deep; the Treadmill Mine on the shoreline of the Gastineau Channel had a glory hole some 450 feet deep leading into a network of tunnels that ran for more than half a mile straight down, while the AJ mine at the base of Mount Roberts had over 100 miles of tunnels stretching over 800 feet down. By the early 1900's seven different mines were operating in the Juneau area and the region rang to their constant, clanging machinery. Evidence of these massive operations is easy to spot. The old pilings and remains of the Treadwell mine still line the western shore of the Gastineau Channel and you can still see the entrances to the AJ mine tunnels in the rock walls along the way as you head into town from the ship. Originally, some 15,000 people lived on Douglas Island and worked in the Treadwell Mine, and the mine was extremely profitable, producing roughly $4 million in revenue per year. A fatal accident flooded the mine in 1917 and led to its closure. The AJ mine closed down in the late 1940's due to labor shortages but not before its tailings had been used to build the network of roads spreading into Mendenhall Valley. As these tailings still contained small but irretrievable amounts of the precious metal, locals still like to mention that the streets of Juneau were paved with gold.

Despite the closure of the mines, Juneau remained the territorial capital and once Alaska became a state in 1959, the city became the capital of America's 49th state. Ever since the very first cruise ships headed north in the late 1890's, Juneau has also been a popular port of call, establishing a somewhat unlikely seasonal cycle. Today, over 50% of Juneau's 30,000 year-round residents are employed in local and state government. Between September and May, when the legislature is in session, the city is a hive of lobbyists and local government officials. Come May each year, the legislators return to their homes throughout Alaska and Juneau takes on a new identity as the gateway city to the best that Southeast Alaska has to offer.

The city of Juneau opens directly to the great outdoors. World-class hiking trails start right from downtown. The Juneau Icefield, stretching over 1500 square miles, sits just above the town and the Mendenhall Glacier, often called Alaska's drive-thru glacier, flows right down to the valley floor, where it nourishes a network of salmon streams, wetlands and wildflower meadows just minutes from downtown. And to top all of this, humpback whales take up residence each summer in the channels and bays surrounding Juneau, providing some of the best whale-watching opportunities in the state. Certainly Juneau has much to offer; the real challenge is choosing what to do.

Mendenhall Glacier

Juneau - Naturalist's highlights

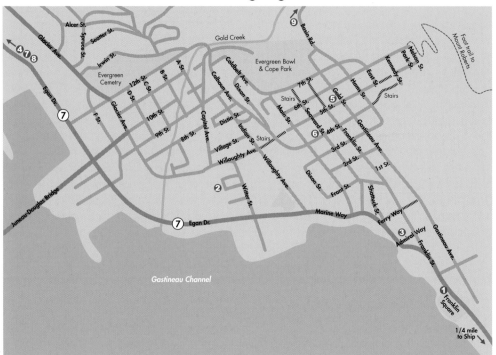

In Town:

PPI 1. Mount Roberts – for great hiking trails and easy access to alpine meadows

PPI 2. Alaska State Museum – displays include artifacts from Alaska's six indigenous groups. Other displays focus on regional Russian and American History

PPI 3. Red Dog Saloon – local bar with Alaskan flavor

PPI 4. Macaulay Salmon Hatchery – see a working hatchery

PPI 5. Russian Orthodox Church – Alaska's oldest church

PPI 6. State Capital building – tours offered daily through summer

Around Town:

PPI 7. Mendenhall Glacier – for wildlife spotting, glacier viewing

PPI 8. Auke Bay – departure point for most whale-watching trips

PPI 9. Perseverance Trailhead – a historical trail offering great views and intriguing history

PPI *See your Port Guide: Princess Points of Interest for more details.*

In Juneau

It's hard to tell, but Juneau sits on the shoreline of the mainland. The bridge across the Gastineau Channel connects the downtown area with Douglas Island, where many residents choose to live as rainfall is slightly lower in the winter months. The Channel is known for strong currents and extreme tidal flows, so don't be surprised to see the angle of the ship to the dock change dramatically over the course of your day in port. Mendenhall Valley, referred to by locals as simply "the valley," lies to the north of town and sits at the foot of the Mendenhall Glacier. Typically, Princess Cruise ships dock at the Franklin dock just to the south of town, where they can plug into shore-side power. The power facility was put in place in 2002 to ensure that the air quality in Juneau is not impacted during ship visits. The main area of town is a short quarter-mile walk along the dockside, and shuttle buses also run into town from here.

Heading into town on Franklin Street, you'll see the remains of the AJ mine on the hillside. You'll also pass by the Taku Salmon headquarters, a good place to find free samples of fresh local salmon. Ahead is Franklin Square, very much a hub of activity on most ship days. There's a well-stocked visitor information center next to the entrance to the Mount Roberts Tramway station where you can pick up city maps. The tramway, which is owned and operated by the Goldbelt Native cooperation, offers a quick 10-minute ride halfway to the summit of Mount Roberts and this short trip is a great way to get your bearings. At the top of the tramway you'll find a network of short nature trails and a nature center. Allow about an hour to get up and back, especially on busy port days. Alternatively, you can start a full day's hiking adventure from Tramway summit; see the "Take a Hike" section for more details.

Franklin Square.

Continuing along Franklin Street will take you past the **Red Dog Saloon**, at the junction of Franklin and Marine Way, and into the downtown area of Juneau. At one time, over 30 bars and saloons lined Franklin Street. Today, the Red Dog Saloon is the best known, while the Alaskan Hotel, a little further up the street is considered the most authentic local watering hole; both make for interesting side trips. Continuing along Franklin Street you'll pass through the main shopping area and on to the **State Buildings** and the **Russian Orthodox Church**, located on 4th and 5th Streets respectively.

If you are interested in visiting the **Alaska State Museum**, bear to the left at the Red Dog Saloon and stay on the shoreline. Follow the docks and pass by the **Patsy Ann Statue**, continue through a little waterfront square, Marine Plaza onto Egan Drive and this will take you to the museum on Whittier Street, just off Egan. It's a pleasant 15-minute walk from the ship and the museum comes highly recommended. Displays include native cultural artifacts, a permanent collection of sketches from the Cook voyages, early photographs of the cities gold mining days and some fascinating details of the first sight-seeing cruises through the region.

The Red Dog saloon sits at the intersection of Franklin St and Marine way. The saloon has some interesting Alaskan memorabilia, including Wyatt Earp's pistol. To get the spirit of the Red Dog Saloon before you go – visit their website at www.reddogsaloon.com.

The Russian Orthodox Church –built in 1894, this is Alaska's oldest church. Inside the church you'll find a small gift shop selling authentic Russian nesting dolls. The church also houses original artwork.

The Patsy Ann Statue – commemorates Patsy Ann, a local, deaf and homeless stray that would arrive on the dock in downtown Juneau during the 1930's, whenever a ship arrived in port. Although ships could head to any of seven docks, Patsy Ann always found the right dock. In 1937, the mayor named her the Official Greeter for Juneau, and exempted her from a dog license requirement.

Mendenhall Glacier and Mendenhall Lake. The park is operated by the U.S. Forest Service and includes an excellent visitor center and a network of short hikes to scenic viewpoints.

Around Juneau
Mendenhall Glacier

As your cruise itinerary may already include a day of glacier cruising, you may be tempted to think that Mendenhall Glacier won't match up. In terms of glacier viewing, this is likely true; on your scenic cruising days, you'll see calving glaciers from the decks of the ship and by comparison the Mendenhall Glacier, visible just across a small lake, is far less dramatic. However, the lake and the surrounding park is a breath of fresh air; scenic, peaceful, and brimming with opportunities for wildlife viewing. The park includes an excellent visitor center and some nice hiking trails. For those with limited mobility, there is an extensive network of wheelchair accessible boardwalks and many of the highlights are within just a short walk of the parking lot. You can see the highlights in an hour or two or you can make a day of it. Regular shuttles leave from Franklin Square by the Mount Roberts tramway station, and the glacier is also included on many tour itineraries.

The Mendenhall Glacier is one of 37 glaciers that flow down from Juneau's 1500 square mile ice field. The glacier stretches some 13.5 miles and flows right down to the valley floor, terminating in Mendenhall Lake. The glacier reached its fullest extent around 300 years ago, in the late 1700's, at which time it reached well out into the valley. Since then it's been retreating, which essentially means it's losing ice at its terminus in the lake faster than it's gaining ice at its source in the ice field. Like most of Alaska's glaciers, the rate of retreat has been increasing in recent years: In the 1990's, the glacier was retreating by about 30 feet per year, by the early 2000's this had increased to an average of 200 feet per year and last year alone the glacier shrank by 540 feet. Park officials have estimated that 40 years from now the glacier won't be visible from the visitor's center. These increasingly rapid rates of retreat illustrate the relentless march of climate change, the effects of which will be keenly seen in high latitudes and cold climates such as Southeast Alaska. Still, as the glacier is so accessible, it offers scientists and park officials the chance to document and record these changes over time and such details are extremely useful in allowing more accurate predictions of what the future may hold. Meanwhile, the retreating glacier frequently spawns large icebergs that drift across the lake. The surrounding peaks make for a spectacular setting on a clear day, and on more overcast days the blue hues of the glacier and the drifting ice glow across the waters of the lake.

Newly colonized terminal moraine, Mendenhall Lake.

Across the lake from the glacier the land is rebounding, literally springing up from under the weight of the ice. As the ice melts back, life moves in quickly and fertile meadows of mean-dering streams, outcrops and small trees develop. Take the Moraine Ecology Trail from the visitor center or the Steep Creek Trail from the parking lot to explore this area. Both trails of-fer wooden boardwalks for easy access and as Steep Creek has an active salmon run from mid-June onwards, there is a good chance of seeing bears in the area. A well-documented group of black bears now regularly feeds on the salmon in the creek and once the salmom runs begins, they are seen daily in the surrounding area. Local park rangers have noted that the males of this group of bears generally feed at times when numbers of visitors are low,

Migrating salmon in Steep Creek, Mendenhall Lake.

An extensive system of boardwalks makes many of the trails accessible. Be sure to heed all bear warnings.

A black bear cub waits for Mom beside Steep Creek.

such as the early hours of the day and after dusk. For females and their cubs, male bears are their primary threat, so they take advantage of the males' skittishness around humans for their own protection and enjoy the premium feeding sites in the Creek during peak visitor times. Be assured though, whenever you spot a bear within viewing distance of the trail, you'll always find a park ranger nearby.

A young black bear poses for photographers.

Meet the Locals: Romeo the Glacier Wolf

Images provided Britteny A. Cioni-Haywood; Black Mutt Photography; blackmuttphotography.com

The story of Mendenhall's most famous wintertime visitor

Romeo's story began one day in April 2003, when a young black wolf was struck and killed by a car within a quarter mile of Mendenhall Visitor Center. Sad as this event was, park officials made the best of it and retrieved the wolf so that at least it could be prepared for display in the visitor's center. They determined that it was a female black wolf, which is a black or tan colored subspecies of the gray wolf, and they also estimated it was a young animal. Young females will generally only leave a family pack with a new mate to start a family of their own, so park officials expected to see the young female's mate in the area. Over the first few months of summer there was no trace, but as winter set in that year, reports came in from residents around the now-frozen Mendenhall Lake that during the long, cold winter nights of November that year, they repeatedly heard the howls of a lone wolf, ringing out across the icy wilderness of the lake.

The first sighting came shortly after the new year, in January 2004. A local naturalist and author, Nick Jans, was skiing across the Lake with his dog Dakota when he noticed a lone set of wolf tracks stretching across the lake. He took Dakota home and returned to the lake, and then encountered the wolf for the first time. It was alone and it was a young male black wolf. A solitary wolf is unusual, especially in winter when wolves typically regroup into their family packs to ensure successful hunting, so when Jans reported the lone wolf sighting, wildlife officials presumed they had found the mate for the young female killed earlier in the year.

As the winter stretched on, the young wolf began to appear regularly, even accompanying Jans and Dakotah on their outings across the lake. The wolf would play with Dakotah, just like any other dog might, and even took to following the duo home. There he waited outside the house for the female lab to appear, leading to his nickname, Romeo. Unbelievably, this went on for many years. Romeo would disappear over the summer but return each winter once the visitors had left and the lake had frozen over.

The iconic appearance of a lone black wolf against the dramatic backdrop of the snow-white lake was enough to draw attention on its own. But Romeo was also sociable, and other visitors to the lake had the same experience as Jans and Dakotah: Romeo would appear and follow at a distance for a while, then, once comfortable, play with the visitors' pet dogs, even fetching tennis balls along with them. He didn't become a pet—no one tried to feed or pet him—but he quickly became a living legend in the region. Juneau residents became fiercely protective of the wolf. In 2006, a group called the Friends of Romeo was formed and Romeo even had a facebook page. Unknowingly, Romeo had came to serve as an ambassador for his species, putting a face to the idea of the lone, wild wolf and putting to rest stories of wolves as crazed, unsociable predators.

In 2009, the story took a sad turn. Romeo failed to reappear that fall and in fact was not seen or heard of again. Eventually a wolf pelt surfaced that was identified as Romeo's, and in May 2010, two hunters were charged with illegally shooting the protected wolf. Unfortunately, there is no happy ending here. Although Romeo's story righted many misconceptions and changed many attitudes, it wasn't in time to save Romeo himself.

For more details on Nick Jans' encounters with Romeo the Glacier Wolf, pick up his latest book, Glacier Wolf. This short but entertaining volume relates the author's life and times in Southeast Alaska and makes for very easy reading.

Within Southeast Alaska sightings of wolves are rare, however if you are traveling on to Denali, the Park has several resident wolf packs, so there is a good chance of sighting wolves in the park. Though hard to spot, they're certainly a highlight of any park tour.

Take a hike

Mount Roberts

Level: easy to difficult, depending on route

Elevation: trails start at 1750ft, summit of Mt Roberts is at 3819ft

Attractions: views across the Mendenhall Valley, wildflowers in season, nature trails and a visitor center

Tip: take binoculars and keep an eye out for bears

Mount Roberts Trail System

One of the very best places to hike in Alaska is up above the tree-line. Evergreen trees give way to cottonwoods and alders and finally to shrubs, berries and wildflowers. The views open up and it can be quite breath-taking, a real on-top-of the world feeling. In most of South-east Alaska, the tree-line sits at around 2-3,000 feet above sea level, so in places where road access is so minimal, getting to this height is also typically quite breath-taking, in a different way. This is what makes Mount Roberts such a unique hiking experience; you can ride the tram and gain 1750 feet in around 10 minutes, leaving you with the time – and energy – to explore above the tree-line.

From the top end of Mount Roberts tramway station, a network of trails leads out across the alpine meadows. A short, 30 minute half mile round route will take you to some of the key viewpoints. This shortest route includes around 60 wooden steps and gains an additional 200 ft in altitude. You'll pass through a range of different plant communities and get some great views along the Gastineau Channel.

Alternatively you can follow the route-markers for Father Brown's cross and head out. Be aware, if you do take to these trails that this is wilderness hiking and you should take appropriate steps. The trail runs around another ½ mile to Father Brown's Cross and then a much longer and more challenging route continues through alpine brush, eventually to the peak of Mount Roberts at 3819 feet. This is a rigorous hike though. A better bet might be to check out the view from Father Brown's Cross, then double-back and follow the network of paths that lead back into the valley.

Keep your binoculars handy, as wildlife abounds up here. Marmots play amongst the rocky outcrops, deer and even bear are all commonly seen in the area.

As you head back to the tram station, a quick detour along the nature trails takes you to the trees with eyes. A common Tlingit practice in the region was to mark ownership of routes and regions with clan crests that were carved into the trees. Several of these can be seen as you trek through the forest around the tram station.

It is possible to hike up Mount Roberts. This trail starts downtown at a wooden staircase on the north-east end of 6th Street and takes several miles of switchbacks to reach Gastineau Peak and the tramway station. As most of the hike is within the secondary growth forest, it's not the most spectacular hike though and the Perseverance Trail is may be a better plan B. However, if you do make it up the trail, you can ride down one-way on the tram for just $5.00. Or spend your $5 on a well-earned beer in the tramway restaurant and then the ride down is free.

View from Mount Roberts.

Take a hike

The Perseverance Trail
Level: easy to moderate
Elevation: trails start at 1750ft.
Attractions: views across the Silverbow Basin
Tip: you can take a taxi up to the trailhead, but the walk talks you through some nice parts of Juneau

The Perseverance Trail

This is a historic trail that takes you along the routes once used by Juneau's first gold miners. To get to the trailhead, take 6th street to Gold Street. Follow this around and bear to the left and this becomes Basin Rd, which takes you to the trailhead. The trail starts at the end of the road and in the same parking lot used for the Last Chance Mining Museum. You can easily get a taxi-cab to bring you to this point if you want to save your time for the trail, but there are great views and plenty to see on the way there.

On the way to the trailhead

The trail winds through evergreen forests dotted with cottonwoods and you'll find several spectacular viewpoints within the first mile. Interpretive signs along the hike add interesting details, explaining that the trail follows the route of Alaska's first road, originally built to allow access to the gold mines in this area.

The trail is a favorite among locals, and you'll see a real variety of people on the trail—even the odd, optimistic gold pannier trying his luck in the creek. For the truly energetic, it's a healthy three mile jog, or a about a three to four hour round trip hike up to Ebner Falls and back.

Gold Creek, Silverbow Basin

Mount Roberts Trail

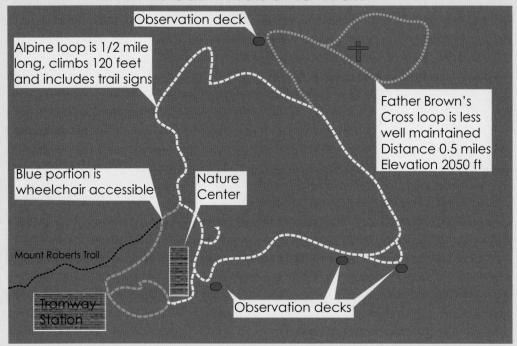

Observation deck

Alpine loop is 1/2 mile long, climbs 120 feet and includes trail signs

Father Brown's Cross loop is less well maintained Distance 0.5 miles Elevation 2050 ft

Blue portion is wheelchair accessible

Nature Center

Mount Roberts Trail

Tramway Station

Observation decks

Perseverance Trail

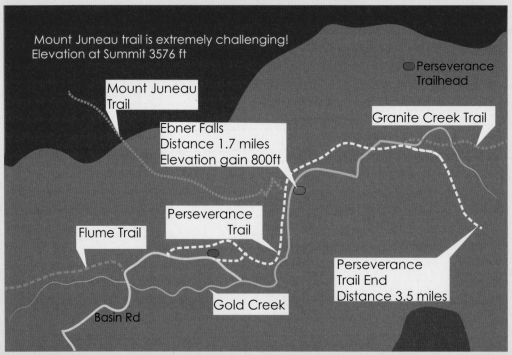

Mount Juneau trail is extremely challenging! Elevation at Summit 3576 ft

Perseverance Trailhead

Mount Juneau Trail

Granite Creek Trail

Ebner Falls Distance 1.7 miles Elevation gain 800ft

Flume Trail

Perseverance Trail

Perseverance Trail End Distance 3.5 miles

Gold Creek

Basin Rd

Mount Roberts Trailhead:

Accessible by the Tramway, running from Franklin Square
Round trip Fare – Adults $31.00, Children
You can reach the tram station via the Mount Roberts Trail, but it's not an especially scenic hike and takes at least 2-3 hours.

For the Perseverance Trail

Take the main road, Franklin St. through town all the way to 6th St. Go right on 6th then left on Gold. From here, you'll see signs to the trailhead. Follow Gold St to Basin Rd, then go left. The trailhead is around 1 mile here, but it's a very pleasant walk.

The Flume Trail, also known as Trestles, is a fun alternate route. You'll see the trailhead marked on Basin Rd. The trail drops down then crosses the river, and then runs along the restored boardwalks of the trolley system that was part of the Gold Creek mining operations. It's around 1 mile from the trailhead to the end of the boardwalks and a very popular run for the truly energetic. At the end of the trail, you can walk back through town (allow 30 minutes) or retrace your steps back to Basin Road.

Field guide to Alaska's wildflowers

Wildflower season in Alaska varies with location and with altitude. Head up above the tree-line on the Mount Roberts Tramway, or out to Mendenhall glacier to see Alaska's wildflowers in full bloom. Keep in mind, July 4th is often considered to be the last day of summer in these regions, so peak wildflower season is in late may and June in this part of the world.

Nootka Lupine

Fireweed

Forget-me-not
(Alaska State Flower)

Chocolate Lily

Salmonberry

Red Elderberry

Devil's Club

Skunk Cabbage

Goldenrod

Alaska's Weather Barometer: Fireweed

"Once the fireweed turns to cotton, summer soon will be forgotten."

An iconic photo of the Mendenhall Glacier shows the glacier fringed in the foreground by a bright pink wildflower. This is fireweed, *Epilobium angustifolium*, and you'll see its bright pink blooms throughout Alaska. This bright flower thrives in areas where the land has been disturbed, so typically it's the first to appear, for example after a fire, hence the name of the flower. It lines many of the main highways around the region, blooms brightly from June through the summer and the pink petals are used by locals in jams, honey and even ice-cream.

These bright blooms are also an Alaskan weatherclock. As summer arrives, the first flowers appear at the bottom of the stem. Blooms slowly move up the stem as the summer progresses, and by the time the top of the stem is flowering, the flowers on the lower portion of the stem have turned to cotton-like seeds. For Alaskans, fireweed in full flower means that the summer is here, but as fields of fireweed turn to cotton, this is a sure sign that fall is just around the corner.

Spring   Summer   Fall

Hoary Marmots

If you're headed for Mount Roberts and have a few minutes to spare, spend a moment or two quietly watching among the boulders and wildflowers in the alpine meadows and you will mostly likely spot one of Mount Robert's most charismatic residents, the hoary marmot.

This small, ground dwelling mammal is fondly referred to as a squirrel on steroids, and if you do spot one, you'll soon see how fitting their nickname is. Marmots will stand or sit completely still, seemingly under the entirely misguided assumption that they are well camouflaged. Then suddenly they'll leap into action, and with a shrill whistle they will make a mad dash into a patch of wildflowers or down into their underground burrows.

In fact, these small mammals are highly sociable and renowned for their vocals. Like other ground dwelling mammals such as meerkats, they have an extensive and remarkably sophisticated repertoire of whistles which they use to alert family members to incoming predators. Different whistles are used to identify different predators such as eagles, wolves and bears. As yet, no specific whistles have been identified for incoming hikers, but that doesn't mean there isn't one. One common whistle they use sounds remarkably like a wolf whistle, which is certainly a strange sound to hear on a hiking trail. Typically, you will often hear these little guys before you see them but take a moment to watch and they will usually reappear. Favorite hoary marmot trivia: they are especially prevalent in British Columbia, and that's how Whistler, B.C. got its name.

A hoary marmot stands guard in an alpine meadow.

Meet the Locals: Libby Riddles, Juneau's First Lady

Libby Riddles, the first female winner of the Iditarod, joins Princess Cruises ships in Juneau and tells her story.

During the summer months, Juneau is home to one of Alaska's living heroes, Libby Riddles. In 1985, Libby became the first woman in history to win the Iditarod Sled Dog Race. This grueling dog sled race runs from Anchorage to Nome each year. It covers 1,049 miles, and the mushers and their sled dog teams travel across some of the most remote regions of Alaska's Interior. Contestants race through blizzards, whiteout conditions and gale force winds. Temperatures frequently drop below zero and the race lasts anywhere from nine to sixteen days, depending on conditions out on the trail. In many ways, the race is seen as a true test of the best of Alaskan character, requiring strength, determination and a willingness to take on any kind of weather. In Alaska, the winners of this race, both the mushers and their dogs, become Alaska's own rock stars.

The route of the race follows a historical trail that was originally used by native Athabascans and Inupiaqs. The first Europeans to use the route were most likely Russian fur traders and once gold was discovered in Nome in 1898 many optimistic miners followed in their footsteps. The most famous run along the route was the Great Race of Mercy, the 1925 serum run to Nome. Over the winter of that year there was an outbreak of diphtheria in Nome, and local children had not been vaccinated. As this was a "white man's disease," native children had no immunity, so the vaccine would be life saving. The nearest supplies were in Anchorage though and the port of Nome was ice bound during the winters. This meant that the only route into Nome was overland by dog-sled. A team of twenty mushers and over 100 dogs was assembled. The serum was shipped from Anchorage by train to Nenana, the town at the end of the train line and from there, the dog teams worked in relays to get the serum to Nome, 674 miles away. It arrived in five days despite the worst of weather conditions—and in time to save the young children of Nome.

Today's Iditarod race commemorates this epic run and is no less challenging than that first time. A single musher runs the race with a team of up to 24 husky dogs. The race lasts up to 12 days and runs whatever the weather; in fact, that's part of the challenge. Many participants who start the race don't finish and even experienced race veterans will say that they never can predict what the course—and the weather—might have in store for them. All of this makes Libby's win all the more remarkable. She was just 27 years old, it was only her third time in the race and she finished in record time, becoming the first woman to take the gold.

You'll have a chance to meet Libby when she comes aboard in Juneau and hear her story firsthand. For now, here are a few highlights and insights from Libby herself.

Qu: You traveled to Alaska for the first time at the age of seventeen. What set you off on that trip and what did you imagine Alaska to be before you arrived?

I came up for the wilderness and was not disappointed! I had a very narrow vision of what I was getting into. Alaska is full of surprises and contradictions.

Qu: When you first arrived in Alaska, what surprised you most?

I had no idea of the size of Alaska and the variety of climates and landscapes. I've spent many enjoyable years experiencing it now. I was surprised by how hard I fell in love with living in the mountains!

Qu: There's a rumor that you arrived wearing high heeled sheep skin boots. Is that true?

They were low heeled high top sheepskin boots. Look at it this way—with Uggs being so popular now, I was just ahead of my time!

Qu: It seems like many avid Alaskans weren't actually born in Alaska. Is there any particular way you would describe a true Alaskan? What special qualities do you associate with Alaskans?

Alaskans refuse even to be defined! Self-sufficient, hard working, independent, a little crazy…. And they will give you the shirt off their back in an emergency. That's a good start!

Qu: What makes a dog special to you?

All animals are amazing, and the dedication that dogs display to us makes them ALL special, if you ask me. I love the old dogs, the relationship built over many years, and dogs that have really fun, outgoing personalities, like Iceworm.

Qu: Do you have any specific explanations as to why you can connect so well with your dogs?

I've always connected well with animals. Probably the main reason I connect so well with my huskies is the time and effort of years and years of learning by working side by side with my dogs and being observant. I like the challenge of helping a dog understand how to learn and grow and develop confidence and pride.

Qu: Many Princess Cruises passengers plan their trips far in advance, but they are in Alaska only for a week. If you could offer passengers one piece of advice to make the best of their vacation, what would that be? Is there one thing you really think they should see or do during their vacation?

GO SEE THE SLED DOGS!

Whale Watching in Alaska

If there is a single image that captures the spirit of Alaska, it might just be the view of a whale's tail as a great whale dives deep into the cool, Alaskan waters. Whales complete the scenery of Alaska, both above and below the water. John Muir describes whales as the heartbeat of the ocean, and they also add the soundtrack, as their songs and sounds echo across the vast, deep, icy fjords of the Inside Passage.

The "big two" whales you're most likely to see in Alaska are humpback and killer whales (or orca). Currently, the waters of Alaska's Inside Passage are home to around 1500 humpback whales and between 3-400 killer whales. Considering the thousands of miles of waterways that make up Alaska's Inside Passage, finding a whale could be like finding the proverbial needle in a haystack. However, like the rest of Alaska's wildlife, these whales are in search of food and that makes their location a little easier to predict; find the food and you will find the whales.

Humpback whales are mysticetes, or baleen whales. They have large plates of baleen that hang from the upper jaw and assist in capturing prey. Their prey of choice is small; they feed on amphipods that look like tiny shrimp or small schooling fish such as herring and pollock. Favored hotspots for humpbacks along the Inside Passage include Snow Passage just north of Ketchikan, Frederick Sound (particularly in the second half of the season), some areas of Chatham Straits and Icy Straits and the headwaters at the entrance to Glacier Bay.

Killer whales are quite different from humpbacks, both in their feeding choices and their distribution in Alaska. They are odontocetes, or toothed whales, equipped with sharp teeth. Their diet varies between the three recognized ecotypes. Resident killer whales choose salmon as their favored prey; transient killer whales look for young seals and sea lions, sea otters and when they can catch them, Dall's porpoise; and offshore killer whales feed on large fish, including shark. Resident killer whales are occasionally seen in the lower waters of Glacier Bay and have been sighted as far south as Ketchikan in recent years. You might see them in any area with a healthy silver salmon run. If you're fishing, watch out—when the chance presents itself, a resident orca will never say no to an easy lunch and there are many reports of killer whales snagging salmon from a fisherman's line.

Sightings of transient killer whales are harder to predict. They roam freely along Alaska's coastlines in summer, and in winter may venture as far south as California in search of favored prey. They are often seen close to ice packs in College Fjord or Tracy Arm, where seal "snacks" resting on the ice become easy prey.

Offshore whales, which make up the third group of killer whales, are only rarely seen in coastal regions, as their name implies. Scientists have recorded offshore whales feeding on Pacific sleeper shark that live on the edge of the continental shelf. The whales dive deep to catch the shark and feed on their oil-rich livers.

The range and prey preferences of these different whales means that whale-watching in Alaska is a lofty goal. Notwithstanding, the waters around Juneau are one of your best bets. Blooms of tiny shrimp bring in hungry humpbacks, healthy salmon runs attract resident killer whales and the abundance of seals, sea lions and small dolphins, such as the Dall's porpoise, occasionally draw transients in too.

You'll have a very good chance of spotting whales from the ship as you cruise, but to see them up close and personal—to watch their behavior, to hear them spout and maybe even hear them sing—you'll need to jump onboard a smaller vessel and take a wildlife cruise. And the best place to do that is from Juneau.

Whale-watching tips

- In Alaska, whales are active all day long, so early morning trips are just as good as sunset trips.
- The longer you spend on the water, the more you're likely to see. Designated whale-watching and wildlife trips may offer more time with whales but all commercial boats are allowed to spend no more than 30 minutes with each group they see.
- Federal guidelines require that vessels don't approach within 100 yards of whales, so take binoculars with you. It's quite fascinating to watch the whales up close and binoculars give you that view.
- Dress in layers as it can be quite cool and breezy out on the water.

A pair of killer whales cruise the waters of the Lynn Canal.

Wildlife Profile: The Humpback Whale

Fast Facts:

Common name: Humpback whale

Scientific name: *Megaptera novaeangliae*

Best areas for sightings: Snow Passage, Frederick Sound, the entrance to Glacier Bay, waters around Juneau.

ID: Large, high blow, usually several in quick succession. Very small, curved dorsal fin and wide fluke or tail that is thrown in the air as the whale dives.

Size: Males up to 40 feet in length, females up to 45 feet. They weigh around a ton per foot.

Lifespan: Up to 50-60 years for both genders, possibly longer.

Mating and reproduction: Whales migrate to tropical waters to mate. Pregnancy lasts 10-11 months, and calves are born in warm waters the following season. Females produce a single calf every 2-3 years.

Typical group size: Lone adults may be sighted, mother-calf pairs common and feeding groups of 4-16 whales frequently form in Southeast Alaska.

Diet: Krill and small schooling fish such as herring, pollock, sand lance.

Recommended websites: Alaska whale research foundation – www.alaskawhalefoundation.org; Juneau area fluke catalogue: http://www.afsc.noaa.gov/ABL/Humpback/JuneauCatalog.htm

Wildlife in Focus: The Humpback Whale

To best understand humpback whales, you must look first to the land. Fossil records indicate that the early ancestors of modern whales that were land-based mammals headed back into the oceans around 60 million years ago. In the transition from land to ocean, some remarkable adaptations evolved. Over millennia, nostrils migrated from the snout to the top of the head to become blowholes and allow for easier breathing at the water's surface. Lungs increased in size and efficiency, and whales developed the ability to store extra oxygen in muscle tissue so they could stay submerged for longer periods of time. Meanwhile, the back legs of their original land-based ancestors disappeared completely, the forelimbs lengthened to become fins and the tail became flat, wide and covered in cartilage, making whales into world class swimmers.

Approximately 25 million years ago, whales differentiated into two groups. While one group of whales, the toothed whales, kept their teeth, within another group of whales a chance mutation led to the loss of tooth enamel. Subsequently the teeth themselves disappeared, to be replaced eventually by large plates of baleen, made of keratin—just like human fingernails and hair. These whales retained the grazing habits of their land ancestors, and the baleen plates worked perfectly to sweep up small prey in concentrated protein-rich mouthfuls that could sustain them. As today's baleen whales, they range in size from the blue whale, which reaches a gigantic 80 to 100 feet in length, to the diminutive minke whale, measuring about 30 feet in length. The humpback whale is the fifth largest baleen whale, with a current maximum length of about 45 feet. Humpbacks are also the most acrobatic in this group, known for their showy displays of breaching and other surface activities. And additionally, humpback whales are the crooners; unique in their production of a mesmerizing repertoire of songs and social sounds that echo across the oceans, bays and fjords that they call home. Humpback whales

A humpback whale tail slaps in the waters around Juneau.

A Whale's Tale

You might be wondering how researchers have compiled such detailed histories of humpback whales. Well, their principle tool is actually the whale's tail. The underside of each whale's tail—or fluke—has a distinct pattern of black and white markings. Some may be entirely black, others entirely white. The pattern sets around age 2 or 3, so that individual whales can be identified. Scars, cuts, scrapes and rake marks also accumulate, and these also provide further details of the travels and tales of the different whales.

are a conservation success story. Like most populations of great whales, they were heavily exploited in the early days of whaling in the late 1800's and again during modern whaling days in the 1940's, 50's and 60's. When commercial whaling was finally halted in 1982, their numbers were so low that researchers believed they were headed for extinction. Today, with protection in place, humpbacks are making a strong and steady comeback. The humpbacks you'll see in Alaska are part of the Central North Pacific population, specifically the Southeast Alaska population, numbering around 1500 individuals. The larger population of the entire North Pacific is currently estimated to be around 20,000 and may soon be taken off the endangered species list. While this would be as a true conservation success story, biologists are concerned that such a move would reduce protection for this recovering population.

Humpback whales are in Southeast Alaska to feed, consequently the distribution of food is a reliable predictor of whales in any particular region. Their food ranges from small, shrimp-like amphipods called krill to schooling fish ranging from herring to small salmon. Along with the baleen plates in the mouth, baleen whales also have huge, expandable ventral pleats on their underside, a two ton tongue and a pretty amazing repertoire of feeding techniques.

Essentially, whales use different methods to catch different prey. When krill blooms are deep but concentrated, single humpback whales dive down to depths of around 200 feet or so. There, they open up their huge mouths and take massive gulps of water into the ventral pleats. They then close the jaws, collapse the ventral pleats and use their two tonne tongue to force the water back through the baleen plates. The tiny shrimp get caught on the bristle-like ends of the plates, and the whale then licks the plates clean. When krill blooms are close to the surface, whales will lunge or side-skim through regions rich in prey. When catching fish or krill less densely concentrated, the whales produce bubble nets, diving down and exhaling a circular string of bubbles that works as a net, catching and concentrating the prey. As the bubbles rise, they expand and the net gets tighter. The whales also make loud, high-pitched sounds that frighten their prey into a tight ball. Once the prey ball reaches the surface, the whales rush up from below with their large mouths wide open. They catch the prey in a single, huge gulp and then strain them out of the water using their huge baleen plates.

Some whales will bubble-net individually, but more frequently this is a group activity, with as many as 20 whales working together to spin a huge bubble net. Group membership is consistent from year to year, however the whales are not related in any way and neither gender is more common. Within the groups, the whales surface in a distinct and orchestrated routine each time, and feeding for hours at a stretch. It's hard to imagine just how much food 12 to 15 large whales would consume. One estimate is that each whale needs around a ton of food per day. Since this collaborative feeding behavior persists, it must be cost-effective and deliver sufficient food for each whale in the group. It is certainly one of the most spectacular sights to see in Southeast Alaska. Most frequently, you'll see humpbacks feeding this way in the waters around Juneau, in Chatham Straits and in Frederick Sound. Watch for birds as they frequently gather overhead of the feeding humpbacks.

As humpback and other large whale numbers resurge, many fisherman are concerned about the impact this could have on regional fish stocks. However, recent research shows that large whales play a crucial role within the ecosystem in these waters. In fact, large whales act as nutrient pumps. They feed at depth, below the point where sunlight penetrates, but return to the surface to breathe. At the surface, for want of a better biological term, they poop. This increases nutrient levels which in turn enhances productivity in the upper light-rich layers. And more productivity means more fish—and more food—for the entire ecosystem.

This photo was taken under NMFS permit 10018-1 during permitted research activities. For more details go to www.caringforcalves.org

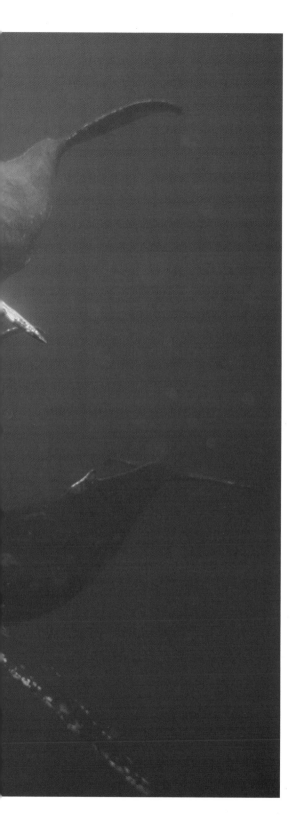

As fall arrives, days shorten, the light dims and food stocks dwindle. For humpback whales, the food available doesn't warrant the energy needed to capture it. In addition, at this time of year pregnant females are about to give birth to small, naïve calves that would be perfect snacks for transient killer whales. So the mothers-to-be head south to warmer waters that lie beyond the range of these hungry predators. Non-pregnant females and males follow, as the lure of romance and mating in warm, tropical waters easily outweighs the prospect of meager food supplies and cold waters on the feeding grounds.

Roughly 80% of Southeast Alaskan humpbacks choose Hawaii for their winter vacation. Because they are so large, swimming doesn't take much energy, and the huge stores of energy laid down as blubber during the summer that will sustain them during the winter breeding season. After a three thousand-mile swim, humpbacks arrive in their winter home, Hawaii. The first whales may be seen in November and numbers increase from there. Mating activity peaks in January and early February, then newly pregnant females quickly return to Alaska to make the most of the next feeding season, while males persist through February and March, making sure they cover all their mating bases. Females that have given birth stay also linger until their calves are strong enough to fight off the hungry transient killer whales they'll meet as they head north.

Around 30% of first season calves arrive in Alaska with tell-tale tooth rake scars on their flukes, scars that speak of close encounters and lucky escapes from killer whales on their first migration. By mid-summer most calves arrive safely in the food-rich waters of Alaska alongside their hungry mothers. Over the first season they'll learn to feed and find their way around their Alaskan home, the next generation of Alaska's gentle giants, a living testament and a future challenge to our commitment to the conservation of the wild and pristine waters of Alaska's Inside Passage.

A humpback whale mother cradles her calf in the warm Hawaii waters.

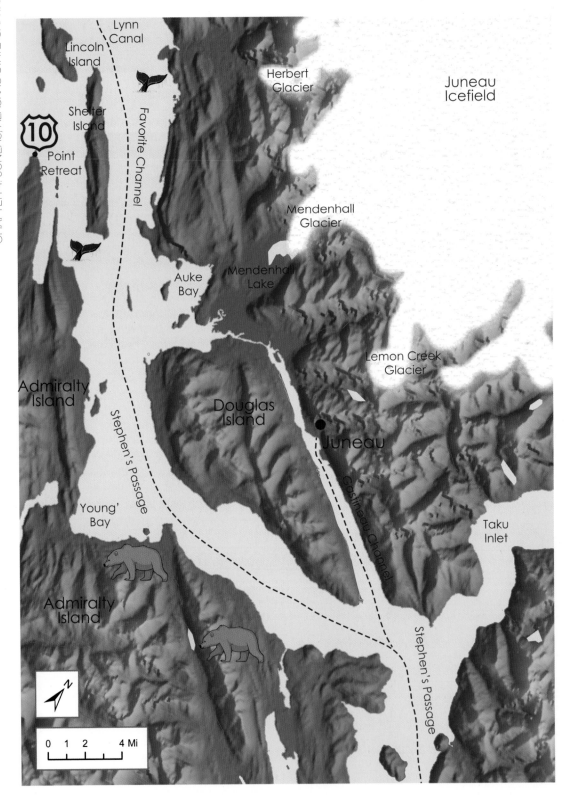

Lynn
Canal

Lincoln
Island

Herbert
Glacier

Juneau
Icefield

Shelter
Island

Favorite Channel

10

Point
Retreat

Mendenhall
Glacier

Auke
Bay

Mendenhall
Lake

Admiralty
Island

Stephen's Passage

Lemon Creek
Glacier

Douglas
Island

Juneau

Gastineau Channel

Young'
Bay

Taku
Inlet

Admiralty
Island

Stephen's Passage

N

0 1 2   4 Mi

Cruising highlights

All ships leaving Juneau will initially head south along the waters of the Gastineau Channel. Douglas Island lies on starboard side of the Channel and the town of Juneau, along the portside, is located on the mainland.

From the starboard side of the ship, you'll have a good view of the remains of the Treadmill Mine, a huge mine that once operated on Douglas Island. On the port side, look out for Sheep Creek, around 15 minutes after departure. By mid-summer, as salmon start to run, bald eagles congregate at the mouth of the Creek.

Juneau sailaway - Northbound. Once clear of Gastineau Channel, northbound cruises will turn to starboard, heading north into the Upper Lynn Canal towards waypoint 10.

Juneau sailaway – Southbound. If you're headed south, you'll sail through Stephen's Passage and into Frederick Sound; the Sound is a very popular area for humpback whales especially in the later portions of the summer.

Juneau Sailaway

Whichever direction you're traveling, all ships sail south out of Juneau down the Gastineau Channel. Most (but not all!) ships sail from Juneau in the evening, so be sure to check your Princess Patter for your departure time. Either way, there's still plenty of daylight in mid-summer, even at 9:00 and 10:00 p.m., so whatever time you sail, the departure from Juneau can make for a very pleasant hour or two on the open decks. Roughly 15 minutes from the dock you'll pass Sheep Creek, visible from the port side of the ship. Hatchery-raised salmon are released at this location yearly and bald eagles congregate in the area, making the most of an opportunity for an easy snack. You might also spot mountain goats on the sides of the cliffs in this area. Originally mistaken for sheep, it's these creamy-white mountaineers that gave their name to the Creek.

If you're sailing during the afternoon and headed south, expect a very scenic sail ahead. From the Gastineau Channel, you'll pass by Taku Inlet approximately 30 minutes after leaving the dock, and from there you'll sail into the waters of Stephen's Passage. By early evening you'll be in Frederick Sound. You can read more about this area on page 127; it's a hotspot for humpback whales, especially as the season progresses.

Northbound cruise ships will make a turn to starboard at the end of the Gastineau Channel into the waters of the northern portion of Stephen's Passage. At this point the west coast of Douglas Island will lie to starboard and the northern coastline of Admiralty Island to port. Around an hour and a half after departure, as you round Douglas Island, the Eagle Glacier comes into view on the starboard side. You will also be able to see the lights of Juneau. This area is a promising area for humpback whale sightings, but on a clear evening, the mountain range to the northeast will catch your attention too. These are the mountains of the Chilkat Range; they line the route to Skagway and the icy wilderness of Glacier Bay lies just over the ridge line to the west.

Sheep Creek, Gastineau Channel.

Waypoint 10: Point Retreat Lighthouse

Point Retreat Lighthouse marks the northern tip of Admiralty Island. You may pass by this lighthouse on wildlife tours out from Juneau and as you sail north from Juneau for Skagway.

When Captain George Vancouver first explored this area, he sent a small boat ashore here to explore, but when his men encountered native people engaged in a celebration, they quickly retreated to this point, and so the point was named "Point Retreat".

The light was installed in 1904 and resident lighthouse keepers manned the station until 1973. Today, the light is automated and plans are underway to refurbish the remaining buildings and open them up as a bed and breakfast.

Point Retreat lighthouse, Auke Bay, Juneau.

Chapter 5

Skagway: Gateway to the Yukon

The Golden Hotel on Broadway, Skagway.

Skagway

Located at the northern tip of Alaska's Inside Passage, Skagway lies nestled at the base of the snow-capped mountains of the Coast Range. Typically, most ships arrive here in the very early hours and as you step ashore in the morning, you'll notice straightaway that this is a town with character.

Generally, your ship will dock out on the railroad dock and as soon as you disembark you'll see the railway carriages of the White Pass and Yukon Railroad. Bound for the Yukon, these parlor carriages run along narrow gauge tracks and come complete with Harry Potter-esque train guards in full period regalia. At the end of the dock, you'll be greeted by the ladies of the Skagway Streetcar Company; they too sport their finest turn-of the century outfits. To get into town, your choices include a short walk, or alternatively you can travel by horse drawn carriage or pedi-cab. You'll pass by carefully trimmed planters and brightly colored flower displays. Once in town you'll find yourself walking down wooden boardwalks and past buildings that have been authentically restored to their hey-day of some 100 years ago.

The bright gold dome of the Golden Hotel on Broadway is easy to spot and though somewhat unusual for Southeast Alaska, it's typically glistening in the sunshine. Unlike its close and sometimes soggy neighbors, Skagway gets only 26 inches of rain a year, so it's warm and sunny through most of the summer. All in all, this is Southeast Alaska's own Shangri-La.

The ladies of the Red Onion Saloon recreate the atmosphere of Skagway in the days of "98.

The town itself is compact and easy to navigate. Broadway runs through the center of town with cross streets organized numerically, just like the lower 48. Set off to explore, and you'll soon see that Skagway truly celebrates its glory days of the Klondike Gold Rush. Between 1896 and 1898, the town grew from a registered population of two to 20,000. It's estimated that some 40,000 gold prospectors passed through Skagway on their way to the Yukon gold fields. During these exciting times only a few got rich; those supplying the optimistic gold rushers with gold-pans and mining equipment made a lot more that most of the miners themselves. But for all who made the trip, it was the adventure of a lifetime. The Klondike gold rush is often billed as the Last Great Adventure, a time of huge risk, hard work, but potentially great rewards. Today, much of Skagway falls within the Klondike Gold Rush National Historic Park and both the larger history and the local stories of these times are re-told here in Skagway. If you have ever wanted to immerse yourself in the life and times of Alaska's greatest adventure, then this is the place to do so.

Along with its history, Skagway is also surrounded by spectacular scenery. There are some excellent hiking trails into the hills around town. The train ride takes you out of Skagway, over the Coast Mountains and into the Yukon. Aerial tours let you fly over the adjacent ice-fields of the Chilkat Mountains, where you can skirt the border of Glacier Bay while Haines, which is just a short ferry ride away, offers great opportunity for wildlife viewing. And if you have time to spare after your adventures and would like some cool souvenirs, then Broadway, the main street in Skagway, is home to some of Alaska's oldest and most authentic gift shops and art galleries.

Skagway

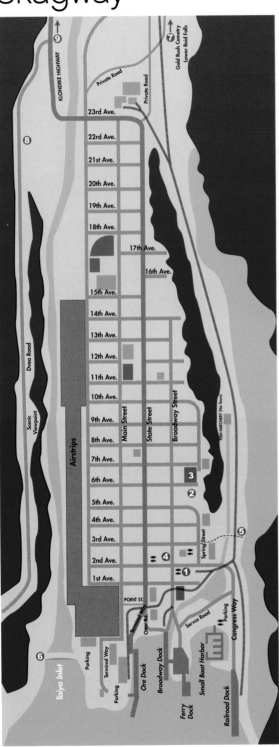

Naturalist's highlights

In Skagway:

PPI 1. Klondike Gold Rush National Historical Park Visitor Center – for walking maps and guided tours.

PPI 2. Moore's Cabin – Skagway's oldest building.

3. Skagway Museum – Fascinating details of local history.

PPI 4. Arctic Brotherhood Hall – houses Skagway's Visitors Bureau. Officially the most photographed building in Alaska.

PPI 5. Deer Mountain Trailhead – a moderately strenuous hike to a peaceful lake setting.

PPI 6. Yakutania Point – an easy hike to a beachside picnic spot.

Around Skagway:

PPI 7. Gold Rush Cemetery – final resting place for Gold Rush heroes and villains. Paths lead to Lower Reid's Falls.

PPI 8. Dyea – originally the start of the Chilkoot Trail, now deserted

PPI 9. Klondike Highway – road access to the Yukon and Canada.

PPI *See your Port Guide: Princess Points of Interest for more details.*

In Skagway

As you head into town from the Railroad Dock, you'll find a recently renovated rest area at the end of the dock. This houses a visitor center, where you can pick up maps and other information. From there, it's around a 10 minute walk into town. There's also a shuttle service that runs in and out all day, or alternatively, there are bicycles for hire here and they provide a great way to explore the town and the surrounding area.

On your way into town, you'll pass over the railway tracks for the White Pass and Yukon railroad, and then over a small stream that has an active salmon run by mid-summer. As you continue into town, the road you are on becomes 2nd Avenue and on the left-hand side, just past the railroad depot at the junction of Broadway and 2nd, you'll see the **Klondike Gold Rush National Historical Park Visitor Center**. This is a good spot to start your day. The park provides a plethora of information and walking tours led by very well-informed park rangers offer a great introduction to the town.

At the cross section of 2nd and Broadway is the **Red Onion Saloon**. Built in 1897, this was one of Skagway's most famous bordellos in days gone by. Though times have changed, the current owners aim to keep the spirit of the Red Onion intact. It might not be the place to stop on your way into town, but its well-worth a few minutes if you have time at the end of your day.

Going north on Broadway will take you to the **Arctic Brotherhood Hall**. In the days of "98, once you had hiked over the trails to the Yukon and made it back to town, you could join the Brotherhood and tell your tale. The driftwood façade makes this officially the most photographed building in Southeast Alaska. The original driftwood, all 8833 pieces, was attached to the building in 1899 and the building was very carefully renovated in 2005.

The Arctic Brotherhood Hall, Broadway, Skagway. In the days of the gold rush, this was the gathering place for those who had successfully returned from the Yukon.

Continue along Broadway to 6th Avenue and take a left there to reach **Moore's House**, the oldest house in Skagway. Originally, this was the home of Captain William Moore and his son Bernard, who founded Skagway in 1887 and became its first two residents. The house is fun to see and has quite a story; the interpretive signs provided by the park will fill you in. The **Skagway Museum** is next door and this is also a very worthwhile stop; this little museum is quite the hidden gem. It provides some fascinating details of day-to-day life during the gold rush, there are some very insightful short films you can watch and you can pick up a copy of the Skagway News from 1897.

Around Skagway

The Gold Rush Cemetery lies just outside town. You can take Broadway or State Street all the way north and the cemetery is well signed. Eventually both roads lead to 23rd Ave and from there you'll see the signs that take you behind the train depot, across the train tracks and over to the cemetery. It's around 1.5 miles from downtown and definitely a worthwhile side-trip. Original gravestones decorate the mature forest floor and it's really quite atmospheric. Soapy Sam, the villain of Skagway's stories, was buried outside the cemetery after his demise in 1899, but as the graveyard has expanded and new pathways have been put in place, it's now one of the first graves that you see. Take a few moments to read the headstones; they give real insight into what life was truly like in the days of the Gold Rush. Also, if you have an extra 20 minutes or so, follow the signs back to **Lower Reid's Falls**. A short but well-marked trail meanders through the forest and takes you back to a beautiful waterfall that cascades down a 300 ft cliff face. It's a really pleasant moment of quiet in the hustle and bustle of a day exploring Skagway.

The Gold Rush Cemetery, Skagway.

Skagway Centennial Park, at Broadway and 1st St. A bronze statue forms the centerpiece of the park, and depicts an experienced Tlingit guide and a naïve young stampeder headed for trails.

The original railroad depot building now houses the headquarters of the Klondike Gold Rush National Historic Park. Other sites in the park include regions of downtown Seattle and portions of the Chilkoot trail and the White Horse Pass.

If you chose a bicycle as your mode of travel for the day, then a good plan for the day is to head first to the cemetery, then return to 23rd Avenue, follow the road over the bridge around to the right and take the first left for Dyea. Originally, this was the starting point for the Chilkoot Trail, the infamous trail that took prospectors on foot over a 3500 ft high pass and down to the Yukon. You can still drive to Dyea, although the town has long since been abandoned, it's around 9 miles from the Bridge. If you're cycling, there is a scenic over-look around 2.5 miles along this road that makes a great turnaround point.

As 23rd Avenue crosses the bridge it officially becomes the Klondike Highway and this is Skagway's land connection to the outside world. The highway leads to the Canadian Border. From there, the next stop is Carson City, Whitehorse and the Yukon. The highway parallels the White Horse Pass and tops out at 2883 ft. Once you reach summit of the Pass, you're in a very different environment; you're above the tree-line and surrounded instead by rolling alpine meadows, interspersed with miniature streams and waterfalls. Stunted trees in this area may be two-three hundred years old but are only four feet tall. It's a very magical area with its own unique atmosphere of wilderness and serenity. Often, by the time you arrive at these high, alpine regions you'll literally be in the clouds. The mists give the region a very ethereal feeling, and it's really quite beautiful. Alternatively, if you reach this area on a sunny day, the views last forever.

There are a wide variety of tours to the summit of the White Horse Pass. Riding the White Pass and Yukon train is certainly the most popular, and you'll get to hear tales of the gold rush days as you travel. Bus tours also run to the Summit and these give you a chance to get out at scenic points along the route. Whichever way you go– don't forget your ID or your passport as you will cross into Canada along the way.

One of the most popular excursions in Southeast Alaska. Ride the train to the summit of the White Horse Pass, and don't forget to bring ID as you will cross the border into Canada.

Views above the treeline at the summit of the White Horse Pass.

The Alaska-Yukon Border.

Take a hike

The Dewey Lake Trails

Level: Lower lake – moderate, Upper Lake and Devil's Punch-bowl – very demanding

Elevation: Lower Lake - 1250ft, Upper lake – 3200ft

Attractions: scenic lakes, wild-flowers, forest

Tip: take a picnic and enjoy the lower lake

Dewey Lakes Trail System

The Dewey Lakes Trail System starts right in town; just take a right at the train tracks on your way into town from the ship. If you're already in town, there's a footbridge at the east end of 3rd Avenue. Cross over to the east side of the train tracks and you'll see the trailhead. The trail is well marked and maintained and certainly moderate exercise, as switch-backs meander through spruce forest on the way to Lower Dewey Lake. The lake itself is a little under a mile, but it's quite a hike as it's quite steep in places.

Once at the lake, the path circumnavigates the lake. Its rough going on the far side, but passable. An alternative plan is to take a picnic and head for an extensive grassy area at the far end of the lake. This is a perfect spot on a sunny afternoon. If you want to continue on, you can follow the path at the end of the lake through more mature forest and eventually out to a very scenic viewpoint, Sturgill's Landing. From here, you can see all the way down the Taiya Inlet, to the Cathedral Mountain Range. This is a long hike though (4.5 miles) and the trail is not well-maintained in some places. It is nice to venture a short way in though, as you'll soon notice a distinct change in the ground layer in this region – see inset box. Alternatively, you can return to the head of the lake and continue uphill – as the name implies, there is an Upper Dewey Lake.

Upper Dewey Lake

This is a considerable hike, and should not be taken on lightly. The route starts at the north end of the Lower Dewey Lake, so watch for trail signs as you reach the first lake. Upper Dewey Lake is another 2.5 mile climb to a total altitude of just under 3000 ft. It is very steep and rough in places. Devil's Punchbowl is an additional 1¼ miles further on from Upper Dewey Lake, and another 200 feet gain in altitude.

This is the sort of day hike that takes advance planning. Keen cruise-ship crew and Skagway residents may attempt it once per season, however if you are experienced hikers, you have a full day in port and you set out early, it is feasible. If you do make it all the way to the Upper Lake, there's a rustic cabin with a logbook you can sign. If you continue on to the Devil's Punchbowl, the views are tremendous. And romantic too; look back down on Upper Dewey Lake, and you'll see that it is heart-shaped. It's actually a popular spot for wedding proposals. After such a hike, who could say no?

Lower Dewey Lake.

Seeing the woods for the trees

If you have done some hiking in Southeast Alaska before hitting the trails for Dewey Lake, you'll immediately notice how different the forest is in this area. The reason for this is the recent history of logging in the region. As a result, the trees are much younger and comprise even age stands. At the start of the Dewey Trails, you'll notice an open canopy and verdant ground layer in the forest, but as you get further up, you'll see that the canopy closes in and the forest is composed of densely packed, young slim trees. Look at the ground layer and here you'll really see the difference. Under the young trees, the ground layer is entirely comprised of a dense layer of decaying pine needles. Typically, pine needles break down very slowly and render the soil acidic so that few other plants can get a foothold. Only once some of the trees die, or the forest is thinned out, does the ground layer start to develop. The moss blanket and diverse understory that characterize mature forest won't develop until the forest has been un-touched for over 50 years, and it takes 200 years before a region officially comprises frontier, or old growth forest.

Even age stand

Mature forest

Take a hike

Yakutania Point
Level: easy to moderate
Elevation: sea level
Attractions: great views
down Taiya Inlet, good
chance of seal sightings
Tip: take a picnic!

Yakutania Point

If a pleasant stroll sounds more appealing than an arduous hike, head to Yakutania Point. To find the trailhead, go all the way west along 1st Avenue, past the airport and over the bridge. From there, follow the trail to the left. It's a short half mile out to Yakutania Point, and another half mile through the woods to Smugglers Cove. Both areas are perfect for a picnic; trails lead you to a variety of picnic tables and small, hidden beaches and bays. Be sure to keep an eye out as harbor seals frequent the sheltered bays along the shoreline here. From the point, you can see right down the Taiya Inlet and on really sunny days Smugglers Cove, also clearly signed, becomes a popular swimming spot for truly hardy locals.

Trail to Yakutania Point.

Hiking in Skagway

Dewey Lakes Trailhead:

From the railroad dock, follow the road to town, cross the railway tracks and then take the first right on Springer Street. Cross back over the tracks and you'll see the trailhead...heading up!

You can also follow along the riverbank of Dewey Creek, but you should heed all signs regarding crossing the rail tracks.

The trail for Lower Dewey is steep in places and you should allow at least 2-3 hours to reach the lake and complete the trail around the Lake. For Upper Dewey and the Punchbowl, plan on taking a full day and be prepared; this is a very strenuous hike.

Yakutania Point.

To reach this trail system, head into town, then stay on 2nd Avenue over to Main Street. Take a left there and follow the road around, in front of the airport then over the river. The trail to Yakutania Point is flat and very passable. The views from the point are spectacular on a clear day, and from the point you can follow the signs back to a very peaceful, scenic spot, Smuggler's Cove.

On a sunny day, this is a favored swimming spot for locals, and just fyi; swimming gear is typically optional...

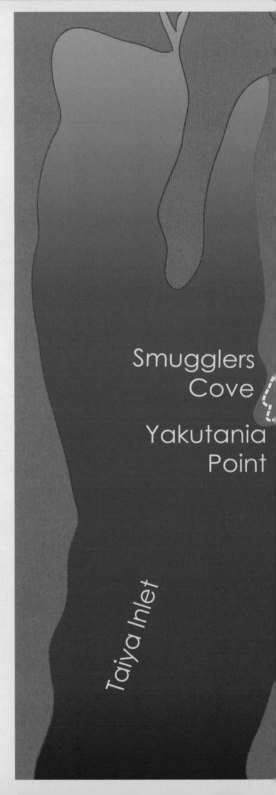

Smugglers Cove

Yakutania Point

Taiya Inlet

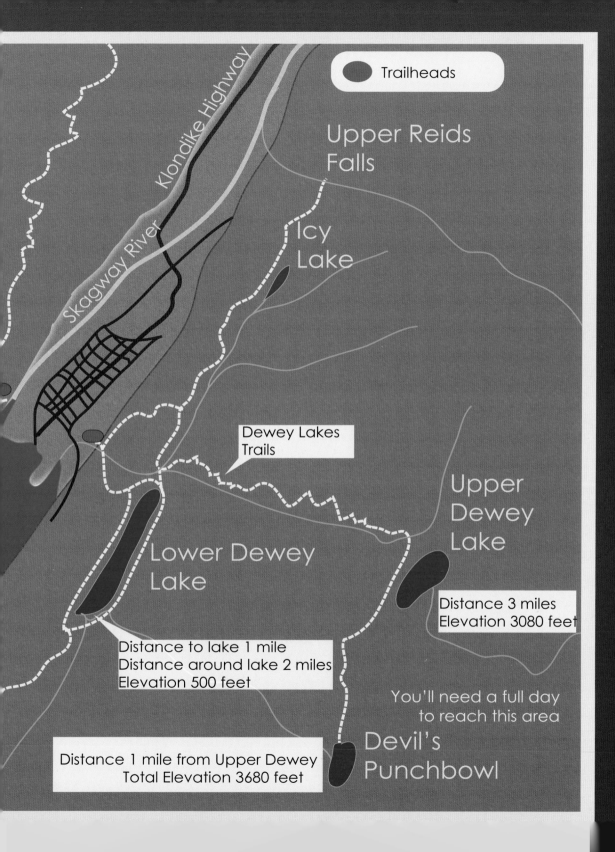

Trailheads

Upper Reids Falls

Klondike Highway

Skagway River

Icy Lake

Dewey Lakes Trails

Upper Dewey Lake

Lower Dewey Lake

Distance 3 miles
Elevation 3080 feet

Distance to lake 1 mile
Distance around lake 2 miles
Elevation 500 feet

You'll need a full day to reach this area

Distance 1 mile from Upper Dewey
Total Elevation 3680 feet

Devil's Punchbowl

In Focus: The Klondike Gold Rush

The infamous story of the Klondike Gold Rush begins in August 1896, when a small group of miners working along the confluence of the Yukon and Klondike Rivers, in North-west Canada struck gold. The first lucky miners worked their claim through the winter that year and set off back to the lower 48 the following summer. On July 14th 1897, a ship carrying the first of these miners docked in San Francisco and three days later, on July 17th, a second ship docked in Seattle. This second ship, the Portland, carried 68 miners and over 2 tons of gold. Word spread like wildfire and the rush to the North was on.

Every possible passage north was booked, but the location of the gold strike, in the Yukon Territory of Canada was hard to reach. The "rich man's route" was all by water; by steamer to St Michael on the coastline of Alaska then by riverboat down the Yukon River. Around 3,000 of the more affluent prospectors took this route. For those with fewer resources, the poor man's route was entirely overland, starting from Edmonton, Canada. Of the few who took this route, only a handful made it and they arrived years after the gold rush was over.

By far the most popular route was to take passage on a ship from Seattle to Skagway. From there, two different routes led over the Coast Mountains. The Chilkoot Trail was shorter but steeper; the pass was at 3,525 feet. The White Horse Trail was longer, but summitted at 2885 feet, and was potentially passable with pack horses. Once over the mountains, stampeeders would reach the official border with Canada and were only allowed to pass if they could show they had enough supplies with them to last a year. So, for most stampeeders their trip began with multiple journeys up and down the Chilkoot or White Horse trails, ferrying their supplies to the border. This was done over the winter months and the stampeeders then camped at Lake Bennett, they built rafts and then they waited for the ice on the Yukon River to melt. Once the spring came and the ice melted, they sailed down the rapids of the Yukon River into gold territory.

SCALES AND SUMMIT OF CHILKOOT PASS

University of Washington Special Collections: Hegg 105A

One thousand feet up and two feet wide; the famous golden staircase led over the highest peak of the Chilkoot Trail. If a stampeeder stepped out of the line, they might wait days to get a place again.

The real-life saga of Soapy Sam

Skagway in the days of '98.

University of Washington Special Collections: Hegg 20A

Once the gold rush began, Skagway grew up almost overnight as stampeeders thronged through the town. Over the course of a single summer, hotels, stores and saloons sprang up. A town was quickly surveyed and laid out, but by all accounts that may have been as far as orderliness went. The lure of gold brought more than honest miners and adventurers to the North. It also brought con men, thieves and opportunists. Notorious among them was Jefferson Smith, a.k.a. Soapy Sam, whose gang of over 100 ruffians ruled Skagway in 1897 and 1898. He ran telegraph offices that had no telegraph link and freight companies that dumped their freight as soon as they were out of sight. He set up crooked gambling halls and even ran an "army enlistment" tent where the victim's clothes and possessions were stolen while a "doctor" administered a physical on the would-be recruit. Soapy also maneuvered himself into the position of town's mayor, his gangs ruled the streets and the town quickly developed a notorious reputation. His men would meet newcomers at the docks and use a wide variety of tricks to rob and cheat them out of any wealth the newcomers carried before they even made it into town.

Eventually though, this practice led Soapy to his demise. When he and his thugs fleeced a newly arriving miner of $2,800 in gold, the miner turned to the honest citizens of Skagway. They formed a vigilante committee, called the committee of 101, headed by Frank Reid who was the town's civil engineer. On the evening of July 8th 1898, another dispute led them to decide that the time had come for action. They went in search of Soapy Sam. In true western style, a shoot-out in the streets followed. The details remain vague and in dispute, but shots rang out and at the end of the gunfight, both Frank Reid and Soapy Sam lay dead. Soapy Sam was 38 years old.

The Women of the Gold Rush

While most of the tales of the gold rush tell the stories of intrepid, male gold-seekers, in fact one in ten of those headed for the Klondike gold fields were women. They came from every walk of life, from housewives and shopkeepers to dancers and barmaids; even a group of nuns made the trip. Some found gold in the goldfields; the famous Mrs. Willis made over $300,000 on her claim in the Yukon. Others bedazzled the lucky miners out of the hard won riches in the dance halls. Popular showgirls quickly rose to movie-star status; one of the most famous dance girls of the time was Klondike Kate, known across the region for her "flame of the Yukon" dance.

But other women became well-known for their homeliness amongst the rough and tumble of the gold rush camps. One such girl was Mollie Walsh. Mollie arrived in Skagway 1897, along with a Presbyterian minister. Overwhelmed by the chaos of Skagway, she chose to set out for the trails and set up a mess tent at Lake Bennett. To hungry miners fresh from the tortuous trails, a home cooked meal served by a bright-eyed pretty Irish girl was as close to heaven as they could hope for, and Mollie got the nickname "Angel of the Klondike Trail". She had many suitors and unfortunately died young, at the hands of one of them, Mike Bartlett. Still, other suitors never forgot her and one of them, Packer Jack, fashioned a very pretty bronze statue in remembrance of her. The statue was installed in the 1930's and is still on display today, in Children's Park.

A group of brave dancers set out for Dawson City.

University of Washington Special Collections: LaRoche2012

Panning for gold

Ever wonder where the expression "It didn't pan out " came from? In fact, this goes back to gold rush days. The gold that was discovered in the Klondike Gold Rush was placer or alluvial gold, found within long meandering ribbons of quartz in the bedrock. These veins of gold were forced to the surface by volcanic action, then weather and erosion would release the gold from the quartz as small gold nuggets and gold dust that would wash into nearby waterways.

Optimistic miners would sample the stream bed in promising regions in the hopes of finding "pay dirt". Miners used large, open pans to sluice through loads of gravel and sand. Because gold was heavy it would sink to the bottom, and as it was bright, it was easy to spot. Groups of hard-working miners would spend months sifting through the stream bed. Sometimes a miner would be rewarded with the sight of tiny flecks of gold, but this wasn't always the case. Either way, this lead to the use of the expression "panned out", as in an area did, or didn't pan out.

All a gold miner really needed was a pan, determination and some luck. It was shrewdly observed by commentators of the time, "never have so many fortunes been made by men whose outfits cost so little".

Haines

Haines is located 16 miles south of Skagway and is easily accessed via the ferry system that runs between the two towns. Most Princess ships call at Skagway and run a variety of excursions to Haines, however on other itineraries your ship may dock in Haines, so conversely Skagway is easily accessible for the day.

In many ways, the defining natural feature of Haines is the Chilkat River. While Chilkoot, as in Chilkoot Trail, is the Tlingit word for big fish, Chilkat, as in Chilkat River, means many fish in the Tlingit language and this is certainly the case. The Chilkat River and surrounding tributaries host a bountiful salmon run that includes five different species of salmon. Runs persist from mid-summer, all the way through fall and into early winter. The winter salmon run is possible because the waters in the river are slightly warmer than in surrounding regions. As a result, the river stays ice-free and in November each year, dog salmon running up the river comprise the latest salmon run in the whole of North America. This provides a welcome winter food source for wildlife across the region, and it's also thought to explain why this region was one of the first settled by indigenous people.

Originally, Haines was the home of the Chilkat Tlingit, a group that has always been known for its great arts and crafts within the Tlingit culture. Chilkat blankets, first crafted in this region, remain world renowned and recognized as one of the iconic artifacts of the Tlingit culture.

The town of Haines sits at the base of the cathedral mountains. The Victorian houses at the back of town originally comprised Fort Seward. Today, they house a Tlingit art center along with an array of authentic craft stores.

Today, Tlingit art is again finding a new center of innovation in the town, as craftsmen and artists from throughout Alaska gather at the Alaska Indian Arts Center of Haines. The center is also home to the Chilkat Dancers, who have won international recognition for the authentic dances and costume. The Arts Center is housed in an old Victorian building that was originally part of the army installation built here, Fort Seward. This was built just after the turn of the last century, in 1904, and was essentially designed mostly as a showpiece; the fort comprised a row of typical Victorian homes, built around a parade ground. After the fort was decommissioned in 1946, the buildings were purchased by a group of local retirees, and one of the buildings was given over as the Arts Center. The other buildings have also been kept up and they now comprise an unusual Southeast Alaskan neighborhood.

For wildlife sightings, the hotspot in this area is the Chilkat River, just outside town. Most notable are the bald eagles that congregate each winter along the shoreline of the river, but in the summer months bears, moose, lots of eagles and a wide variety of birdlife can also been seen in the region. There are several different types of tours offered that explore the region; to see wildlife, choose those that are focused on the river, such as the floats or the jet boat tours. Either of these options explores the spectacular Chilkat River Valley. The Valley is a natural wildlife corridor and the one place in Southeast Alaska where you may just see a moose on the loose.

In Focus –Chilkat River Bald Eagle Reserve – Valley of the Eagles

The Chilkat River Bald Eagle Reserve was established in 1982 to protect the world's largest gathering of bald eagles that occurs each year along the banks of the Chilkat River. At the confluence of the Tsirku, Kleheni and Chilkat Rivers, in an area known as the Tsirku fan where the three rivers meet, the substrate comprises a deep, fan shaped accumulation of gravel and glacial debris. Water from the surrounding glaciers and snow-banks flows onto this huge fan each spring and trickles down into the massive gravel bed. As water flows in faster than it can flow out, a large underground reservoir forms. When winter arrives and surrounding waters freeze, the water in the rocky reservoir stays warm and slowly percolates up, warming the waters of the river by some 10-20°F, and keeping the river ice free.

It's this warm water that leads to the late salmon run; dog salmon enter the river in November, comprising the last salmon run of the year. This late pulse of food draws bald eagles from across the area and as many as 4,000 eagles may congregate along the banks of the confluence each winter.

Even in summer though, the area sees large numbers of eagles. The best viewing areas are between mile markers 18 and 22 on the Haines Highway, which is the main road out of Haines, where you'll find spotting scopes and lots of interpretive signs and information. Most tours to Haines will include a stop here on their itinerary and it's not unusual to spot 20-30 eagles in the area at any one time.

For information on pretty much anything to do with bald eagles, visit the website of the American Bald Eagle Foundation, http://baldeagles.org/. Based out of Haines, this group is very active and the website really does cover everything you might ever need to know about bald eagles.

Wildlife Profile: The Moose

Fast Facts:

Common name: Moose

Scientific name: *Alces alces*

Best areas for sightings: Interior Alaska. Occasional sightings in the Haines area and along the shorelines at the entrance to Glacier Bay.

ID: Long legged, with a drooping nose and a "bell" or dewlap under the chin. Males sport large antlers.

Size: Males up to 6 feet tall to the shoulder, maximum weights may be up to 1600 lbs. Females are slightly smaller, standing up to 5 feet tall and reaching up to 800 lbs in weight.

Lifespan: Typically 5-6 years, rarely more than 15 years.

Mating and reproduction: Females mate in the late summer and give birth the following May or June. Twins are common. Calves grow extremely quickly. Newborns may weigh between 28 – 35 lbs, and by the end of their first summer, most weigh over 300 lbs. Many females will breed annually.

Typical group size: Lone adults typically sighted. Mother-calf pairs stay together for a year.

Diet: Graze on willow, birch, aspen and wetland vegetation.

Recommended websites: http://www.mooseworld.com - For everything you need to know about moose

Wildlife in Focus: The Moose

By the time you've reached Skagway, you may be wondering why you haven't seen moose wandering down the streets of Southeast Alaska. Certainly, that's one of the most memorable images from shows such as "Northern Exposure". Well, the reason is that moose are actually quite rare in Southeast Alaska. They are interior animals, most closely associated with boreal forest, a.k.a. the pine forest that characterizes the inside Passage. On the far side of the Coast Mountains moose are very plentiful—and prone to wandering through small towns. However moose are terrible mountain-climbers and consequently, the mountains have been a barrier for dispersal into coastal areas. Rivers provide an easier avenue of migration where moose can easily traverse the shoreline regions, and in fact moose are now slowly moving into Southeast Alaska. Over the last 10 years or more, numbers have been increasing and moose are now quite regularly seen around Haines, where the Chilkat River provides easy access and movement around the region. They have also dispersed along the shorelines of the area and they are also seen now in increasing numbers in the lower reaches of Glacier Bay.

Rather unkindly, moose are often referred to as "God's Mistake". It's true that at first glance, moose seem ungainly and ill-prepared for the challenges of life in the wilds of Alaska. On closer inspection though, moose are in fact very well equipped for life in Alaska. Their large size means that, like many arctic animals, they have a low surface to volume ratio and this keep them warm in winter. Additionally, their coat comprises a dense soft undercoat overlaid by a rough outer coat of hollow hair; this method of insulation is used by polar bears and is extremely efficient. In fact, warm temperatures are more of a challenge for moose. They start to pant as soon as the mercury hits a balmy 23°F, and on warm winter days in Alaska, they will roll in the snow, making moose versions of snow angels, all in an effort to cool down.

The long legs are also an Alaskan adaptation, providing easy mobility in snowy weather. Adult moose can move easily through snow banks as deep as 36 inches and in the boggy shore-lines of wetlands, which comprise some of their favored feeding regions. With such a large body on thin legs, moose are known for the arthritic knees and also their preference for a therapy for this. Moose frequently browse on willow, which contains salicylic acid, the active ingredient in aspirin. Long ago, native people took a cue from the moose and started to use willow as a painkiller themselves and today of course, aspirin is in widespread use.

Growing a new set of antlers each year is all part of the methods male moose use to attract the fairer sex.

Romance in the wild

The mating habits of moose offer a noteworthy example of the lengths males go to in the pursuit of females. Male moose have what's known biologically as enhanced secondary sexual characteristics. Essentially, this means that they develop extreme and pronounced characteristics that seem to have no apparent survival function; in some cases these traits may even be a challenge to their survival. In fact, the purpose of these pronounced traits is to attract females. For traits such as these, bigger, louder or brighter is always better, which brings us to the rack (or antlers) of the male moose.

Each year male moose drop their antlers in the fall and then start to grow a new rack each spring. The rack grows fast; as the food supply increases with the spring thaw, male moose antlers become the fastest growing animal organ known. They develop their own blood supply in the form a soft, velveteen coating and continue to grow through summer. At full size, the male rack might measure 3-4 feet across and may limit the male's ability to move through dense scrub and forest. Come the fall, the velveteen breaks down, it begins to fall off the antlers and eventually the males shed the velveteen completely. Once the velveteen has been shed, the rut begins. Old bull males usually shed first and then construct a rutting pit. The pit is around 2-3 inches deep and 2 feet wide. The bull first urinates in the pit, then splashes his new cologne (yep—urine) all over, especially in the dewlap below the chin, which is especially designed to efficiently disperse his new "cologne". His bright new rack gets a good coat too and with that, he's ready to find his mate. Now, where are those lucky females....

A female moose with a young calf—considered by most Alaskans to be one of the most dangerous animals to encounter in the wild.

Skagway

Dyea Inlet

Taiya Inlet

Chilkat River

Lutak Inlet

Chilkat Inlet

Haines

11

Katzehin River

Chilkat Mountains

Rainbow Glacier

Davidson Glacier

Chilkat Peninsula

Upper Lynn Canal

Coast Mountains

Sullivan Island

12

Eldred Rock Lighthouse

N

0   1.25 2.5   5 Mi

Cruising highlights

Skagway Sailaway – North and Southbound Cruises
The sailaway from Skagway is certainly one of the most scenic along any cruise of Alaska's Inside Passage. The ship pulls away from the dock into the waters of the Taiya Inlet. This is the deepest fjord in the North America, waterfalls cascade down to the steep shorelines on either side of the ship and the Cathedral Mountains at the end of the Inlet provide a spectacular backdrop.

Waypoint 11 – Haines & the Upper Lynn Canal
Approximately 45 minutes after leaving Skagway, the ship passes by Haines on the starboard side and turns into the Upper Lynn Canal. The view down the canal is considered to be one of the best in Southeast Alaska.

Waypoint 12 – Eldred Rock Lighthouse
This picturesque lighthouse will be on the starboard side of the ship. It's visible around 2 hours after leaving Skagway. The Davidson and Rainbow glaciers will also be in view at this point.

Look for Steller sea lions along the shoreline just past the Katzehin River. Humpback whales may occasionally be sighted in the lower reaches of the Upper Lynn Canal.

The Taiya Inlet with the Chilkat Mountains in the distance.

Skagway Sailaway

Most Princess ships sail from Skagway in the early evening, just as twilight falls. The ship pulls back from the dock into the waters of the Taiya Inlet, from the stern of the ship you have a great view of the town nestled in among the mountains. All the predominant architecture that you can see dates back to the days of the Gold Rush and it's easy to imagine the town in those exciting times.

The Taiya Inlet is the longest, deepest Fjord in North America. For more on fjords, you can take a look ahead at the section on glaciers. In a nutshell, a fjord is a deep U-shaped channel that was carved out by an advancing glacier and subsequently flooded with saltwater as the glacier retreated. The glacier that created the Taiya Inlet is the Dyea glacier, and it has long since receded back into the Dyea Inlet on the far side of the channel. But the handiwork the glacier left behind is remarkable. The fjord is over 1000 feet deep and its steep sides rise to almost 3000 feet high on either side of the ship. The slopes are covered with deep evergreen forest and a myriad of waterfalls carrying fresh snow melt cascade down to the shoreline on either side. One of the most prominent is the Carvelle falls, named for a local ferryboat captain. You'll see these falls around 20 minutes after Sailaway on the port, the left hand side, but there are numerous un-named waterfalls along the way. So, now's your chance; pick your favorite and you can give it a name.

Waypoint 11 – Haines and the Upper Lynn Canal

Around 30 to 45 minutes after leaving Skagway, as you cruise down the Taiya Inlet, the cathedral mountain range, which lies just behind the town on Haines, comes into view from the bow of the ship. If the weather is good, it's well worth finding a spot where you can see forwards, as the view that emerges as the ship turns from the Taiya Inlet into the Upper Lynn Canal is considered by most to be the best view in Southeast Alaska.

As the ship passes by Haines and makes this turn, the Chilkat Mountains reach to the skyline on the starboard or right side of the ship, the Davidson and Rainbow Glaciers will come into view on the starboard shoreline and the Coast Mountain Range lines the shoreline on the port side. If it's a clear evening, as the sun sets to the west the last rays of light bathe the mountain tops in alpenglow, a deep orange color that persists through to midnight in mid-summer. So, wander out to the decks, take a drink and maybe a loved one. Evenings such as this are Alaska's true gold.

Humpback whales at sunset.

Katzehin River

Around 30 mintues beyond Haines, you'll see the Katzehin Rover on the port, or left side, flowing into the waters of the Fjord. The river flows down from the Katzehin glacier and the grey color of the river is due to the glacial silt that the river carries. As the river is freshwater, it's less dense than the saltwater and consequently, it sits on top of the water of the fjord and only mixes slowly. This leads to the distinct color differences. You'll see this phenomenon again while cruising glacial regions.

Waypoint 12 – Eldred Rock Lighthouse

Eldred Rock Lighthouse is officially the most photographed lighthouse in Southeast Alaska and if there is still sufficient light as you cruise by, you'll see why. The lighthouse sits against the backdrop of the Chilkat Mountains and truly meets all the stereotypic requirements of a view of an Alaskan Lighthouse.

The rock was named by Marcus Baker in 1880, after his wife Sarah Eldred. The lighthouse was erected in 1906 and was automated in 1973. Several famous shipwrecks have happened in this area, the most tragic being the sinking of the Princess Sophia in October 1918. During a vicious storm in October 1918, the Princess Sophia, carrying 353 passengers and crew, and one dog ran aground just south of here on Vanderbilt Reef. As winds reached 100 mph and waves were over 30 feet high, the weather was too rough to deploy the life boats and passengers stayed onboard. After 40 hours grounded on the reef, a large wave dislodged the ship, the hull of the ship broke apart and the Princess Sophia quickly floundered. All souls onboard were lost. Only a small dog managed to swim to shore.

> The Princess Sophia, a popular steamboat offering sight-seeing cruises in the waters of Alaska's Inside Passage, sank shortly after this picture was taken, in October 1918. All 353 passengers were drowned. The lone survivor was a dog, that escaped by swimming to shore.
>
> Source: Alaska State Library, William Norton Photograph Collection, Identifier: P226-747

Waypoint 13 – The entrance to Glacier Bay

After passing the Eldred Rock lighthouse, you'll continue cruising south through the Upper Lynn Canal. Ships bound for Glacier Bay will then take a turn to starboard into the waters of Icy Strait. This channel was named by early mariners for the huge bergs that they frequently encountered here. Most of these came from the Grand Pacific Glacier in Glacier Bay, but now that the Grand Pacific glacier has retreated icebergs are infrequent through here. The entrance to the bay lies on the northern shoreline of Icy Strait, shortly beyond this turn.

Ships leaving Skagway and headed for Juneau will continue south, cruising through Favorite Channel and around Douglas Island into Juneau, while ships headed for Tracy Arm or for points further south will take Chatham Straits. Take a look at the map that accompanies this book and you can follow your route through the region.

Eldred Rock lighthouse. You'll pass this point around 2 hours after leaving Skagway.

Chapter 6

Glorious Glaciers: Cruising Alaska's Wilderness Bays

Yale Glacier, College Fjord.

Wilderness Cruising

"A picture of icy wilderness unspeakably pure and sublime"
John Muir, 1879, recounted in "Travels to Alaska" 1915.

With these words, written in his journal following a day spent exploring Glacier Bay in 1879, the Scottish-born naturalist John Muir placed the wilderness bays of Alaska on the map. The picture that he painted, with words not photographs, inspired the first wave of tourists to head north and Alaskan-bound sight-seeing cruises became a fashionable choice. Since then, many millions of people have visited the very regions that John Muir first described. And thanks also to the work of John Muir, much of Alaska's land and coastline remains protected and intact. As you cruise through these areas and look out from the decks of the ship, your view of these regions is unblemished. You too can experience the icy splendor of Alaska's wilderness bays, thanks in large part to the long shadow cast by the naturalist John Muir.

Princess itineraries include four different wilderness bays on their Alaskan cruise routes and each bay offers something slightly different: In Tracy Arm, huge, azure-blue icebergs drift along the shorelines of a narrow and delicate fjord. In Glacier Bay, the wilderness of the park is rich in wildlife and the Margerie Glacier is both approachable and active. In Yakutat Bay, the splendor of the Hubbard Glacier is hard to match; its face stretches six miles across the bay and the Wrangell St. Elias Mountain range provides a breath-taking backdrop. And in College

Fjord, Prince William Sound, six tidewater glaciers tumble down the shoreline along a single stretch of coastline, comprising the largest accumulation of tidewater glaciers anywhere in the world. In this chapter we'll explore each bay in turn, providing full details of the times and places to be out on deck to see the wildlife and to enjoy the especially scenic viewpoints in each bay. But first, let's get to know a little more about glaciers and the wildlife of these regions.

Alaska's Glaciers

The glaciers of Alaska are in many ways a defining characteristic of coastal Alaskan eco-systems. In Southeast Alaska, most terminate in bays and fjords within the Inside Passage, bringing a steady flow of freshwater and minerals into the system. The calving of glaciers mixes the water column and the icebergs they produce serve as refuges for wildlife. Alaska's glaciers range widely in size and length and while some are world famous, most of the 100,000-plus glaciers to be found across the state are unnamed and undocumented. But they all begin life in the same way, high in the icefields above the Alaska shoreline.

Ice at the source

In vast, snowy, silent icefields up above 4000 feet, Coastal Alaska's ample rain falls as snow. Where temperatures stay cool enough the snow persists year-round, accumulating year after year. Each year, as new snow is added, the weight of the accumulating snow increases, compacting the snow below. Eventually the combined pressure of the accumulating snow-pack leads to the formation of firn, an intermediate, rice-grain like material. Over long periods of time, the firn cleaves into huge sheets of **glacial ice**. The glacial ice is heavy and dense; between 15 to 30 feet of snow may compact down to produce just one foot of glacial ice and 90% of the air that was in the original snow is squeezed out by the intense pressure.

Ice in motion

The glacial ice accumulates in the natural basins within the mountain range. Glacial ice has a degree of plasticity and a consistency like putty. Eventually, it overflows from the basin and slowly starts to slip down the mountain side. Due to the weight of the ice above, the very low-est layer within the ice melts and this layer of water acts as lubricant on the underside of the glacier. Augmented by the pull of gravity, the ice slips into motion and so becomes a **glacier, a river of ice in motion**.

The birth of a glacier; ice overflows from the ice-field above. Glaciers are ice in motion. Look for the tell-tale crevicing or cracks that indicate the ice is on the move.

Crevices on the top of the glacier are a reminder that the glacier is in motion. Crevices from as the uppermost portion of the glacier cracks as the glacier weaves it's way down the mountainside.

As the glacier makes its way down the mountainside, ice flows through the glacier just like water flows through a river. Flow rates are usually slow. A typical rate of movement would be around one to two feet per day, but when glaciers start to surge, or gallop, rates of up to 1000 feet a day have been recorded. The glacier finds the easiest route through the mountain range, flowing around curves and over obstacles. The lower portions of the glacier remain cold and plastic so it can flow through the route, but in the top 150 feet, the ice is warmed by the air above and starts to melt. As the glacier twists and turns, the top layer starts to crack; this is how crevices form. Looking for crevicing is actually a great way to distinguish glaciers from the surrounding snowpack. Where you see deep cracks or crevices in a pack of snow or ice, this indicates that the ice is in motion and you are in fact looking at a glacier.

The tell-tale moraines

As the growing glacier advances, it scrapes over the bedrock below. Boulders and rocks are embedded in its undersurface so it literally sculpts the regions that it flows over. The broken down rock, finely ground to the consistency of baking flour, is called glacial silt. The silt serves as a testament to the strength and power of glaciers; essentially, it's all that is left of the mountains that the glaciers flow over on their relentless march to the ocean or to the valley floor. The silt accumulates in large stripes within and around the glacier, called moraines. **Lateral moraines** form down each side of the glacier and when two glaciers merge, flowing together just like streams would in a river system, the lateral moraines mark the point where

the merging takes place, and form a stripe down the center of the glacier called a **median moraine**. The moraines tell the story of the glacier as it flows, leaving signs of points where glaciers join or where tributary glaciers flow into major glaciers high within the mountain range.

The Smith Glacier, College Fjord, boasts a clearly defined median moraine.

The U-shape of this valley is a clear indication that the valley was created by an advancing glacier and later exposed as the glacier retreated. You can see the remnant glacier, far back in the recesses of the mountainside.

Advancing and retreating glaciers

The advance or retreat of a glacier depends on three key factors; the supply of snow in the ice field, the year round temperature and the location of the terminus or tip of the glacier, often referred to as the snout of the glacier. In advancing glaciers, plentiful snowfall means that snow accumulates in the ice field each year. As more ice accumulates at its source, the glacier advances. However, when the glacier receives less snow, if the weather warms and the ice and snow melt, or if the glacier meets the ocean and the ice at the snout of the glacier starts to melt, then the glacier may halt in its advance. If the rate of loss and gain of ice are equal, the glacier may stay around the same length for a while. During this time, ice continues to flow along the length of the glacier but the glacier doesn't change in overall extent. Only when the rate at which ice is lost exceeds the rate at which ice is gained will the glacier start to shrink or retreat. As it does, the glacier's handiwork on the rock below is revealed. As the glacier shrinks back into the route it once created, a deep flat bottomed U-shaped channel is exposed. Where the glacier has reached the ocean, saltwater moves in as the glacier retreats. This is a fjord; a natural conduit and a perfect pathway by which to explore these icy bays.

Eagle Glacier, outside Juneau. Clearly defined sharp peaks, called nunataks, have always been above the ice. Gently rolling profiles, like the island in front have been shaped by glaciers that flowed over top of them in years gone by.

Glacier footprints

Retreating glaciers leave clear footprints to tell of their former presence. Typically, the glacier halts before starting to retreat. At this point, the flow of ice continues through the glacier and debris, glacial silt, even rocks and boulders are carried along in the flow. It's as though the glacier becomes a rocky conveyor belt. All the rocks and debris are deposited in a single spot and accumulate as a ridge of debris that may be hundreds of feet high. This is called the **terminal moraine**, a clear footprint in the substrate that marks the point where the glacier once stood. Glaciologists can provide dates for different terminal moraines and in this way they can track the exact size and extent of the glacier during prior times.

Look around in glaciated areas and you'll see other glacier footprints too. While V-shaped valleys are formed through the flow of water, U-shaped valleys are the work of glaciers. Hanging valleys with clear U-shaped walls have been formed by glaciers long gone. Sharp mountain ridgelines indicate areas that have always remained above the ice and snow. These are called nunataks, peaks that once would have been islands as a sea of snow and ice surrounded them. Look a little lower down and you'll see gently rounded summits. This is another glacial footprint; at one time, glacial ice flowed over the tops of those mountains, smoothing their sharp ridges into the gently rolling profiles you see left behind.

The wavy appearance of the ice in the background reflects year round variation in ice accumulation.

Rocks and boulders are embedded into the ice along the length of the glacier. The undersurface looks like this too and gives advancing glaciers the ability to sculpt the mountains and scenery they flow through.

The face of the glacier

The vertical view of the glacier at its snout is the face and by all accounts, this is the most exciting point of the glacier. Here is where the glacier calves, as the push of ice from behind and the melting of the ice below cause chunks of ice to fall from the face. Calving is most dramatic where glaciers terminate in saltwater but it is always a very unpredictable event. Sometimes you may spot a tell-tale ripple of icy debris falling from the face of the glacier. These areas of instability are always promising and worth watching. At other times, a spire that defies gravity may stubbornly remain suspended for hours on end before finally crashing into the water below. That generally happens the minute you look away! As you stand in front of the glacier, you can hear the clap of "white thunder" as it splits and splinters. As it creeps towards you, you'll feel a very cool breeze of air. These are glacial winds that flow down from the ice fields along the course of the glacier. Few experiences rival the moment when you see the glacier calve. But keep the camera ready; these special moments are easy to miss....

The face of the Margerie Glacier, Glacier Bay.

Field guide to Glaciers

Essentially, glaciers are rivers of ice. Glacial ice accumulates in the ice field at the glaciers source. Eventually it overflows, and propelled primarily by gravity, the ice starts its slow motion slide down the mountainsides and across the landscapes of Alaska. Once in motion, the glacial ice officially comprises a glacier. Currently, there are more than 100,000 glaciers in Alaska and they come in a wide range of shapes and sizes.

The ice field

Ice fields are high, smooth plains of ice that may stretch across entire mountain ranges. Ice in these regions may be many hundreds of years old and thousands of feet thick. Generally, multiple glaciers will flow from an icefield. The Juneau Icefield is the source for more than 40 different valley glaciers.

The tall rocky peaks that rise above the icefield are called nunataks.

Cirque Glaciers

Cirque or hanging glaciers form in the natural hollows and basins high in the mountain slopes. The name "cirque" comes from the French word for bowl.

The accumulated ice moves into motion as it spills out or overflows from its cirque, but cirque glaciers remain high in the mountain range, rather than flowing down to the valley floor.

Valley glaciers

Valley glaciers flow down to the valley floor. Just like a river, they find the easiest route through the mountain range and terminate on the valley floor. In many cases, the meltwater from the glacier accumulates to form a small lake.

Crevicing in these glaciers will be pronounced around sharp corners and in regions of steep incline as the uppermost portions of the glacier cool and crack as the ice flows along it's course.

Piedmont glaciers

Piedmont glaciers occur where valley glaciers flow down on to flat land. The name comes from a French word meaning "foot of the mountain".

The flowing glacier may have been hundreds of feet deep as it flowed down the mountainside but once it reaches flat land, the ice spreads out like spilled milk and forms a thin but extensive layer of ice across the landscape.

Tidewater glaciers

Tidewater glaciers are valley glaciers that flow all the way down to the ocean. As saltwater intrudes underneath the glacier, this causes rapid melting and dramatic calving, as the glacial ice falls from the face of the glacier into the water below.

The blue green color of the seawater at the face of the glacier is due to glacial silt carried along in the massive amounts of meltwater that flow through the glacier.

Icebergs

Tidewater glaciers give rise to icebergs, and they come in all shapes and sizes. In summer most will melt quickly but large ones may last up to one month. Their color changes from deep blue to white as they melt and they're moved around by tides and currents.

In Alaska's wilderness bays icebergs are havens for wildlife, especially popular with harbor seals and sea otters.

Once the ice falls: Icebergs, shooters, bergy bits and growlers

The name iceberg comes from a Dutch word meaning "ice mountain" and in many ways, that's exactly what an iceberg is; a mountain of ice floating freely in the open water. They float because they're composed of freshwater and this is less dense than saltwater. Rocky debris and glacial silt are often caught within the ice that forms the iceberg, giving the iceberg a range of colors and stripes. This also means that the berg is a little heavier and the saying is true; only the tip of the iceberg, around 10%, is actually visible above the surface.

Shooters are large icebergs that have calved from the underwater portion of a tidewater glacier. While watching the glaciers on your cruise, you may occasionally see one of these bergs appear. Frequently, they generate substantial waves as they emerge like sleeping giants from below the water's surface. The ice in shooters has not been exposed to the air so it is more intact. It's often a steely blue color and the texture is like steel too. All vessels, from large ships to small craft, give these bergs a wide berth. Shooters tend to be heavy with debris and often float very low to the surface of the water so they can be hard to spot and as they gradually melt, they may roll at any time.

Bergy bits, or **growlers**, are smaller pieces of ice produced as icebergs melt or as icy rubble falls from the face of the glacier. Though smaller in dimension, this type of ice can be just as much of a hazard to shipping. Typically, growlers flow on predominant currents; on incoming tides they accumulate in front of a tidewater glacier, while out-going tides will disperse the bergs across the fjord or bay. You'll see your captain carefully navigating the ship through fields of growlers and bergy bits. Still, these types of floes are popular pupping sites for sea otters and harbor seals as the icy debris makes it hard for predators, such as transient killer whales, to echolocate and track down their prey amongst all the ice.

A sightseeing vessel passes by a large ice-berg at the entrance to Tracy Arm.

Why is the ice blue?

Glacial ice forms under intense pressure and cold conditions. As a result, it has different properties than ice that forms simply under cold conditions, such as in a refrigerator. Glacial ice is dense, containing only small amounts of air, and as a result of that increased pressure it's comprised of larger crystals. When the spectrum of visible (white) light hits these large crystals, the light is broken down into its spectrum of colors and the lower energy portions of the light spectrum, the red and yellow colored light, is trapped within the large crystals. Only the high energy (blue) light is reflected back and this makes the ice appear blue. The deeper the ice, the more intense the color will be. The color is called lapis lazuli and though many an artist has tried, it's said that this is a color that can't be replicated. And it's ephemeral too; as the ice warms in the surface layers of the glacier, the large crystals break down and glacier blue hues fade to white.

Bergy seltzer – snap, crackle and pop!

As your ship makes its way through the growlers and icy debris, listen for a moment or two and you'll often hear a persistent popping sound. This is bergy seltzer, the snap, crackle and pop of the glacial ice melting. With each pop, a small pocket of compacted air is released. This air was trapped as snow that fell in the ice-fields compacted down to become glacial ice. Given the age of the ice, some of this air may be hundreds of years old. In fact, scientists are using the ice from these pockets to learn more about our atmosphere in years gone by.

Wildlife viewing in the wilderness bays

The wilderness bays offer some of the best opportunities to see wildlife from your ship. Each bay has its own highlights but there are also some common features to all the bays that will influence where wildlife may be found. All four of the bays visited on Princess itineraries were originally formed by the advance and subsequent retreat of a glacier and all four bays have quite clearly defined terminal moraines. Of course, these will be submerged but on the ships navigational equipment they are surprisingly evident. While the fjords and channels of these regions are typically between 600 and 1000 feet deep, terminal moraines at the entrances to major bays may rise to within 50 feet or less of the surface. These submerged ridges direct currents underwater and cause upwellings that bring deep, cool nutrient rich waters to the surface and into the portion of the water column where light is available and photosynthesis is underway. The winning combination of light and nutrients fires up the food chain and means that these areas at the entrance to the bays are typically rich in wildlife.

Viewing from the ship, you'll often see an accumulation of debris such as kelp fronds, spruce needles and plant debris along current lines created by these upwellings. This is a clear sign to grab your binoculars and keep a lookout. All forms of marine life, from birds to sea otters, even baleen whales, will forage along these current lines.

The wilderness bays offer great opportunities for bird enthusiasts. Although the state is the year round home for only a small number of species of marine birds, many more use the state seasonally as a summertime feeding ground and/or a nesting region. The puffin is probably the most popular bird in Alaska. Like many seabirds, typically it's the males that display bright colors during the summer months in the hopes of attracting a female. You'll see some of these birds in open water across the mouths of the bays. Most nest and roost along the shorelines or on rocky outcrops in the bays so keep the binoculars trained on these areas too. A guide to Alaska's shorebirds is provided on page 238.

Horned puffins nest in upper reaches of Glacier Bay but they are most frequently sighted at the entrance to the bay. Tufted puffins, such as those shown here, are also frequently sighted in these regions.

A sea otter warms up on an iceberg in Prince William Sound, a bull moose forages along the shoreline and a mountain goat takes a rest up above the treeline.

Typically, the lower portions of the wilderness bays will offer better chances of seeing marine-based wildlife. As you head into the bays, the meltwater from the glaciers carries huge amounts of silt with it. This silt is important in the overall system here in Alaska but where it accumulates, it makes feeding more challenging for many marine species. The exceptions are those species that use the bays as sanctuaries for exactly this reason. Those species that feed on other marine mammals, specifically transient killer whales, will not usually venture into the silty headwaters of the bays. As you reach these areas you'll see that the ice-floes are well populated with sea otters and harbor seals, especially during the pupping season, when this areas offer a safe sanctuary, beyond the reach of predators

The key to spotting land-based wildlife in these regions is to keep your binoculars trained on the shoreline and the region above the treeline. Look for moose along the shorelines, especially at the entrance to the bays, brown and black bears will use shorelines as well as regions above the treelines and if you look above the tree-line to the most inaccessible rocky outcrops, that's where you'll see the ultimate mountaineer of these regions, the mountain goat.

Wildlife Profile: The Brown Bear

Fast Facts:

Common name: Brown bear, grizzly bear

Scientific name: *Ursus arctos*

Best areas for sightings: Shorelines of Glacier Bay, especially upper regions and along Tarr Inlet.

ID: Dish shaped face, prominent snout, long claws and a hump between the shoulders.

Size: Varies widely with location and season. During summer, Southeast Alaskan males typically weigh between 500-900 lbs, maximum on record 1400 lbs. They may stand up to 9 ft tall when raised on hind feet. Females weigh 500-700 lbs, interior grizzlies much smaller than coastal browns.

Lifespan: Males up to 22, females up to 25 years.

Mating and reproduction: Pairs associate for up to 1 week in late May, early June. Males mate with multiple females. Females give birth every 2-3 years. Typical litter size; 2-3 cubs.

Typical group size: Males solitary, females remain closely associated with cubs for 2-3 years. Browns may concentrate around food sources such as salmon streams.

Diet: Varies through the season, around 80% vegetarian.

Recommended websites: www.defenders.org/wildlife__and__habitat/wildlife/grizzly__bear.php

Wildlife in Focus: The Brown Bear

The brown bear holds iconic status among Alaska's wildlife. It's certainly high on most visitors "must-see" list and Alaska is the place: while brown bears are endangered or even extinct across most of their range in the lower 48, in Alaska, brown bear populations are holding their own. Currently, the population across the state may number 30,000 and numbers in Glacier Bay alone are nearing 300. Still, territory size varies widely with area. On the Northern tundra, male bears may each have a territory of over 100 square miles, while on Admiralty Island in Southeast Alaska brown bear density is estimated at around 1.2 bears per square mile.

Perhaps the key explanation for the continued success of brown bears in Alaska is the wide open spaces and functioning ecosystems that are available to them. That may well explain why the sight of a brown bear is so iconic; it implies so much about the world around the bear. Brown bears are easily disturbed and displaced by human activities. When you see a bear in the wild, in many ways it defines the wildness of the place itself.

In their interactions with humans, brown bears get a bad rap. Dogs, bees, lightning and other humans are far more dangerous and account for many more fatalities per year than brown bears. Since 2000, there have only been 5 fatal brown bear attacks recorded across Alaska and this figure includes the famous Timothy Treadwell and his partner, Amie Huguenard, who spent many years living with the brown bears of Katmai National Park prior to the fatal attack in October 2003. However, brown bears deserve respect for sure. They are fully equipped to defend themselves and their territory. They become aggressive when startled or threatened and as male brown bears frequently attack cubs, female brown bears are especially easily roused. The golden rule to remember if you do come across a brown bear in the wild is not to run. This makes you look like prey to the bear and as bears have been tracked running at speeds of up to 45 mph, things are unlikely to end well!

Brown bears may not always look threatening, but should always be treated with respect and caution.

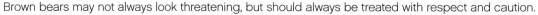

In terms of their diet, brown bears are mostly vegetarian. When first emerging from hibernation, they feed on roots to jumpstart their digestive system. The large hump and long claws of the brown bear are actually adaptations for digging up food items of this type. The salmon runs in Southeast Alaska provide the protein in their diet but even when salmon streams are in full flow, brown bears will still seek out berries and grasses. In inland regions, the protein of the bears' diet may come from lemmings and ground squirrels. Brown bears may also attack live prey on occasion; moose or caribou calves are typical targets.

Mating in brown bears occurs between May and July. Typically, a female establishes a home range which includes all the resources she needs to raise her cubs while males roam across the home ranges of several females. Females with cubs generally don't mate, which is why males may be aggressive towards a female's existing cubs; the loss of a female's cubs will bring her into estrus. Once the female has mated, she goes into a state of suspended pregnancy called diapause. If she has a good feeding season and retires to hibernate with sufficient fat resources, the pregnancy will continue to develop. Bears enter hibernation around October and females give birth around Christmas time to small, one pound cubs that are blind and hairless. The licking of the female stimulates hair growth and that's thought to be where the phrase "licking into shape" comes from.

By May, when the female and her new cubs emerge from their den, the cubs will be strong, mobile and ready for the challenges of Alaska. They will stay with the mother bear for two to three years until moving off to find territories of their own.

A female and her cub forage along the shoreline. Barnacles and blue mussels are favorite food supplements for brown bears.

Wildlife Profile: The Sea Otter

Fast Facts:

Common name: Sea otter

Scientific name: *Enhydra lutris*

Best areas for sightings: Entrance to Glacier Bay, Point Packenham, Prince William Sound.

ID: Large, prominent head, typically swimming on their backs, with fore and hind limbs visible.

Size: Males slightly larger than females, may reach 5 feet in length and weigh up to 100lbs.

Lifespan: Up to 20 years in the wild.

Mating and reproduction: Breeding occurs year-round. Females give birth to a single pup after 5 months gestation. Female-pup pairs remain closely associated until pups reach 6 months in age.

Typical group size: Large rafts are common, 15 to 20 animals may move as a group.

Diet: Bottom feeders so crab, abalone and sea urchins all popular food items. Typically take around 25% of their body weight in food per day.

Recommended websites: http://www.montereybayaquarium.org/cr/sorac.aspx

Wildlife in Focus: The Sea Otter

Watch a raft of sea otters for just five or ten minutes and you'll soon see that sea otters are lively, animated and basically pretty adorable members of the marine community. Their bright eyes, blond facial hair and deep, thick fur make them especially photogenic but unfortunately, this beautiful fur almost led to their demise. The fur or pelage of the sea otter is widely recognized as the finest in the animal kingdom. Perfectly adapted to the cool temperate waters where they dwell, sea otter fur is dense, soft and incredibly warm. It more than makes up for the fact that sea otters, as the largest member of the weasel family, are not true marine mammals and do not have an insulating layer of blubber. Once you spot sea otters in Alaska you'll see that they spend hours grooming their fur between dives in order to keep it in tip-top condition. The alluring pelt of the sea otter was one of the driving forces behind the early exploration of Alaska, drawing in traders and hunters from across Europe. Pelts became the currency of early Russian traders in the region and by the late 1700's, a good quality pelt could fetch the equivalent of a year's wages in Russia.

The early popularity of sea otters led them to the brink of extinction. It's estimated that over a 150 year period, Russian fur traders harvested between 150,000 and 300,000 otters from along Alaskan coastlines. Consequently, numbers quickly dwindled to the point where these sleek sea mammals were a rarity. There were efforts to raise them in farms, but once captured, the otters would refuse to eat and would quickly starve. In July, 1911, the United States, Japan, Russia and Great Britain entered into a treaty "for the protection of fur seals and sea otters in the North Pacific by outlawing the killing of fur seals and sea otters in these waters by any Americans except Alaska Natives." The U.S. Navy was charged with enforcing the treaty and the sea otter in Alaska made a remarkable recovery. Today an estimated 150,000 occupy Alaskan waters and relocations of sea otters from booming populations in regions such as Prince William Sound, to areas in Southeast Alaska where sea otters were locally extinct, have met with great success. Some 400 otters were relocated to Southeast Alaska in the late 1960's and numbers in the region now top 15,000.

Female sea otters form co-operative groups and frequently baby-sit each others offspring during feeding.

A mom and pup pair maintain close contact during an afternoon nap. The mom will be the silver-haired member of the pair and her over-sized offspring stay closely associated for the first 3-6 months of life.

This is especially important as sea otters are a keystone species; a species that is essential in maintaining balance within an ecosystem. Essentially, sea otters feed on sea urchin and abalone and these organisms in turn feed on kelp, which is the primary producer in the marine system in this region. Lose sea otters and urchins will overrun the kelp beds, eating through the holdfasts that anchor the kelp forests in place. This causes the kelp to float free and then die. Sea otters feed voraciously, taking over 25% of their own body weight in food per day. This keeps the urchin population in check and in turn ensures a healthy kelp forest. Often, fishermen view sea otters as competition for their valuable crop but the truth is, these little mammals play a crucial role in maintaining the overall health of the marine system.

Sea otters in the wild are highly sociable. Rafts of sea otters may number up to the hundreds, though this is a safety in numbers approach that serves to reduce predation risks. Typically you'll see large numbers of sea otters at the entrance to Glacier Bay and around Point Pack-enham, as you approach College Fjord. However, if there is no trace of the sea otters, don't be surprised to see a large, darkly colored high standing dorsal fin cruising by....

Wildlife Profile: The Harbor Seal

Fast Facts:

Common name: Harbor seal

Scientific name: *Phoca vitulina*

Best areas for sightings: Commonly seen along the Inside Passage. Large breeding colonies in front of actively calving glaciers.

ID: Large, dark, forward facing eyes, a bowling ball shaped head in the water and curved body profile when hauled out.

Size: Up to 5-6 feet in length, males may weigh up to 230 lbs, females up to 180lbs.

Lifespan: Males up to 25 years, females up to 35 years.

Mating and reproduction: Mating is rarely seen, but gestation lasts around 8 months and most pups are born between May and July.

Typical group size: Large groups are commonly seen. Favored haul-out sites may hold 200 to 300 seals.

Diet: Varies in response to availability – may include pollock, herring salmon, octopus and squid.

Recommended websites: http://www.alaskasealife.org/New/research/index.php?page=harborseal_research.php

Wildlife in Focus: The Harbor Seal

Harbor seals are actually one of six species of true (haired) seals found in Alaskan waters. The hair is short and bristly and changes in color from dark brown to golden as harbor seals dry out on land. They are usually spotted, with light spots on a darker background or vice versa.

One of the most notable features of harbor seals is their diving ability. When seals dive, most dives last around 4 minutes and go to a depth of around 20m. However, on occasion harbor seals can join the ranks of elite divers, making dives to over 1500 feet and staying submerged for up to 20 minutes. They have a suite of adaptations that allow them to dive like this: they have high blood volume and during these long dives, they direct blood circulation away from extremities and concentrate blood flow in the vital organs. They can also slow down their heart rates to around 12 beats per minute. High levels of muscle myoglobin allow them to store extra oxygen and they are perfectly proportioned to minimize drag and maximize their swimming efficiency. They use their hind limbs for propulsion and their fore limbs to steer; viewed underwater their dives are truly elegant. Also, scientists have discovered that just like human divers, they make safety stops at shallower depths at the end of long dives to ensure that they don't succumb to "seal bends".

Perhaps reflecting their incredible swimming talents, you'll find that seals in the water are curious and often quite bold. Don't be too surprised if you're kayaking and turn around to find you have a buddy! On land though, seals become the original sitting duck. The accumulation of insulating blubber that keeps them toasty warm at 1000 feet down in Alaskan waters doesn't work so well on land. Harbor seals can't quite get their hind flippers underneath them, so when hauled out they have to roll along like a very animated caterpillar. Consequently, at haul-out sites, seals are very vulnerable to predation. They typically will stay close to the water's edge and flee back into their watery realm at any sign of disturbance.

Specific groups of harbor seals use glacial fjords as a home base, retreating to ice floes that lie beyond the range of their main marine predator, the transient killer whale, especially during the pupping season. Seals are notoriously hard to count but it is estimated that over 1000 harbor seals pup each year in Glacier Bay, most using the ice-floes in front of the John Hopkins Glacier as their safe pupping sanctuary. Notwithstanding, you'll still see the odd transient killer whale cruising these waters and sending seals into a spin. In the waters of Tracy Arm, transient killer whales have been observed working co-operatively and taking turns creating waves to literally "wash" seals off the ice floes and into the jaws of eagerly waiting accomplices.

This is just one aspect of predation. Within the Alaskan eco-system, harbor seals have a whole host of potential predators. Bears will come down to rocky shorelines to steal pups and eagles will swoop down from the sky to snatch an unsuspecting pup from the ice. In Alaska there is a saying that harbor seals are the Twinkies of the food chain. Potentially, they look like lunch to just about every possible predator. No wonder they always look so worried.

Seals vs. sea lions

Trying to tell one from another in the water can be tricky but just look closely at the shape of the head. Harbor seals have a round, bowling ball shaped head, while sealions have an elongated snout and a much flatter head.

Wildlife Profile: Mountain Goat

Fast Facts:

Common name: Mountain Goat

Scientific name: *Oreamnos americanus*

Best areas for sightings: Southeast Alaska, especially the shorelines of Tracy Arm and Misty Fjords National monument. Look high above the tree-lines in the sub-alpine meadows.

ID: Long, shaggy white coat and small, pointed back horns.

Size: Females may weigh up to 180 pounds, males up to 250-350lbs.

Lifespan: Possibly up to 15 years, typical lifespan around 12 years.

Mating and reproduction: Males compete for access to females and mate with multiple females in one season. Mating takes place in October and November, kids are born the following spring.

Typical group size: Adult males may be solitary, young males form bachelor groups and females with kids form large nursery bands during the summer months.

Diet: Entirely herbivorous. Summer graze includes grasses, herbs and shrubs. Wintertime; lichen, anything green!

Recommended websites: www.adfg.alaska.gov/index.cfm?adfg=goat.main

Wildlife in Focus: The Mountain Goat

Mountain goats are officially the least studied large mammal in North America. Their over-all range is extremely limited with nearly all the world's wild mountain goats being found in Southeast Alaska and British Columbia. The population is split into small breeding groups and one of the largest of these is found on Revillagegedo Island, Ketchikan. Their numbers are thought to be stable but accurate population estimates are hard to establish.

The most distinctive features of mountain goats are their short black horns. These are es-sentially made of a keratin like substance comprised of twisted and matted hair. Both males (billies) and females (nannies) have horns. Female horns are slightly more slender than male horns and males use their horns during the rut to battle with other males for access to the best females.

Mountain goats are the single representative of a unique group of mountain ungulates called rock goats; though closely related, they're not true goats and fall into an antelope-goat group. Their unique adaptations come to the fore when they are viewed in their favored habitat; the high mountain slopes and rocky outcrops of Southeast Alaska. Mountain goats are the mountaineers of this system. Their specially shaped hooves allow them to gain a foothold on the steepest of slopes and the narrowest of crevices. Their long coats equip them to stay high in the mountains through the winter and it's only in Southeast Alaska where you'll see mountain goats on the upper margins of the forest during the winter months.

In the springtime they shed their heavy coats to reveal a soft, light summer coat, but by October each year, they re-grow their wintertime pelage. They even grow hair right down their legs, to increase the effectiveness of their insulation and their ability to withstand the coldest of the winter weather.

A male billie goat in full wintertime pelage.

Separating the sheep from the goats

Looking up to the very highest outcrops it can be hard to make out the fine details of the small, white dot in the distance. Is it a Dall's sheep or a mountain goat?

Well, if you are in Southeast Alaska, it's a mountain goat. According to Alaska Fish and Game Dall's sheep have yet to be seen in Southeast Alaska. Of course, that doesn't explain the plethora of creeks and other landmarks named for the sheep of Southeast Alaska. I guess Goat Creek doesn't have the same ring....

Dall's sheep – found only in central and interior regions of Alaska.

Following the rut in the fall each year, nanny goats have a full six month gestation period and give birth to their offspring each spring. They don't breed untill age four so it's a narrow window in their short 10+ year life span. Nannies will stay solitary to birth, but soon join large, boisterous nursery bands that roam across the alpine meadows over the summer months. They may be predated by wolves, bears or lynx so these large groups carry the benefit of safety in numbers while allowing the young kids to interact.

Mountain goats can be surprisingly laid back. When climbing they can leap 12 feet or more between high mountain ledges but even when alarmed, they'll continue to travel at a relaxed gait. You are more likely to see them if you hike high above the treeline than during aerial tours as they have been found to be quite sensitive to helicopters. Alternatively, you have a good chance of sightings from the ship in specific regions such as Tracy Arm. Look to the highest ridges to see them. When you find that spot that only the bravest of mountaineers would venture out to, then you're in mountain goat territory.

Wildlife Profile: The Steller sea lion

Fast Facts:

Common name: Steller sea lion

Scientific name: *Eumetopias jubatus*

Best areas for sightings: Traditional haul-outs across Southeast Alaska. Bachelor groups common around Juneau.

ID: Thick neck, especially in males, long whiskers and pointed snout.

Size: Males up to 10 feet in length and 1200 lbs, females up to 8 feet in length and 600 lbs.

Lifespan: Males live to 20 years old and females live to around 30.

Mating and reproduction: Dominant males establish harems of females. Females start to breed between age 3 and 7, then spend the next 20 years either pregnant or lactating. Mating takes place in November and pups arrive the following May or June.

Typical group size: Large colonies may include 200-300 animals.

Diet: Quite varied; may range from cod and salmon to squid, herring and pollock.

Recommended websites: See a live stream from the Chiswell Islands sea lion haul out at: /www.alaskasealife.org/New/research/chiswell.php

Wildlife in Focus: The Steller sea lion

Steller sea lions are the largest of the true "eared seals". They have external ear flaps, long forelimbs that resemble flippers and rotatable hind limbs that are used for propulsion in the water and for climbing on land. Their coat of dense black fur lightens to reddish brown as they age and while the females have a somewhat more slender profile, the males have a large, thick neck with small eyes and large teeth. There's not much getting around it, Steller sea lions are really not designed for fund-raising posters, but what they lack in physical appeal they more than make for with personality. These lions of the sea are rambunctious. You'll usually hear them before you see them and you only need observe a group of Steller sea lions for a short length of time to quickly see what "lively" characters they are.

While you may occasionally encounter a lone sea lion, typically they travel in two types of groups. First, there are the male "bachelor" groups. Steller sea lions operate on a harem mating system; this means that dominant males do most—though not all—of the mating and younger males spend large portions of their lives with minimal access to females. So, single males form bachelor groups or grapples. Come across a tiny marker buoy and a crowd of 20+ Steller sea lions vying for the same spot and these are the bachelor groups. You'll also see them on surprisingly high rocky outcrops along the shoreline, and they have even been known to climb trees, all in an attempt to be above their counterparts. All the play fights and dominance displays of young adulthood serve a purpose though, as useful practice for the challenges of adulthood.

A bull Steller sea lion keeps a watchful eye on his harem.

Steller sea lions in the Gulf of Alaska

One of the real biological mysteries in Alaska surrounds the precipitous drops in Steller sea lions numbers in the Gulf of Alaska over a forty year period that started in the late 1960's.

Numbers of Steller sea lions at that time were estimates to be around 140,000, but declines were noted in their favored haul outs. These declines continued to the point where previously inundated haul-outs would host just 50-60 animals. The Gulf of Alaska population plummeted to 30,000 and was placed on the Endangered Species List. All possible causes were investigated, from food shortages to changes in the predatory behavior of transient killer whales. As yet, the cause of the dramatic drop has yet to be explained, but the population is now holding steady and biologists continue their investigations.

The second type of group commonly seen in Steller sea lion society are harems. Typically, you'll see these groups at well-known haul-outs across Southeast Alaska, many of which have been used for over 100 years or more. The sea lions find a spot that allows for easy access to the water and for the dominant males, a good vantage point is essential too. Within each haul-out you can usually spot the dominant male; look for the thickened neck and they're roughly 30% bigger than the females around them. Males attempt to maintain large harems of receptive females and for a long time scientists believed that the dominant male was responsible for siring all the next year's offspring. The dominant male will haul out and may stay out of the water for 30-60 days during the period when females are receptive. During this time he fends off other males, thus deflecting aggressive behavior towards himself rather than the females. Other males will station themselves around the periphery of the group but were not previously thought to achieve any mating success. However, DNA studies have revealed that the dominant male is not in fact always the "baby daddy". It turns out that whenever the dominant male is engaged in a fight, or even just taking a nap, peripheral males will sneak in unnoticed and mate with the females. In many ways though, this is a good thing for the group as a whole as it ensures genetic diversity and luckily, all baby Steller sea lions look basically the same...

Field guide to Alaska's Shorebirds

The protected rocky shorelines of the Inside Passage make great feeding and nesting areas for many of the region's shorebirds. Over 70 different species have been recorded along Alaska's shorelines and waterways. The entrances to the wilderness bays, especially Glacier and Yakutat Bay, are especially good bird-watching areas. Upwellings in these areas lead to rich food supplies, attracting diving birds such as puffins, murres and scoters. Right at the face of the glaciers, look out for kittiwakes and arctic terns swooping in to skim insects from the water's surface as the glacier carves.

Horned Puffin

Tufted Puffin

Common Murre

Black Oyster catcher

Arctic Tern

Black-legged Kittiwake

Surf Scoter

Pigeon Guillemot

Marbled Murrelet

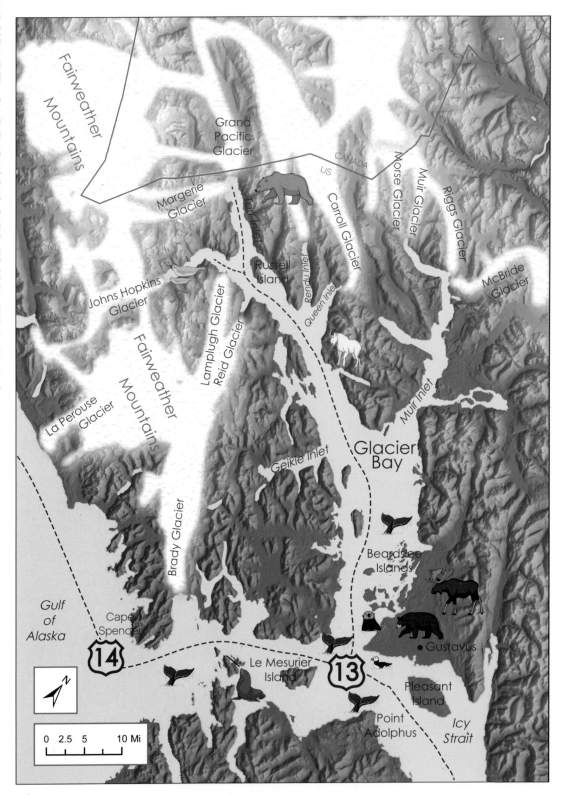

Fairweather Mountains

Grand Pacific Glacier

CANADA
US

Morse Glacier

Muir Glacier

Riggs Glacier

Margerie Glacier

Tarr Inlet

Carroll Glacier

Russell Island

Rendu Inlet

McBride Glacier

Johns Hopkins Glacier

Queen Inlet

Fairweather Mountains

Lamplugh Glacier

Reid Glacier

Muir Inlet

La Perouse Glacier

Geikie Inlet

Glacier Bay

Brady Glacier

Beardslee Islands

Gulf of Alaska

Cape Spencer

14

Gustavus

Le Mesurier Island

13

Point Adolphus

Pleasant Island

Icy Strait

N

0   2.5   5   10 Mi

Glacier Bay

Highlights of your day

Entrance to the Bay
Look out for all types of marine life. Humpback whales, harbor porpoise and sea otters typically seen. Marine birds also plentiful; watch for puffins in mid-channel waters.

Queen Inlet
Ranger narration begins. Grand Pacific Glacier in view.

Tarr Inlet
Approach to Margerie Glacier. Sightings of brown bears common along shoreline.

Glacier viewing Margerie Glacier
The Margerie Glacier is the most active glacier in the park. Grand Pacific Glacier is adjacent. Tufted and horned puffins nest on the rock face to the left of the glacier. Keep an eye out on the opposite shoreline for bears.

Jaw Point
Best viewpoint in the park. John Hopkins Glacier in view. Harbor seals use the ice floes as a pupping area. Shoreline opposite the point is also good for bear sightings. Look for the Lamplugh Glacier on the right as you leave Jaw Point, known as the blue glacier.

Lower Bay
Look out for whales, porpoise, sea otters and puffins as you leave the park.

Icy Strait
One of the best areas for humpback whale sightings. Look out for Steller sea lions on the rocks to the starboard side of the ship as you pass Inian Point.

Ask your onboard naturalist, park rangers or check the Princess Patter for the times for these locations

View from Jaw Point, Glacier Bay.

Cruising Glacier Bay

Glacier Bay, the original icy wilderness of John Muir's musings, is a park that lives up to its reputation. With 16 different tidewater glaciers surrounded by snow-topped mountain ranges, over 3 million acres of protected wilderness and a lacy network of pristine fjords and bays, Glacier Bay offers stunning scenery and amazing wildlife viewing opportunities which combined, make for a great day of wilderness cruising.

On entering the park, your ship will pick up a pair of park rangers for the day. They will work with the ship's captain and bridge crew to determine the best route through the park, based on weather and wildlife sightings. You'll see all the key areas but the order may change from week to week. You can find out the exact times to be out on deck for the key highlights of the park by visiting the information desk that the rangers set up, or alternatively, ask your ship's naturalist; they will also have the most up-to-the minute details of the ship's route through the park.

As a general rule, the lower waters of the bay tend to be richer in marine life such as sea otters, whales and porpoises. The silty waters found up-bay are less well suited to these species but at the entrance to bay waters are clear and upwellings augment nutrient flow to produce great feeding sites. Humpback whales frequent the waters of the lower bay and sea otter numbers have recently resurged in this area. As recently as 1995, only a handful of otters would be seen at the mouth of Glacier Bay. Official counts were in single figures. Today, most recent counts range over 6,000. This is higher than the numbers for the whole of the California Coast. As sea otters are a keystone species, this is a good sign for the park.

On shore, numbers are also rising. Moose were rarely seen in the Park 50 years ago. Around 40 years ago, a single moose showed up in Gustavus, the small town at the mouth of the Bay. Today, moose outnumber year-round residents (though to put a figure there that means more than 300; Gustavus is a very small town). Black bears are typically seen in the Lower Bay while the upper reaches of the bay are the domain of brown bears. Numbers of brown bears are also increasing, and at last count over 300 brown bears were using the bay. Unfortunately, not all species are fairing so well. The most notable decline is in the number of harbor seals. This is a trend that is mirrored across many regions of Alaska and as yet, scientists have no explanation for the cause of this decline. With this in mind though, you will notice that the ship's crew is especially cautious in maneuvering around John Hopkins Inlet as this is one of the main harbor seal pupping areas within the park.

Changing landscapes in the park

Glacier Bay Park is a changing landscape. Shaped by the movements of glaciers over the last two centuries, fjords have opened up in regions where previously glaciers flowed. This is a part of the dynamics of these regions. Retreating tidewater glaciers reveal fjords, and where retreating glaciers terminate on land, new terrain is opened up and the process of success takes hold. Tough, resilient pioneer plants are followed by serial stages comprising small bushes and shrubs, fast growers that fix nitrogen. More sturdy woody plants such as alder and birch follow, and finally forests move in. These changes in plant life pave the way for changing animal life as regions that once were covered in ice become fertile landscapes. Typically you need to wait several hundred years to see these changes, but as you cruise back into the park you'll see these changes as you travel. The furthest point you'll reach is the face of the Margerie Glacier at the head of the Tarr Inlet. Deep water in front of the glacier means that your captain can maneuver your ship directly in front of the glacier. As the glacier calves, this begins the processes that have built Glacier Bay.

Front row seats at the Margerie Glacier.

Glacier Bay and the Grand Pacific Glacier
How an unsung glacier built a bay of world renown.

The Glacier Bay of the 1600's could not have been more different than the Glacier Bay of today. A wide, green valley of aspen brush, meadows and streams rich in salmon, the valley was home to a flourishing community of Tlingit people. The Grand Pacific Glacier lay in the background lining the high ridges that surrounded the valley. But as the Little Ice Age tightened its grip on northern landscapes the Grand Pacific, along with many other glaciers in the region, began a final surge. Surging "faster than dog could run", according to local Tlingit people, the Grand Pacific moved irrevocably forward. A surging glacier is one of the earth's unstoppable events and so the Tlingit homeland was lost, covered by ice up to 4000 feet deep in places. The ice surged on to what is now the mouth of Glacier Bay. At its peak, in the early 1700's it stretched right into the waters of Icy Strait but there, the glacier slipped over the top of its own terminal moraine. The snout of the glacier now lay unprotected in the salty waters of Icy Strait and as temperatures rose, the glacier began to melt. As more and more ice melted away into the saltwater, the Grand Pacific started to shrink and as it did, the mighty glacier revealed its handiwork; a huge, broad, deep U-shaped trench dug deep into the mountainsides and below the valley floor. As the Grand Pacific retreated, the U shaped trench filled with water creating the stark, natural beauty that is Glacier Bay today.

In 1791, Captain George Vancouver mapped out a bay that extended some 5 miles back from the mouth of Icy Strait before meeting a huge 20 mile expanse of ice; the face of the Grand Pacific. In 1879, some 85 years later, John Muir retraced the steps of Captain Cook. John Muir's trip was somewhat less auspicious than Vancouver's early explorations. John Muir chose an open canoe as his vessel, hired a Tlingit captain and set off in mid- October

to explore the waters of the Bay. Their trip included icy storms and near (but not surprising!) mutiny. Still, this infamous crew reached the face of the Grand Pacific on November 24, 1879. They had travelled some 30 miles into the park and 26 miles beyond the point at which Captain Cook had U turned.

Today, the trip may be somewhat more comfortable but the views are the same as those that met Captain Vancouver and his crew, as well as John Muir and his companions. Today, ships travel around 65 miles into the Park before they reach the face of the Grand Pacific Glacier. This true dame of the park now sits at the head of Tarr Inlet in one of several newly revealed fjords that comprise the waterways of the park. Beside the Grand Pacific is the Margerie Glacier. In the world of glaciers, the Margerie is the latest Hollywood starlet. The most active and perhaps one of the prettiest glaciers in the park today, the Margerie grabs all the attention. A bright, clean-blue glacier of young ice flowing 23 miles down from the Fairweather Mountain Range, the Margerie is surging forward overtop of its protective shoal of moraine. Consequently, calving is frequent and can be dramatic, especially in spring time when spring melts augment the flowing water below the glacier.

As your ship pauses in front of the Margerie, be sure to take a moment and give the Grand Pacific glacier your attention. As evidenced by her low profile and silt-covered surface, the Grand Pacific glacier continues to retreat. As it does, Glacier Bay grows a little each day. At the current rate of retreat, by 2025 the park may extend another 12 miles. So, the Grand Pacific, the unsung glacier, continues to quietly expose her handiwork; world renowned Glacier Bay.

Port
Snettisham

Snettisham
Peninsula

Big
Bend

Hole in the
Wall Falls

Mud
Flats

Williams
Cove

The
"S" turn

North
Sawyer
Glacier

Tracy Arm

Sumdum
Glacier

9

The Bar

Harbor
Island

Holkham
Bay

Wood
Spit

South
Sawyer
Glacier

Endicott Arm

Bushy
Island

Dry
Bay

N

Fords Terror

Windham
Bay

0 1 2   4 Mi

Tracy Arm Highlights

Highlights of your day

Holkham Bay	Good chance of humpback whale sightings.
Crossing the bar	Terminal moraine of the Sawyer Glacier. Time to start looking for ice-bergs.
Big Bend	As your ship turns to starboard, the Hole-in-the Wall Falls is on the port side and Icy Falls comes up shortly on the starboard side.
Mud Flats	Look out for black and brown bears foraging on the beach. Check mountainsides for mountain goats.
The S turn	Dramatic turns through steep sided portions of the Fjord.
Glacier viewing	Your ship's final position depends on the amount of ice in the area. The South Sawyer Glacier lies off the bow and the North Sawyer Glacier becomes visible during your approach on the port side of the ship. Look for harbor seals on the icefloes and mountain goats above the treeline on the steep cliff faces.

Ask your onboard naturalist or check the Princess
Patter for the times for these locations

The Sawyer Glacier, Tracy Arm.

Cruising Tracy Arm

"Surrounded by sublime Yosemite cliffs, nobly sculptured, and adorned with waterfalls and fringes of trees, bushes, and patches of flowers"; this is John Muir's description of Tracy Arm, written in 1880 as he toured the region with his companion, Mr. Young, the earnest young missionary and two native guides, Captain Tyeen and Hunter Joe. As you cruise through Tracy Arm today, the very same views await you. The entrance to the Fjord opens up dramatically, giving a real "lost world" feel to your cruise through this area; it's easy to imagine John and his crew appearing from around one of the jack-knife bends as you sail the still waters of the fjord.

Tracy Arm is one of two sister fjords that lead off Holkham Bay on the northeast shoreline of Frederick Sound. Endicott Arm lies to the south and Tracy Arm to the North. As you head into the bay you pass over an area that locals refer to as The Bar. This is the terminal moraine of the Sawyer Glacier, the glacier that originally created Tracy Arm, and the prominent ridge is actually visible at extreme low tides. The waters here are nutrient rich and often teeming with food on the ocean side of the bar so look out for humpback whales - Frederick Sound is one of their favored areas along the Inside Passage. You'll also encounter the other attraction for which Tracy Arm is famous; beautiful, blue icebergs.

The Sawyer Glacier at the head of Tracy Arm is a short, steep glacier. As a result, ice that flows through this glacier is intact and deeply frozen when the glacier reaches the waters of the fjord. Like most of Alaska's glaciers, the Sawyer Glacier is retreating quite rapidly at this time and ice falls are dramatic and continuous throughout the summer months. As exciting as this is to watch, it's actually calvings that occur underwater from the submerged portions of the glacier that give rise to best bergs. These are the huge, blue bergs that drift across the waters of the fjord. A little cloud cover enhances the colors of the bergs so that they truly seem to glow from within.

The cruise through the fjord is spectacular. Tracy Arm is 32 miles long, but only 1 mile wide so it really seems like the forest and the shoreline are right beside you. Add to this the soaring cliffs and cascading waterfalls and you have all the makings of a spectacular wilderness cruise.

As you enter the fjord, the first glacier in view is the Sumdum Glacier and Mount Sumdum just beside it reaches 6,600 feet high. Sumdum is a Tlingit name, inspired by the sound of ice falling from the glacier. You'll pass by a small cove on the port side which is another good spot for icebergs. Depending on currents and tides, large bergs will often beach along this shoreline. A hard turn to starboard takes the ship around Big Bend and the view into the fjord opens up. Hole-in-the-Wall Falls can be seen on the port or left side here and Icy Falls is the most prolific falls on the starboard side, just past Big Bend. An outcrop of silt on the port side comes up next known as Mud Flats. This is a great bear-spotting location so keep the binoculars handy. From here the ship will proceed cautiously through two sharp bends known as the S-bends. Granite walls to the front of the ship rise over 2000 feet and justify the "Little Yosemite" comparisons.

As you approach the glacier, your progress really depends on the amount of ice that is present in the bay. Take a look on the ice-floes for the area's most abundant wildlife; harbor seals number over 1000 in this area and the ice floes in the furthest reaches of the fjord here are a favorite haul-out. In the distance, their distinct curved profile makes them look a bit like 5 day old bananas. Reputedly, this keeps their un-insulated hind flippers off the ice and prevents cold toes!

On several ship itineraries the cruise into Tracy Arm starts early in the morning allowing for maximum time in the ports of the day. The good news is that the route into the fjord is the same as the route out so as the ship retraces its route along Tracy Arm, find a good view point on the stern of the ship and you can still enjoy the spectacular views of Southeast Alaska's little Yosemite.

Blue berg on the Bar, Tracy Arm.

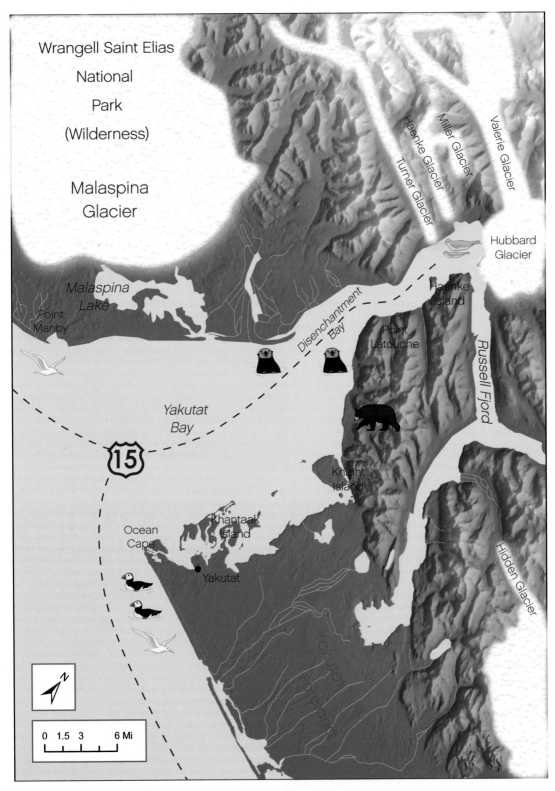

Wrangell Saint Elias

National

Park

(Wilderness)

Malaspina
Glacier

Turner Glacier

Haenke Glacier

Miller Glacier

Valerie Glacier

Hubbard
Glacier

Malaspina
Lake

Point
Manby

Haenke
Island

Disenchantment Bay

Point
Latouche

Russell Fjord

Yakutat
Bay

Knight
Island

Khantaak
Island

Ocean
Cape

Yakutat

Hidden Glacier

Yakutat Forelands

15

0 1.5 3   6 Mi

Yakutat Bay Highlights

Highlights of your day

Entrance to Yakutat Bay	Favored area for keen birders. Horned puffins nest along the outer coastline to the north of the Bay. Good chance of humpback whale sightings and killer whales are also seen in this area.
	Malaspina Glacier visible from the port side of the ship.
Point Latouche	Point Latouche marks the entrance to Disenchantment Bay.
Haenke Island	Haenke Island is nesting colony for Kittiwakes. Arctic terns also common in the area. Watch out for sea otters on the ice-floes in this area.
Glacier viewing	Hubbard Glacier is the biggest and the best when it comes to glacier viewing. The face extends 6 miles and the glacier is advancing, so large calving events are frequent. Large numbers of seals may be seen on the ice-floes in front of the glacier.

Ask your onboard naturalist or check the Princess
Patter for the times for these locations

The Hubbard Glacier and surrounding mountains.

Cruising Yakutat Bay

When it comes to scenic cruising, Yakutat Bay offers the biggest, best, and some of the most exciting scenery in Southeast Alaska. The bay is home to the longest tidewater glacier in North America, the Hubbard Glacier, which stretches 72 miles in length from its source on the slopes of Mount Logan, Canada's tallest mountain, to its snout in Yakutat Bay. The Wrangell-St Elias Mountain Range comprises the world's tallest coastal mountain range. With 16 peaks that rise over 10,000 feet, the mountains provide a spectacular backdrop for the Hubbard Glacier. Add to this the world's largest piedmont glacier at the mouth of the bay, along with beaches that are home to some of Alaska's richest summertime bird populations, and Yakutat Bay quickly becomes a highlight of your cruise.

The dramatic coastal scenery is a direct result of the underlying geology of the region. The Yakutat block, a piece of the earth's crust called a terrane, broke off the edge of the Continental plate around 25 million years ago. It hitched a ride on the Pacific Plate and ended up here at Yakutat. Now, the block lies sandwiched between the Pacific and Continental Plates and as the Pacific Plate drifts, it pushes the dense Yakutat block underneath the lighter Continental Plate. As the mountains sit on top of the Continental Plate, they are slowly rising, albeit by around two and half inches per year. On a clear day, the string of peaks that is in view is quite breath-taking. On other days, clouds and fog may fill the lower bay but the expanse of white terrain across the mountains and at the foot of the glacier reflect back the heat of the sun, creating a microclimate right at the face of the glacier. The clouds lift directly over the glacier and under these conditions, the true blue of the glacier shines through.

As you cruise into the bay, the little town of Yakutat lies on the right or starboard side of the ship. The town was first settled around 250 years ago and today it is home to some 300 people. The Malaspina Glacier is on the left or port side of the ship. This piedmont (foot-of-the-mountain) glacier spills down from the surrounding mountains. Over two dozen small

Hubbard Glacier calves into the waters of Disenchantment Bay.

tributary glaciers join the main glacier along its route and once the glacier meets the valley floor, it spreads across the flat terrain like spilled milk to become the world's largest piedmont glacier. Measuring 45 miles from east to west, the Malaspina Glacier has a 60 mile long face. It's bigger than Rhode Island and even a small country such as Switzerland would fit within its borders. Admittedly, from sea level it's not so easy to appreciate this as the glacier is low lying but if you ever fly across this area, the glacier is quite an incredible sight.

The Malaspina Glacier was named after a Spanish Explorer, Alejandro Malaspina, who visited the bay in the summer of 1791. He had sailed from Mexico and like many of his counterparts of the day, he was in search of the elusive Northwest Passage. Financed by the then King of Spain, King Carlos III, Malaspina was charged with exploring Yakutat Bay which at the time was known as the Straits of Anian. Sailing into the 16-mile wide entrance of the bay, the hopes of Malaspina and his crew were high, but as they made their way into the depths of the bay they soon encountered the huge wall of ice that was the face of the Hubbard Glacier. At this point the glacier reached down to Point Latouche and it was here that Malaspina realized that his hopes would not be realized. In light of his dashed hopes, he renamed the bay Disenchantment Bay.

Around 3000 years ago it's estimated that Hubbard Glacier filled the entire extent of Yakutat Bay. In Malaspina's day, the lower portions of the Bay were navigable but the inlet leading from the lower portion of Yakutat Bay to the face of the ice was just a small ice-filled basin. However, Hubbard Glacier was in the process of a massive retreat at this stage and today you'll sail some 14 miles back into Disenchantment Bay. Then you too will meet the mighty face of the Hubbard Glacier.

The Hubbard Glacier and surrounding mountains.

The Galloping Glacier

As glaciers go, the Hubbard Glacier is a pretty exciting glacier. Today it's one of the few remaining glaciers in Alaska that is still advancing and currently, it's a very active glacier well known for frequent calving and huge ice-falls. However, it's the Hubbard's propensity for unpredictable surges that gets this glacier in the news.

In a healthy glacier, ice flows smoothly from the source in the ice field to the snout, the face of the glacier. Rates of flow are usually quite slow, around a foot or two a year is typical, and though flow rates may increase to some degree in springtime as meltwater lubricates the flow, overall they are quite consistent. In a surging glacier something interrupts or blocks this flow. Ice accumulates in the ice field and in glaciers that are already advancing, substantial amounts of ice may pile up over the course of the winter. Come spring when meltwater flows freely, glaciers move into action again. Stockpiles of ice can suddenly be "unplugged", leading to dramatic surges and rapid advances.

Accumulations of ice over winter have led to dramatic surges like this in the Hubbard Glacier. Until recently, the most well-recorded of these surges was in early summer of 1986, when the Hubbard surged right across Disenchantment Bay to hit the cliff face opposite. This closed

Big Waves in Yakutat

The area around Yakutat Bay not only boasts the longest tidewater glacier, the largest piedmont glacier and the tallest coastal mountains, it's also the site of the largest wave ever recorded. Events that led to this Big Wave story took place in Lituya Bay, around 50 miles south of Yakutat Bay. Generally, this entire region has a history of geologic activity. On September 3rd 1899, a violent earthquake equivalent in magnitude to the 1906 earthquake in San Francisco rattled the Bay and its residents. No lives were lost, but according to eye-witness accounts "the trees waved like stalks of grass" and the hill above town was renamed Shivering Hill after the quake.

The Lituya Bay earthquake happened on July 9th 1958. It measured 7.9 on the Richter scale and shook free some 40 million cubic yards of debris from the surrounding mountains. This debris roared down into the bay, creating the huge wave. The wave scoured the trees from the surrounding shorelines of the Bay, leaving behind a clearly defined measure of its true height; 1720 feet above the bay. Three fishing boats were anchored in the bay and amazingly, two boats rode out the wave as it sloshed back and forth across the bay so there are eye witness accounts of this monster wave.

off the entrance to the upper portion of the Bay and Russell Fjord, which lies just beyond the glacier, became Russell Lake as it was no longer connected to the open ocean. The huge ice dam stayed in place all through summer, trapping seals and other marine life in the rapidly deepening freshwater lake. It was only in October of that year that the ice dam gave way. On October 8th 1986, the whole six mile extent of the face of the Hubbard Glacier started to calve from one end to the other. The dam broke releasing vast amounts of flood water and some rather perplexed seals back into Disenchantment Bay. For the next several years, the Hubbard retreated but in 2007 it once again surged across the bay. This time it came within 170 yards of the cliff face at what is now known as Russell Gap. Glaciologists continue watching to see the next installment of the exciting life and times of the Hubbard Glacier.

Wildlife sightings in Yakutat Bay

Arctic terns that mate successfully may stay together for life; evidently, one good tern deserves another...

Look for sea otters in the lower portions of the bay and harbor seals on the ice at the face of the glacier. The area is also rich in birdlife. Some 200 different species and yearly counts of 300,000 shorebirds have been recorded for the bay. The richest birding areas are along the shoreline at the entrance to the bay but birdlife is prolific in the upper reaches of the bay too. Here, two arctic terns rest in the upper waters of the bay. Arctic terns migrate between the Antarctic and Alaska each year. It's a 22,000 mile round trip, and the longest bird migration on record.

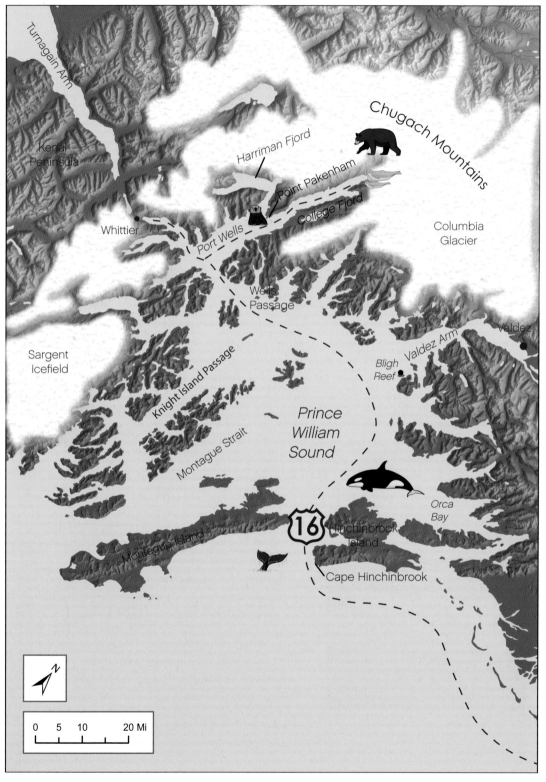

Turnagain Arm

Kenai
Peninsula

Whittier

Sargent
Icefield

Harriman Fjord

Point Pakenham

Port Wells

College Fjord

Chugach Mountains

Columbia
Glacier

Wells
Passage

Valdez

Knight Island Passage

Bligh
Reef

Valdez Arm

Montague Strait

Prince
William
Sound

Orca
Bay

16 Hinchinbrook
Island

Montague Island

Cape Hinchinbrook

N

0 5 10 20 Mi

Prince William Sound and College Fjord Highlights

Highlights of your day

Cape Hinchinbrook	The narrow passage through Hinchinbrook Entrance is a great place to look out for humpback whales. Some chance of killer whale sightings in this region too. The Chugach Mountain range lines the horizon to the north of the Sound.
Port Wells	This is one of the best areas in Alaska to see sea otters. Notably, they are not early risers, so numbers increase as the day progresses. If you don't see sea otters, keep a look out for their predators, transient killer whales.
Point Packenham	A ghost forest extends out onto the point at Point Packenham and along the shorelines too; this is a remnant of the damage of the Good Friday Earthquake of 1962. Go to the bow of the ship for outstanding views of College Fjord.
Glacier viewing	Six different tidewater glaciers tumble down right from the ridgeline into the waters of the fjords. This is the largest accumulation of tidewaters anywhere in the world.

Ask your onboard naturalist or check the Princess Patter for the times for these locations

Yale Glacier, College Fjord.

Cruising Prince William Sound

Marking the northern point of most cruise itineraries is Prince William Sound. The Sound is often referred to as the crown jewel of coastal Alaska and indeed, it is truly an icy wilderness. The lofty Chugach mountain range surrounds the bay and much of the bay lies within the Chugach National Forest. Dozens of glaciers wind their way down from the Chugach Mountains into the waters of the Sound and College Fjord is remarkable as the site of one of the greatest accumulations of tidewater glaciers. Abundant wildlife is to be found across the Sound. Both resident and transient killer whales cruise the waters of the Sound. Rafts of sea otters are to be found in the waters of Point Packenham at the entrance to College Fjord, and huge colonies of harbor seals haul out to pup in the relative safety of the berg-laced waters of College Fjord.

Human populations in the Sound date back to around three to four thousand years ago. Most likely, people came by boat in a chain migration extending into Alaska along the Aleutian Islands and the outer coast of the Kenai Peninsula, so this is an entirely different native group to the Tlingit and Haida people of Southeast Alaska. The early Chugach people did venture south and encountered the Yakutat Bay Tlingits but by all accounts interactions weren't too neighborly and comprised principally of attacks and reciprocal raids on native villages. By the time Europeans arrived in the Sound, records indicate around seven to eight hundred people in the region. Vitus Bering is credited as the first European in the region. Cook followed shortly after and charted the area for the first time. He named the Sound for Prince William Henry of England who later became King William IV and following his tradition, Cook also named prominent features in the Sound for crew members onboard. In an interesting case of serendipity, a small reef to the north of Goose Island on the eastern side of the Sound was named for William Bligh, a low ranking officer onboard Cook's vessel. William Bligh later became well known as Captain Bligh, the villainous captain in the saga of the Mutiny on the Bounty. The reef that was named for him also had its day in the headlines; this was the reef that the Exxon Valdez struck, leading to one of the largest marine oil spills in US history.

Following in Captain Cook's wake, the Harriman expedition cruised through the Sound some 100 years later, in 1899. This was one of the most focused and productive scientific expeditions to Alaska of its day. The cruise was organized and funded by Edgar Harriman, a successful railroad executive. He chartered a steamship, the Elder, and assembled an elite scientific crew. Along with some 30 geologists, other participants included America's favorite naturalist of the day, John Muir, biologist William Dall and noteworthy anthropologist and photographer Edward Curtis. The cruise set sail from Seattle to much fanfare and headed north, navigating Alaska's Inside Passage then heading across the Gulf of Alaska to Prince William Sound. At this time much of the Sound remained unchartered and the glaciers were un-named. As the expedition members constructed detailed charts and maps of the region, each participant got to name a newly discovered glacier within Prince William Sound for their alma-mater. Consequently, cruising across the Sound becomes something like a tour of the Ivy League universities of the day. But the true legacy of this cruise was the detailed scientific journals that the scientists compiled. Documenting everything from glaciers and wildlife to native people, twelve volumes of papers were compiled, providing an unmatched picture of these regions at this time. Today, as climate change continues to alter the contours and scenery of Alaska, these journals have become an invaluable resource.

As shown here, the weather in Prince William Sound is extremely unpredictable. These photos were taken onboard Sky Princess during her first sail of the season through Prince William Sound in early May, 1998. Sightseeing was a little limited that day, but the ever-inventive cruise staff organized other activities. Update: Snow also recorded in PWS on July 5th 2012.

A raft of sea otters.

Heading into College Fjord, you'll pass through the waters of Port Wells. These lower waters are the favored region for rafts of sea otters. Diving down an incredible 500 feet or more, the otters feed on the crabs, urchins and abalone to be found on the bottom of the bay. Watch them feed and you'll see that many employ a small rock while feeding, to help open the tough shells of their prey. After prying open the shell, they will stash their rock in a little "pouch" in their fur for later use before feeding and then diving again. Sea otter numbers here dropped drastically during the days of the fur trade, however a remnant population survived, tucked away in the hidden recesses of Harriman Fjord over on the west side of the Sound. Once the fur trade came to a halt, they spread out and repopulated the Sound. Today, they are prolific in these waters and it's estimated some 12,000 may make their home in the Sound. If you do see large rafts of sea otters in this area, grab your binoculars as they officially win the poster child contest for Alaskan marine mammals. However, if otters are scarce, keep an eye out, as that is often an indicator that their main predator, transient killer whales, may be cruising nearby.

Sea otter with a tasty lunch. Sea otters may consume up to 25% of their body weight per day.

The Glaciers of College Fjord

If you're sailing from Vancouver, then your cruise through College Fjord will be on your last sea day. Generally you'll spend your afternoon in the Sound with pre-dinner glacier viewing in College Fjord as a fitting final highlight of your cruise. Be sure to head to the bow of the ship to see the magnificent views as you enter College Fjord, and of course as you leave, you can enjoy these same views from the stern of the ship.

The first landmark is Point Packenham. This prominent spit of land marks the terminal moraine for the Harvard Glacier that will now be in view over the bow of the ship. You'll notice the ghost forest out on the spit and along the western shoreline of the fjord here. This is a result of the Good Friday earthquake which shook the entire Sound on March 27, 1964. The quake measured 9.2 on the Richter scale. It generated 3 huge tidal waves that wiped out the town of Valdez and caused extensive damage and loss of life in Seward along the coastline. Here in the completely undeveloped regions of the Sound, the effect of the earthquake was actually to tilt the Fjord. The eastern shoreline rose by 6 feet, and the western shoreline sank by 8 feet, sufficient to drown the trees along the shoreline. The resulting ghost forest stands today, a gentle reminder of the overwhelming power of Mother Nature.

As you cruise to the head of the fjord, the glaciers lie along the port side on your way in and the starboard side on the way out.

Point Packenham, Prince William Sound.

The glaciers of College Fjord are truly a textbook set of glaciers. First you'll see two hanging glaciers, the Holyoke and the Barnard, just below the ridgeline on the port side. Next is the Wellesley Glacier sporting beautifully defined lateral moraines. These are the accumulations of glacial silt, literally ground up mountains that line the sides of glaciers. The Vassar Glacier just beyond, demonstrates the process of a glacier in retreat. You can see the accumulation of debris at the terminus or snout; this is a terminal moraine. Small plants and shrubs are starting to move in on the new land that is deposited by the glacier, starting the process of succession. Wait around 200 years or so and we should see new spruce forest here. Beside the Vassar Glacier is the Bryn Mawr Glacier. Clearly defined in this glacier is the median moraine, the thick dark stripe of glacial silt that forms when two glaciers merge. The final glacier along the port side of the fjord is the Smith Glacier. This steep glacier tumbles down the cliffs to the waters of the fjord, perfectly demonstrating the formation of crevices. You can see the deep cracks, towers and pinnacles that form on the surface as the underside of the glacier negotiates the slope. The underside is cold and still plastic enough to flow but the upper, cooler side of the glacier becomes brittle and literally snaps as the glacier flows.

Finally, at the head of the fjord is the Harvard Glacier. This massive glacier incorporates some 27 tributary glaciers along its route. Harvard Glacier created College Fjord, grinding a deep, U shaped channel out of the bedrock as it advanced and then allowing saltwater to flow in and fill the channel as the glacier subsequently retreated. Nestled deeply within Prince William Sound, College Fjord is still tidal but fully protected from ocean swells. At its deepest point, the fjord is more than 900 feet deep and few features disturb the water column. As a result, the meltwater from the glaciers, which is freshwater, sits almost as an intact lens on top of the saltwater below and the glacial silt within the freshwater has remarkable mirroring capacity. On a still day, the glaciers are perfectly reflected in the surface waters of the Sound.

The glaciers of College Fjord.

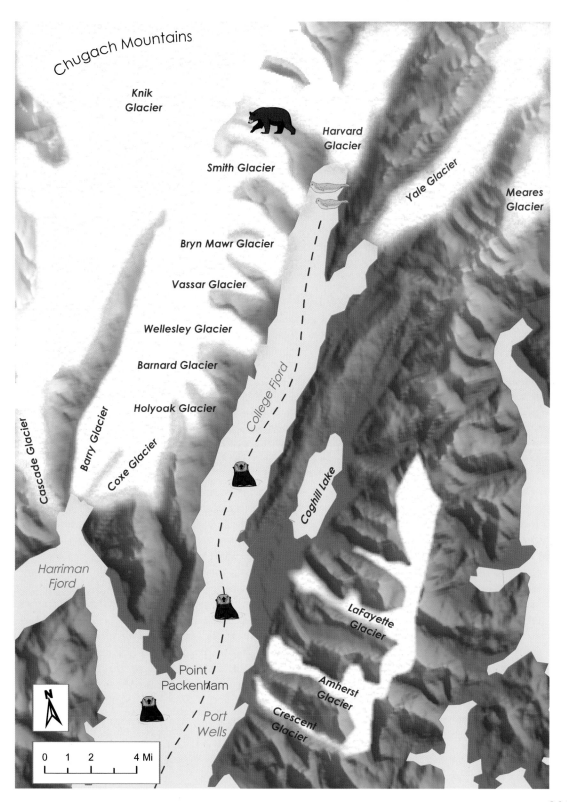

Chugach Mountains

Knik Glacier

Harvard Glacier

Smith Glacier

Yale Glacier

Meares Glacier

Bryn Mawr Glacier

Vassar Glacier

Wellesley Glacier

Barnard Glacier

Holyoak Glacier

College Fjord

Cascade Glacier

Barry Glacier

Coxe Glacier

Coghill Lake

Harriman Fjord

LaFayette Glacier

Point Packenham

Amherst Glacier

Port Wells

Crescent Glacier

N

0   1   2   4 Mi

In focus: The Exxon Valdez oil spill

"We fetched up hard on Goose Island, north of Bligh Reef and we may be leaking some oil". With these words, Captain Joe Hazelwood alerted the world of the disaster to come in the waters of Prince William Sound.

The date was March 24th 1989, the time just after midnight and so began another eventful Good Friday in the history of Prince William Sound. Hazelwood's ship, the Exxon Valdez, had been on its way out of Valdez harbor on a typical run and the ship was fully loaded with Prudhoe Bay's thick, sticky crude oil. The ship left the dock in a violent storm but that wasn't unusual at the time. After piloting the ship out of the harbor, Captain Hazelwood left the helm in the charge of a young third mate and went below. This too was not an unusual sequence of events at that time.

The Columbia Glacier, adjacent to Valdez, was in retreat then as it is now and was known for producing large icebergs. As the young and inexperienced crew attempted to maneuver around the icebergs, they inadvertently left the shipping lanes and ended up on the reef.

By daybreak the next day it was easy to see the extent of the spill as the stain of thick crude oil leaked out across the Sound. Unusually for this region at this time of year, the weather was calm and the oil at least formed a clearly defined slick. Clean-up at this stage might have been quite efficient, but supplies were not at hand and the remote location of the nearest port, Valdez, hampered the progress of organizing supplies and clean-up crews. By the time the clean-up was underway, the weather had changed, the wind was blowing, the waters were rough and the oil had been mixed into a toxic seawater-oil mousse.

After four days of waiting for supplies, clean-up began in earnest. Booms were used to contain the leaking oil, some of the oil was burned and chemical dispersants were deployed. But the damage was underway and as the Hazmat-coated clean-up crews spread out across the Sound, the toll on the region and its wildlife began to emerge. Unforgettable images of rows of oiled seabirds, sea otters attempting to clean the toxic oil mousse of their fur and small armies of clean-up crews in hazmat gear hit the headlines. Between 100,000 and 250,000 seabirds, 2,800 sea otters, 300 eagles, 300 harbor seals and 22 killer whales died at the time of the spill. Over 1000 miles of coastline was oiled and the herring and salmon runs that supported the town of Valdez were devastated.

Exxon Valdez took responsibility for the spill, calling it a tragic accident and expressing their deep regret. The clean-up bill, fines and restitution topped $3 billion at the final reckoning. Joe Hazelwood was charged with criminal negligence and paid a hefty fine. He never went to jail but didn't go back to sea. After a short time teaching maritime navigation he switched to maritime consultancy work.

Twenty years on, scientists still debate the degree to which the Sound has recovered. Oil is no longer seen on most of the beaches, but when sea otters dive to feed and pull up shellfish from the bottom of the Sound, small droplets of oil escape. The numbers of resident and transient killer whales in the area has not rebounded and transient killer whales have not produced any offspring since the spill. As for Valdez, the fishing industry continues to struggle and those whose livelihoods were impacted by the spill still talk about life before and after this event.

Some hard lessons have been learned. Now, all tankers leaving Valdez are double hulled, accompanied by tugs and monitored from the harbor to ensure they stay on course. Much has been learned about methods of dealing with oil spills and their aftermath, knowledge which proved all too useful in the aftermath of the recent Deepwater Horizon oil spill episode. In the Great Spirit Bear Rainforest of British Columbia, a similar terminal is planned for the export of bitumen from the tar sand deposits in Canada. Fleets of heavily loaded tankers will ply the narrow channels and fjords that border pristine old growth rainforest. Activists and environmentalists point to the lessons of Prince William Sound in their attempts to halt the development.

Much was lost on that fateful day in the Sound but in cruising the Sound today, perhaps the lingering lesson is the incredible resilience of the wilderness around us. And like many things in life, it may only be when we come close to losing something that we realize it's true value.

Prince William Sound today shows no visible signs of the oil spill, but there are indications that the oil remains within the Sound's ecosystem.

Continuing your cruise

Between Glacier Bay and Whittier, Prince William Sound.

Waypoint 14 – Cape Spencer

Heading out from Glacier Bay, your route from the park takes you into the waters of Icy Strait and for the next hour, you'll be cruising through excellent whale waters. Look out for puffins and sea otters as well as humpback whales.

If you are northbound, you'll pass the low lying Brady Glacier on your starboard side, and on the portside at this point, you'll see a small group of islands called the Inian islands. Right beside the channel marker on the port side is a favored haul-out for Steller sea lions. The sea lions use this area for pupping and between May and July, several large harems are usually in residence along the shoreline here. By the time August comes around the haul-outs are quickly deserted as pups learn to swim and the sea lions leave for open waters. If you're southbound into Glacier Bay, these points of interest will of course be on the opposite side for you; you'll see the Brady Glacier on the portside and the sea lions will be over on the starboard side.

Waypoint 14, Cape Spencer, marks the northern reach of Alaska's Inside Passage and opens to the waters of the Gulf of Alaska. Certainly a welcome sight for mariners, the cape is a key navigational point and marked by a lighthouse. The Cape was named by Captain Cook for the Earl of Spencer, who was the great grandfather of the late Lady Diana Spencer, Princess of Wales.

Cape Spencer and the Fairweather Mountain Range.

The La Perouse Glacier, Gulf of Alaska.

If the weather is co-operating then the La Perouse Glacier is one of the most impressive sights of any Gulf crossing. On itineraries that started out in Whittier where you'll be heading south, the glacier will be in view around one to two hours before you reach Cape Spencer and enter the Inside Passage. For northbound passengers, it's around an hour after you pass this waypoint.

The La Perouse Glacier was named for the early explorer Jean de la Perouse. It's officially the only tidewater glacier that terminates into the open waters of the Pacific Ocean, however like most glaciers in Alaska, the La Perouse is retreating so the snout is now just about land-based.

The glacier is still an impressive sight though, especially against the backdrop of the Fairweather Mountain Range. Several peaks in this range reach over 10,000 feet and both early explorers and modern mariners use the mountains as a weather predictor; a clear view of the top of the mountain range is a reliable harbinger of good weather on a Gulf crossing.

Waypoint 15 – Entrance to Yakutat Bay

Yakutat Bay lies approximately 220 miles south of Cape Hinchinbrook, at the entrance to Prince William Sound. If you're sailing south and your cruise includes Hubbard Glacier, then your ship will make a sharp turn to port to enter the bay. Bounded by the Wrangell St. Elias mountains, this is a place that is truly only reachable by boat and the name Yakutat is derived from a native word meaning "place where the canoe comes to rest". The beaches on the shoreline here are some of the best birding areas in Alaska, so keep an eye out for puffins and other seabirds. You can find full details on the cruising highlights of the Bay on page 250.

Waypoint 16 – Cape Hinchinbrook

This is another key navigational point in this region, as it marks the outer most point of Prince William Sound. For mariners and fishermen working out in the open waters of the Gulf, this brings a welcome promise of calm waters ahead. You will notice a lighthouse on the northern point here. The lighthouse was built in 1906, after several incidents where sailors hit these rocks before they found entry into the Sound. Considered one of the most remote lighthouse stations in Alaska, there are some fascinating accounts of life at the lighthouse before it was automated in 1974. Go to lighthousefriends.com and search for Cape Hinchinbrook.

Whether you're sailing north or south, you'll almost certainly notice a change in the motion of the ocean as you pass this waypoint. For northbound passengers, an afternoon spent cruising Prince William Sound and College Fjord lie ahead. If you're southbound, you'll typically be on open water until around mid afternoon, so you might want to keep that in mind as you plan your day.

Shorebirds on the beaches of Yakutat Bay.

High mountain peaks line the Gulf of Alaska coastline.

Heading south from Glacier Bay

For southbound cruisers, you'll want to plan some time out on the deck just after you leave Glacier Bay, as you'll be passing by Point Adolphus, one of the most well-known humpback whale feeding regions. This area lies to the south side of Icy Straits and whales move freely between here and the lower portions of Glacier Bay over the summer months.

For ships bound for Skagway, you'll pass through Icy Straits and then head north along the waters of the Lynn Canal and the Taiya Inlet into Skagway. If you're headed south to Ketchikan then you'll turn to starboard at the end of Icy Strait and cruise the waters of Chatham Strait.

Chatham Strait is the "freeway" of Alaska's Marine Highway. Around 150 miles in length and 3 to 10 miles wide along it's length, the Strait runs between Admiralty and Chichagof Islands and it's the main conduit between many of the smaller towns of the Inside Passage. Consequently, it's a great place to get a glimpse of the lifestyle of the region— and maybe do a little local "boat-watching".

Alaska receives most of its incoming revenue from the oil industry, tourism comes a somewhat distant second while fishing places third, but provides the largest number of jobs. This is especially true in Southeast Alaska in regions beyond the state capital, Juneau. The majority of Southeast Alaskan residents supplement their income through fishing. Permits and fishing vessels are handed down through families and in many families, first born daughters and fishing boats share the same name.

Fishing in Alaska is micro-managed, with fish stocks protected above all else when man-made disasters strike. Consequently, the industry in this region is flourishing; 95% of the Pacific salmon that is wild caught comes from the waters of Alaska and the industry actively demonstrates that fishing resources can be successfully harvested and maintained through careful management. A visit to one of the salmon hatcheries, either in Juneau or Ketchikan, is a great way to find out more about the industry.

A salmon seiner in the waters of Chatham Strait. Watch out for several of the vessels from the series Deadliest Catch; at certain times of year, they head to Chatham Strait to fish for salmon.

An evening in Victoria, British Columbia

If you're on a cruise out of Seattle, on your last evening at sea your ship will make a short evening stop in the port of Victoria, British Columbia. Located on the southern tip of Vancouver Island, Victoria is probably best known for its British heritage and authentic memorabilia, from bright red phone boxes and double decker buses, to immaculate English Rose gardens. As you disembark the ship, you'll find an eclectic choice of vehicles awaiting you, ranging from horse-drawn carriages to pedi-cabs. All offer a two to three hour tour of the city and the option to stay in town at the end of the tour, and each comes with its own "colorful" guide. There is also fleet of shuttle buses, run by the friendliest bus drivers you'll meet, and as the center of the city is over 3 miles away, it's best to pick one of these options.

The famous Empress Hotel, Victoria, British Columbia, boasts celebrity visitors, British ambiance and world famous traditional afternoon teas.

For the new world, Victoria is an old city. Founded in 1843 by James Douglas as a trading post for the Hudson Bay trading company, Victoria was named for then—Queen Victoria, however, native settlements were dotted through the area and native people of the First Nation pre-dated European arrivals in the region by several thousand years. Once the trading post at Victoria was established, a busy trade in sea otter pelts flourished and Victoria grew to a town of around 450 residents. Tales of gold discovered in the Fraser River in 1958 soon changed the course of the small town's history. The arrival of the first steamboat brought gold miners from California and Australia into the region and the town's population literally doubled as the first ship docked.

Gold prospectors came and went through the region over the next decade. On the heels of the gold rush, in 1866, British Columbia and Vancouver Island united to form a single colony, with Victoria chosen as the legislative capital. Parliament was established and the development of the city began at full speed; much of the architecture of the city today dates back to this era.

The two most prominent buildings, the Empress hotel and the Parliament Buildings, surround the inner harbor of the city and this is the focal point of the city today. Once the sun sets, both the hotel and the Parliament buildings are artfully illuminated, creating a very appealing cityscape, as the lights reflect in the waters of the harbor. Street artists take to the harbor walk and local artists set up alongside, making a stroll along the waterfront a must-do in the city.

As the sun sets, another side of city also emerges; Victoria is reputedly one of the most haunted cities in North America. Ghost walks abound and even the pedi-cab drivers have their share of fairly gruesome tales. One of the most infamous and frequently sighted ghosts is the late Francis Rattenburg. As the architect of both the Empress Hotel and the Parliament Buildings, Rattenburg had already left his mark on Victoria during his lifetime. However, Rattenburg was quite the playboy, and met an untimely demise at the hands of his second wife's lover, as the two men argued over another mutual mistress. Rattenburg was laid to rest in an unmarked grave in England, but is reportedly frequently seen, cane in hand, wandering the halls of the hotel and the Parliament buildings.

Other ghostly tales involve innocent hotel maids, murderous villains and equally vicious judges; there's even a phantom organist in a now long abandoned restaurant who plays requests from "the other side". Choose one of the tours that include a ghost walk for more on these stories. Meanwhile, for the skeptics–or the easily scared—there are plenty of attractions around town that don't include Halloween flashbacks. One of the best of these is the Butchart Gardens. Covering over 50 acres, the gardens offer horticultural displays that are world renowned. The original estate was a quarry, where Robert Butchart had been extracting limestone. Once the quarry was exhausted, Butchart's wife, Jennie, set about reclaiming the quarry pit, importing hundreds of tons of topsoil and eventually establishing a spectacular sunken garden. From here, the gardens have continued to grow, carried on in the family tradition. Today, they rank as one of Victoria's top attractions. You can check out their website at www.butchart.com for updates on the blooms and features of the park throughout the year. Elegant evening light displays are also a feature of the park and make a last, twinkling impression for your final evening.

Butchart Gardens.

Chapter 7
Alaska's Heartland

Alaska's Heartland

Whether you head to Alaska's heartland before or after your cruise, the dramatic landscapes and endless vistas of Interior Alaska are a complete contrast to the protected fjords and blue green waterways of Alaska's Inside Passage. Taking some time to explore this region will undoubtedly enhance any Alaskan vacation plan and provide a whole different perspective on America's northern lands. The big five for wildlife in Alaska's Interior include wolves, moose, caribou, Dall's sheep and of course, berry-guzzling grizzly bears. Some effort is required to get to the places where wildlife resides but once you find yourself in the right place at the right time, you'll get to glimpse life in a world untouched. Grizzlies graze on blueberries, wolves roam in packs and caribou joust, just as they have over the millennia.

Each region of Interior Alaska is markedly different and each offers widely varying experiences. From the bustle of Anchorage, the excitement of the Kenai, the small town life of Fairbanks and the peace and solitude of Copper River, there's certainly something for everyone. The Princess network of lodges offers the chance to compile your own itinerary through the region. When planning your trip, you'll want to keep in mind that long distances separate key towns. Most highways are in remarkably good condition, but not all are paved and portions of the highways travel through extremely remote regions. If you're leaving Anchorage to head to the Interior, the railroad system provides an easy and incredibly scenic access route up to Denali. The easiest way to travel between the different lodges is on the Princess Shuttle bus system. Shuttles connect between all the lodges and all you have to do is sit back and enjoy the view.

View to the horizon, Copper River, Alaska.

Star Princess at the dock in Whittier.

Whittier

For Princess Cruise's guests, Whittier is the first or final port on your cruise as you join or leave your ship. This small town sits at the head of Passage Canal, a deep fjord which opens into Prince William Sound. As it provides easy access to Interior Alaska, the region has a long history as a portage route used by Chugach Indians, Russian fur traders and American gold prospectors. The town was established here during the World War II to allow movement of troops, supplies and cargo in and out of Interior Alaska. To connect Whittier with Anchorage the federal railroad was extended down to Portage, on the Kenai Peninsula, and a tunnel was blasted through the sheer granite rocks of the mountains that surround Whittier. By 1943, Whittier was directly connected to the outside world. Two multi-story buildings, the Buchner Building and the Begich Tower, were constructed to house operations and personnel, along with a network of underground tunnels to ensure easy–and unseen–access around the town during Whittier's cold winters. Set right up against the 3,500 ft peaks, cloaked in clouds and covered in snow for most of the year, the base at Whittier was almost invisible from the air and became a key player in the regional wartime operations.

The army base closed down in 1964, but since then the town has taken on a new life as a premium jumping off point for trips out to explore Prince William Sound. The tunnel has been converted to allow road as well as rail access so now the town is just 90 minutes from Anchorage. Kayaking, fishing and sight-seeing trips are all extremely popular. The town retains a pretty unusual lifestyle though. Most of the town's 180 residents still live in the multi-story Begich Towers. Children play in the corridors of the tower and in winter there are no snow days as the network of tunnels is still in use and allows wintertime access across the town.

If you have time to wander through town, you'll find the people very friendly. There is a small cove of souvenir shops and cafes along the waterfront at Smithy's cove complete with a pet reindeer sporting Christmas lights for that Christmas in July feeling. For a short hike, Horsetail Falls is just around a mile from town.

Kenai Peninsula

Your time on the Kenai Peninsula may just be the coach ride or the train trip between Anchorage and Whittier but even in that small glimpse you'll see why the Kenai Peninsula is known as Alaska's Playground. Although it's the size of small European country, the Peninsula is very accessible and it's also incredibly diverse. It brims with opportunities to hike, watch wildlife or catch your own fish and the main highways and rail routes run through some of the Kenai's most stunning scenery.

The Kenai Mountains cover most of the eastern side of the Peninsula. Rising well over 4000 feet, they fuel a network of glaciers that cascade down the mountain-sides. Lakes and rivers are sprinkled liberally across the rest of the landscape. The eastern and southern shorelines of the Peninsula open to the Gulf of Alaska and these wild and unprotected coastlines are awash with marine life. Boat trips from Seward access this area. Along the western and northern coasts, the Peninsula borders the estuarine shorelines of Cook Inlet and Turnagain Arm. This is the area you'll be traveling through on your way to or from Anchorage. On the land side of the highway you'll see small lakes and brackish wetlands that border the forest; this is perfect moose habitat. Look to the high ridgelines too, as this is the territory of Dall's sheep too. Perhaps the biggest wildlife scoop is to be seen in the waters of Turnagain Arm and Cook Inlet, on the other side of the highway. These shallow estuarine regions are the summertime home of Beluga whales. Keep a good eye out as their bright, white color makes them quite easy to spot. The railroad runs alongside the highway for most of the route to Anchorage so these highlights are all visible from the train route too.

Perfect moose habitat on the Kenai Peninsula.

The Kenai River, Alaska.

Fishing on the Kenai

If landing the big one is part of your plan for Alaska, be sure to include some time on the Kenai Peninsula.

The Kenai and the Russian River are the big salmon rivers. The lower Kenai River is the premium area, and home to the largest king salmon to found in the rivers of Alaska. The record for kings caught in freshwater currently stands at just under 98 lbs, with the legendary 100 lb king salmon still elusive in freshwater regions. Four different species of Pacific Salmon migrate into the rivers of the Kenai to spawn, offering the chance to reel in your own dinner. Alternatively, fish packing services in the area will freeze your fish and ship them home for you. For halibut fishing, head down to Homer or Seward. Either harbor offers a host of charter fishing options.

Catch of the day:
Captain Jack, a vintage sailor and fisherman based in Seward, Alaska, holds up a perfect silver salmon.

Anchorage

As big cities go, Anchorage boasts one of the most scenic settings across the US. Nestled between the waters of the Cook Inlet and the peaks of the Chugach Mountains, the city sits right on the edge of a huge wilderness region and embraces its "wilderness at the end of the street" identity. Anchorage is home to around 40% of Alaska's population and residents share the region with over 2000 Dall's sheep, 1000 moose and 300 bears. City workers can step outside at lunchtime to go salmon fishing in the creeks that run through town and the city's new logo is "Big, Wild Life".

Captain Cook first sailed through this region in 1779, hoping as always that the inlet would lead to a cross continental route, a Northwest Passage. When his search proved fruitless, he named the channel Turnagain Arm as he left and the region around Anchorage remained only sparsely populated up until the turn of the 19th century. Gold prospectors tried their luck in the creeks and rivers in the area but it wasn't until 1915, when Anchorage was chosen as the site for the terminus of the Alaska Railroad that the city truly began to grow. Railroad workers flooded in and on July 9, 1915 President Wilson authorized the "Great Anchorage Lot Sale", a land auction where the first 600 plots of land in Anchorage were sold. With that, Anchorage was officially on the map.

Today, oil money certainly boosts the local economy, but the city is also very visitor friendly. The city layout is quite straightforward; numbered streets run north to south and lettered cross streets run from west to east. The main visitor center, a very distinctive log cabin staffed by extremely helpful local people, is at 4th and F Street. Head here first and you'll be right in the middle of many of the city's attractions, in the heart of a pedestrianized downtown area decorated with flowering baskets and planters. Gift shops sell the usual array of souvenirs but many have quite an artsy twist on things. If you're in town on a Saturday or Sunday, be sure to check out the Anchorage Market and Festival at the corner of 3rd and E Street. You'll find local treats and tastes, live music, great local arts and crafts and pretty much anything you might ever need made from caribou or moose antlers.

Downtown Anchorage nestled between the Chugach Mountains and the waters of the Cook Inlet.

Log Cabin Visitors center, located on the corner of 4th and F Street.

Street vendors sell reindeer dogs. Apparently, they are quite good!

With a day or two to spend in Anchorage, you can choose between staying in town or heading outdoors to explore the region around Anchorage.

In town, the Anchorage Museum is one of the top-rated attractions. The museum is located at the corner of 7th Avenue and C Street and offers a truly comprehensive review of the human history of Alaska. It's an easy place to pass an afternoon but if you're more interested in Alaska's native culture, the Alaska Native Heritage Center is a good choice. It's located slightly out of town but a shuttle service operates from the Visitor Center or from the Anchorage Museum.

Heading outdoors, the city of Anchorage boasts over 100 miles of hiking trails. Kincaid Park is a favorite with locals. Miles of trails meander through lightly forested, rolling terrain and on a clear day, you can see Mount McKinley from the park. If you're newly arrived in Alaska, or you just haven't seen enough salmon on your trip, head to Ship Creek viewing platform, where you can watch king, coho and pink salmon determinedly making their way up the river. Take C street north to the Ship Creek bridge and then take a right turn on Whitney.

If you have hired a car, heading down to the Kenai Peninsula for the day is a very feasible option and if you haven't had your fill of glaciers, then Portage Glacier is a great destination. You can take a boat out to see the glacier which is now across the lake from the visitor center but the main attractions are the huge icebergs that float across the lake and pile up along the shoreline. Portage Glacier is around one hour's drive towards Whittier. Your route takes you along the shoreline of Turnagain Arm so don't forget to look out for beluga on the way!

Captain Cook Monument, Anchorage.

Railroad depot, Denali. Alaska's rail system connects all the key points in the Interior.

Planes, trains and automobiles; traveling around Interior Alaska

There's no disputing it; distances between the major cities and regions of Interior Alaska are huge. Travel between areas therefore requires a little forward planning but Alaska is well set up with a multi-layered transport infrastructure.

If you've been watching the latest reality TV show, "Alaska Bush Pilots", you'll see that small airports are liberally distributed across the region. There are over 10,000 licensed pilots in Alaska, 1 in every 60-odd people. For most Alaskans, hopping on a small plane is quite a typical part of their routine. For visitors, flight-seeing trips offer the chance to see Mount McKinley up close and small planes are the only feasible transport to remote towns such as Barrow and Nome.

The Alaska Railroad, though state-owned, is run as a private corporation and is quite the model for rail systems. Connecting between Seward on the Kenai Peninsula and Fairbanks in the Interior, the railroad carries freight and passengers across Alaska. Last year alone, Alaska Railroad passengers numbered over 500,000. There are two especially scenic routes; the first is between Whittier and Anchorage and the second connects from Anchorage to Denali. With special carriages decked out for scenic viewing, an Alaskan railroad trip can be a real highlight of your vacation.

The road system around Interior Alaska is also well maintained but drives may be long and services, such as gas stations, are rare as roads pass through some really remote regions. Alternatively, the Princess shuttle service provides a relaxing and stress-free way to travel between the lodges and the scenery along these interior routes is stunning.

Mount McKinley

On your first visit to Interior Alaska, one of the most surprising moments of your trip may well be your first view of Mount McKinley. As the tallest mountain in North America, Mount McKinley stands 20,320 feet high and towers above her nearest rivals, rising vertically some 18,000 feet from the foothills at the base of the mountain. On clear days, this huge slab of granite, snow and ice is visible from downtown Fairbanks and Anchorage. As you travel towards Denali National Park from either direction, the mountain looms ever closer, changing in color as the day progresses and even changing in mood as clouds roll in and out.

The mountain is world-renowned for its extreme weather. In winter, temperatures may drop to -95°F and winds may reach 150 mph around the summit. Over 1000 adventurous souls attempt to climb the mountain each year and over 50% fail, mostly due to the unpredictable summit conditions. Mount McKinley is so tall it literally creates its own weather systems, interacting with the flow of moist air coming from the Pacific to the south. The mountain also

Mount McKinley: how the mountain got its name.

Athabascans, the native people who were the first human inhabitants of this area, were the first to record a name for this majestic mountain; they called the mountain Denali, which means "The High One". When early European explorers mapped the area, they used a variety of different names for the mountain. William Dickey a gold miner who was prospecting in the area in the late 1890's, first used the name McKinley on his maps as he wanted to show his support for a new Republican candidate for president, William McKinley. When the Ohio legislator went on to become president, the mountain kept his name, even though McKinley never even saw the mountain for himself. Recently, several attempts have been made to officially change the mountain's name back to Denali but the current congressman from Ohio tenaciously resists all such motions. So for now, Mount McKinley it is.

influences the weather across the surrounding region: nearly all the incoming weather from the south is trapped on that side of the mountain so these regions may be cooler and wetter, while regions to the north, including Denali National Park, are much drier.

The locals will say "the mountain is out" whenever McKinley is visible. Certainly, this is an iconic Alaskan view but McKinley is a coy and moody mountain. Like a burlesque dancer, she reveals a snowy slope here, a tantalizing peak there. Park officials estimate that some portion of the mountain is visible around one day in every three over the summer months. On rare but splendid days, the entire mountain is on display. If you catch one of those days, be sure to take a picture and with luck like that, you might want to head for the Casino when you join your ship.

Denali National Park and Preserve

"We all need the tonic of wildness..."
Henry David Thoreau

Every one of America's National Parks has its key draw. Yosemite conjures up images of waterfalls and high granite peaks. At the Grand Canyon, we marvel at the handiwork of nature and the ever-changing colors of the Canyon. Think Yellowstone and most people will think of Old Faithful, the geyser. For Denali National Park though, the appeal of the park is something a little less concrete, almost more of a feeling: for Denali, it's real draw is it's wildness.

The park offers a chance to step out into a world as it was before man's footsteps; this is truly wild land, untouched and undisturbed. The park covers over six million acres; it's the size of Massachusetts with only one road passing through it. There is a place in the park when you are literally a thousand miles from anywhere. Of course, most visitors to the park hope for the picture postcard view of Mount McKinley, but even if the mountain isn't "out" when you visit, a trip through Denali is your chance to experience wilderness and that leaves a long-lasting impression.

Denali is often called the Serengeti of the North, however such comparisons need to be drawn with care. Denali's "Serengeti" is comprised of taiga and tundra; low, miniaturized trees and dwarf plants finally give way to bare ground as you head north and up above the treeline. Consequently, productivity in the park is low and the animals and plants that make their home in the park are tough and resourceful survivors. Few species can meet the challenges of life in this biome but those that do offer a rare glimpse of life in a world untrammeled. Unlike most of Alaska, in the main portion of the park hunting is prohibited so wildlife typically shows little startle response to human presence. The single road through the park becomes a frequently used corridor for wildlife as well as visitors and a trip into Denali is one of your best bets to see the wildlife of the interior; grizzly bears and even wolves are frequently sighted on park tours.

The park is very carefully managed to allow access for over 400,000 yearly visitors while still maintaining the park as a wilderness area. Over the summer, private vehicles are limited to the first 15 miles of the park road. Beyond this point, the official Denali Visitor Transportation system, comprising an array of tour buses and shuttles, is the sole concession. You can book your tours into the park through Princess, either prior to your trip or once you arrive at the lodges. Be aware that trips book up early, especially in summer.

To choose your trip, consult the map on the next page. This provides full details and highlights the different waypoints along the road. While a day-long bus trip that starts before dawn may seem a daunting prospect, the further you go into the park, the more you see and the better it gets. The buses are equipped with live onboard video systems so that the bus driver can show you exactly what they're looking at. This is especially useful when they spot a bear the size of a pea on a ridge line several miles away. It also works really well when animals are in close proximity to the bus. A word of warning; the bus drivers are quite the cast of characters. Excellent wildlife narration is punctuated with some of the oldest jokes you'll hear anywhere in Alaska. So, hop on the bus. The wilderness awaits.

The two icons of Denali National Park; Dall's sheep and green school buses

Charles Sheldon, recognized as the original pioneer of the park, first came to Denali in 1906 in search of Dall's sheep. His aim was to bag a few rare specimens of these original wild, white sheep but after several days of unsuccessful hunting he was enthralled by the wild beauty of the region. He returned the following year and stayed for six months in a log cabin in the park. During that time, as miners flooded into the area and vast num-

Dall's sheep.

bers of Dall's sheep were hunted, Sheldon saw the pressing need to develop a plan to ensure the future protection of the "immense, living landscapes of Denali". In 1917, Sheldon, along with local resident Harry Karstens and scientist Adolph Murie, eventually secured the establishment of Mount McKinley National Park. In 1980, the park was expanded and renamed Denali National Park and Preserve. The bus service into the park was put in place in 1972, to reduce visitor impact, and today a small and well-organized fleet of shuttle buses transport visitors along the 92-mile road into the park. The use of the bus system is fundamental in maintaining the park as a wilderness region and each time a visitor to the park uses the bus system, they contribute to the preservation of the park.

Dall's sheep saunter along the Denali Park Highway.

Caribou

Wolves

Kantishna

Turn-around for
Kantishna Experience

Turn-around for Tundra
Wilderness Tour when
McKinley is not in view

Toklat River
Contact Statio

Turn-around for Tundra
Wilderness Tour when
McKinley is in view

Wonder Lake

Denali Park Road

Stony Hill
Outlook E

Eielson Visitor Center

"Denali's Big Five"

Highlights along the Denali Park Road

Park Entrance
The 92 mile long Denali Park Road officially starts here. The Denali Visitor Center is at Mile 1.5. Tour buses stop to pick up extra passengers at the Wilderness Access Center.

To Savage River
You'll pass through low taiga forest between the park entrance and Savage River. Stunted, drunken trees lean at crazy angles, due to the cycles of thawing and freezing of the permafrost, and offer perfect cover for moose. Between mile 9 and 11, if it's a clear day, look for your first glimpses of McKinley. Savage River is at Mile 14 and the check point at Mile 15 is the turnaround for private vehicles.

Savage River to Igloo Creek
Trees thin out and then disappear as you head for the subarctic tundra. Primrose Ridge at Mile 17 is the turnaround point for the 4-5 hour Denali Natural History tour. Between here and Igloo Creek at Mile 34, look out for Dall's sheep and wolves are occasionally seen here too.

Igloo Creek to Sable Pass
Igloo Canyon leads to Sable Pass at Mile 38.5. Known as The Gateway to the Wilderness, this is prime grizzly habitat. Look for wolves along the East Fork Tolkat River corridor at Mile 44 and Dall's sheep frequent the mountainsides.

Primrose Ridge

Denali Park Road

Denali Visitors Center

Sanctuary River   Savage River

Riley Creek

Turn-around for Denali
Natural History Tour

Dalls Sheep

Igloo Creek

③

Polychrome
Pass Overlook

Sable Pass

Moose

⑧

Bear

Sable Pass to Polychrome Outlook

Polychrome Pass is named for the many colored rocks of this area. Looking out to the horizon, you'll have a clear view across the treeless tundra. The Polychrome Pass Overlook is at Mile 47 and Tolkat River Contact Station, at Mile 53, is the turnaround for the 7-8 hour Tundra Wilderness tour when the mountain is not visible.

Polychrome Outlook to Eielson Visitor Center

Several pull-outs along this section of the road provide excellent views of McKinley. The first of these, Stony Hill outlook at Mile 61, is the turnaround for the 7-8 hour Tundra Wilderness tour when the mountain is out.

Eielson Visitor Center to Wonder Lake

Newly refurbished Eielson Visitor Center (mile 66) offers spectacular views of McKinley. Kantishna Experience tours that last 11-12 hours include a stop here. They then continue on to Wonder Lake (Mile 84) and turn around at the end of the road (mile 92). Between Eielsen and Wonder Lake the road drops down into taiga. Herds of caribou may be sighted and if the clouds lift, from across the waters of Wonder Lake the view of Mount McKinley, rising 18,000 vertical feet above the surrounding terrain, is worth every minute of the bumpy bus trip.

For more details of trips into Denali go to www.reservedenali.com

Take a hike in Denali

Level: Moderate to difficult depending on trail.
Elevation change: Variable.
Attractions: Incredible views
Tip: Be Prepared!

Hiking in Denali

It takes a little extra effort to get out and hike in Denali. You'll need to use the Shuttle Bus system, which is only accessible within the park, you'll need to be somewhat self-sufficient, armed with lunch, layers of clothes and bug spray, and you'll need to fully aware that this is a wilderness and therefore carries a few more inherent challenges. But whether you are an experienced hiker or a keen beginner, it's actually quite do-able, surprisingly affordable and so worthwhile. There are few feelings to rival that once-in-a-lifetime moment when you gaze across the endless tundra of Denali. The rarified breeze is the freshest air you can find and the only sounds are those of the wild nature of Denali. If you've huffed up the Alpine Trail, the sound of your own puffing and panting may obscure this magical moment for a while, but this is one place where the effort is truly worth the reward.

To the logistics: within Denali National Park there are two bus systems, distinguished by the color of the buses. The green buses are the shuttle buses and the tan colored buses provide fully guided tours. Full details of these tours are included on pages 288 and 289. The tours pick up at the lodges, they feature comfy buses, excellent guides who provide in-depth narration throughout your trip, longer tours include lunch but you do not have time to get off and hike on these tours. Green buses comprise the Shuttle System. To board these buses you will need to book independently (see below) and then ride the free bus that runs from the lodges to the Wilderness Access Center within the park, where you board your (green) shuttle bus.

Park rangers organize shuttle bus loading and departures with military precision. These buses are not quite so comfy, the guides are excellent and these buses will stop when-ever wildlife is sighted along the route, however the narration is not so detailed. There is no free lunch, but tickets are quite inexpensive compared to tour bus tickets and you can get off and on any of the shuttle buses, once you are in the park. If you just have the day, your best option is to head for Eielsen Visitor Center; this takes you through the best areas for wildlife sightings in the park and still gives you ample time to hike.

The visitor center is at mile 66, around 5 hours from the park entrance and if you make it to the visitor center by noon, there are some ranger led tours. Otherwise, you'll be headed to the trails independently. There are two trails from the visitor center; one leads out across the tundra and the other heads to a high alpine ridge. You should plan for your whole day to be spent out in the park, and be aware; the Alpine Ridge Trail at Eielsen really is quite demanding.

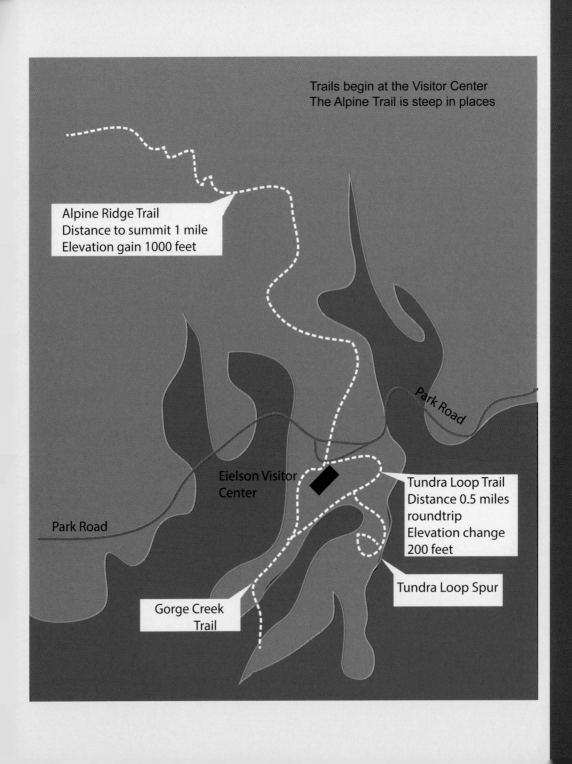

Trails begin at the Visitor Center
The Alpine Trail is steep in places

Alpine Ridge Trail
Distance to summit 1 mile
Elevation gain 1000 feet

Park Road

Eielson Visitor
Center

Tundra Loop Trail
Distance 0.5 miles
roundtrip
Elevation change
200 feet

Tundra Loop Spur

Park Road

Gorge Creek
Trail

Hiking in Denali: Step by Step

- Visit www.reservedenali.com. Under the "play" tab, choose Eielsen Visitor Center and book your shuttle bus ticket. Early to mid morning will work best.
- When you arrive at your lodge, pick up the schedule for the free bus to the park at the front desk.
- On the day of your trip; pack lunch, water and bug spray.
- Dress in layers, include a waterproof.
- Take the free bus from the lodge to the Wilderness Access Center in the park
- Board your shuttle out to Eielsen at the Wilderness Access Center. Once out there, you can take any shuttle back. Shuttles leave every 30 minutes from the Eielsen Visitor Center.

A young wolf lopes across the tundra.

The Wolves of Denali

Of all the mammals that make the "Big Five" list for Denali, perhaps the most poignant is the wolf. Long the subject of mysteries and fairy-tales alike, there are few sights that identify wilderness better than the sight of a wolf in the wild.

Within Denali, the wolf population is estimated at around 100 animals. The East Fork and the Grant Creek groups are the best known and both groups favor the eastern side of the park. They're typically found in the tundra rather than within the forests or Taiga borders and it's their highly efficient travel that allows them to roam far enough to find sufficient food in this sparse landscape. Typically, a wolf may wander over 50 miles or more in a day in search of food; "fed by its feet" as the Russians would say.

Their typical prey include smaller mammals than might be expected. Ground squirrel and small rodents comprise much of their diet. Generally, successful kills of larger prey such as caribou or moose target the young, sick, frail or diseased members of the group and keep these populations strong. Successful kills average around one in ten, and in fact wolves spend more time looking for and chasing prey than actually capturing them.

The wolf pack is a tightly knit, life-long family association, with finely tuned internal hierachy. The howl of the wolf is a way of cementing the social bonds within the group. During the summer months, the family may split into smaller sub-packs; these are the groups most commonly sighted in Denali. Look high on the ridgelines for their iconic, unmistakable profile.

The Willow Ptarmigan

Although seen across the state, the willow ptarmigan is most common in Interior Alaska. This year-round resident is the Alaska State Bird. In summer it sports a rust brown plumage and in winter trades this for white. It adds feathers right down the legs and across the top and bottom of its feet. No cold toes for this little guy.

The beaver is the park's resident architect. Beaver dams across rivers and streams provide habitat for a host of other animals including waterfowl and other migrating birds, along with the park's single frog species, the wood frog.

Meandering glacial rivers like this provide easily passable corridors for large mammals such as bear and moose.

Talkeetna

Talkeetna, a vibrant and peppery end-of-the-road town, leaps out as a bright splash of color against the backdrop of the evergreen landscapes of Alaska's Interior. From the highly decorated moose sculptures and ubiquitous flower baskets liberally scattered throughout the town, to the quirky characters to be found bar-side in the famous local watering holes, an afternoon in Talkeetna quickly becomes a trip into the heart of an "off-the-grid" Alaskan lifestyle.

The sign at the junction of Main Street and the Talkeetna Spur Road welcomes you to town. From there the town is yours to explore, it's easily covered on foot and there is likely something to entertain everyone in your group, Jet-boat and river rafting tours take you out in the surrounding wilderness while flight-seeing trips head to near-by Mount McKinley. Alternatively, plan to spend your time in town where authentically restored historical buildings dating back to the early 1900's nestle in amongst an array of tempting lunch spots, pleasantly eclectic art galleries and refreshingly novel gift stores.

The name of the town comes from an Athabascan word meaning "river of plenty" and in fact three rivers, the Chulitna, the Sustina and the Talkeetna, converge here. Walk to the end of Main Street for a view out across the endless delta. Since the early 1900's, the town has been a key regional supply point; the historic Nagley's General Store which first opened its doors in 1921, has moved with the times, literally, relocating from its original construction site on the Sustina River to the Talkeetna riverside via river barge and eventually, on log rollers, to the main street of Talkeetna in 1949.

The Talkeetna Historic District Walking Tour takes you to 16 different historic sites within a 5 block area of town. Pop in here, at the Three Bachelor's Cabin right at the entrance to town, to pick up a map. The cabin measures 12 x 24 feet and was built in 1934 as an albeit cozy home for three German miners. It was originally situated out at Cache Creek, but later, like many buildings in town it was dismantled, towed to town then reassembled here and it was a private residence until 1985.

While the town swells in summer, only 800 people are registered year-round Talketna residents, and the town proudly retains a pretty eccentric reputation. Summer time events include the moose-dropping festival, where 10,000 actual moose droppings are thrown out from a helicopter, in wintertime the town hosts the Wilderness Women's contest, where local women compete in events such as axe-throwing, water-fetching and sandwich making, and in 2009, Stubs, a local housecat, was elected as the town's mayor.

Let's do lunch!

One great piece of advice if you're heading to Talkeetna is to schedule your trip over lunchtime. The range of restaurant choices in town runs the full gamut, from trendy gourmet food trucks to down home eateries boasting 1910 sourdough and traditional Alaskan game. The famous West Rib Pub and Grill, located at the back of Nagley's store, was featured in the Travel Channel's Man vs. Food show and the Wake and Shake ice cream shop on Main Street comes complete with hand churned ice cream maker out front. Several of the local pubs are especially proud of their wide array range of locally-brewed artisan beer, providing the perfect alternate activity while others in the family head to the eye-catching art galleries and gift stores around town.

At the tasting room on Main Street, Talkeetna, the locally-brewed raspberry beer comes highly recommended.

Fairbanks

The key to enjoying a trip to Fairbanks is to embrace the fact that, although Fairbanks is Alaska's second largest city with a population of just over 30,000, in real terms Fairbanks is a small town sitting right at the edge of a very large wilderness. Just as in Anchorage, the surrounding wilderness shapes the town and Fairbanks retains a pioneering, frontier atmosphere and a rustic lifestyle.

Some of the main attractions of the town are the steamboat trips along the Chena and Tanana Rivers. Refurbished steamboats ply the waters and crews onboard retell the tales of the gold rush days as seen in Fairbanks, when the rivers served as the main conduits to the gold fields of North. Fairbanks first residents, E.T. Barnette and his wife, arrived by river in 1901. They too originally planned to head further north, until the rigors of the journey compelled the couple to settled in this region. They established a trading post and by following year, Fairbanks had officially found its place on the map.

To get a real-life glimpse of pioneer life in Fairbanks, head over to the Morris Thompson Cultural and Visitor Center on Dunkel St, along the Chena Riverfront. The museum is newly opened and focuses on the life and culture of Interior Alaska. Alongside the museum is a small log cabin, dating back to the early 1900's and the very earliest days of Fairbanks. By all accounts, it had been continuously occupied since then. When the museum was planned on the site, it was slated for demolition until local townspeople stepped in. The cabin has now been converted to a living museum, complete with an authentic and historically accurate garden. Record breaking sunflowers surround the cabin and in just 1/8th of an acre, facilities' manager Jason Ferris enthusiastically raises 19 different crops using heirloom seeds and providing Alaskan-sized fresh vegetables to the local food bank through the summer.

Downtown Fairbanks.

The Antler Arch at the Morris Thompson Cultural and Visitor Center, located on the Chena River Waterfront in Fairbanks, contains more than 100 moose and caribou antlers collected from across Interior Alaska. The antlers are woven together to represent the sharing of stories by those who provided the antlers. For locals, it's a favorite wedding location.

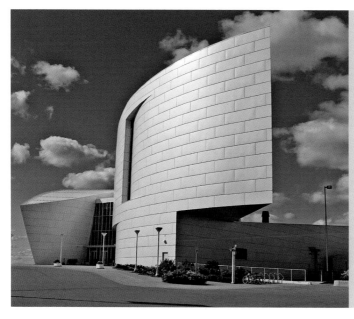

The Museum of the North, Fairbanks. Located out at the University of Alaska, Fairbanks campus, this is considered to be the premier museum in Alaska. Exhibits include a 36,000 year old bison, Babe Blue, that was retrieved intact from the permafrost by a local miner. Displays also cover the natural history of the state, an intriguing look at the science behind Northern Lights and a fabulous viewing deck where you can look out over the endless taiga to the distant Alaska Range.

Aurora Borealis – The Northern Lights

Fairbanks ranks as one of the best places in the world from which to view the Northern Lights. At risk of taking the romance out of such rarified displays, these curtains of night-time color are essentially the result of a basic physical phenomenon. The flow of solar winds across the upper atmosphere causes gas molecules 50-200 miles above the earth's surface to become excited and emit light. Although this happens year-round, you need to have sufficient dark hours of the night to see the lights so typically the best displays are seen in winter. The lights are visible in Fairbanks on more than 200 nights of the year and that number diminishes as you go north or south. One hot new line of tourism in Fairbanks is an influx of Asian visitors who believe that babies conceived during aurora borealis events will be especially gifted and auspicious.

It is possible to see the Northern Lights further south when conditions are right, especially in the early fall when the sun sets a little earlier each night and the hours of darkness lengthen. There is a web-site that quite accurately predicts the lights (www.gi.alaska.edu/AuroraForecast). Alternatively, you can keep the romance and just watch out for a clear, crisp fall day followed by a cold, clear night.

Northern lights across the Fairbanks sky.

Creamer's Field – Fairbanks hidden gem

If you are an avid, or even just an amateur birder headed for Fairbanks, be sure to schedule a side-trip to Creamers field while you're in Fairbanks. Originally, this was an active dairy farm producing cream and milk. When the farmer dug out some watering holes for his cattle, he found that these were wildly popular with all sorts of migratory bird fowl. Geese, ducks, swans, shorebirds and even sandhill cranes were all frequent visitors to the creamery when passing through the region. When the farm ceased operating as a dairy, the owners continued to maintain the ponds for use by all the waterfowl and today it's a bird sanctuary managed by Alaska Fish and Game.

Sandhill Crane.

The creamery is located at 1300 College Road, about 1 mile from the university campus. The 2000 acre site includes interpretive signs and spotting scoops are located in a pull-out right in front of one of the favored meadows. Sandhill cranes, well-known for their elaborate mating displays, are probably the most exciting to see, but huge flights of noisy geese are also impressive.

Creamer's field; popular stopover for migrating waterfowl and other birds.

The Trans-Alaska Pipeline

Snaking its way across the Alaskan landscape, the Trans-Alaska Pipeline stretches 800 miles from the North Slope of Alaska to Valdez on Prince William Sound.

The pipeline essentially transports Prudhoe Bay crude oil from the oil fields on the northern slopes of Alaska for distribution around the world, by tanker from the port of Valdez. Valdez was chosen as the terminus for the pipeline as it is the northern-most ice free port in Alaska, therefore offering the easiest exit point for oil from the Prudhoe Bay oilfields. On its way across Alaska the pipeline crosses three mountain ranges, 30 major rivers and streams, it traverses tundra and wanders through regions of low taiga.

More than half of the pipeline is above ground. This precaution is necessary where the ground is usually frozen because the warm oil in the pipeline would lead to melting of the permafrost, causing buckling of the pipe and increasing the chance of leaks. For a portion of its course, it follows the Richardson Highway between Fairbanks and Copper River and is easily visible from the road.

Oil that enters the pipeline in Northern Alaska takes around 12 days to travel the 800 mile-length of the pipeline, moving at around 4 miles an hour. The pipeline is monitored twice a day by air and by regular foot patrols, but maintenance is mostly done from the inside, by pipeline pigs. These large mechanical devices travel through the pipeline and work just like heavy duty spiral bottle washers, keeping the insides clear of build-up and ensuring that the oil runs smoothly through the pipe.

The pipeline was built in 1977 at a cost of $8 billion making it the largest privately funded construction project of its time. From the time oil first ran through the pipeline, it's estimated some 16 billion barrels have been transported. There is no doubt that oil revenue has had a huge influence on the economy of Alaska. Thanks to the Alaska Permanent Fund, everyone benefits so career-minded politicians generally support the oil industry.

Environmentalists have other concerns. While large oil spills inevitably hit the headlines, smaller, but more frequent spills can do more damage. Across the oil fields and along the length of the Trans-Alaska Pipeline there were some 4,530 spills of more than 1.9 million gallons of diesel fuel, oil, drilling fluid and other materials, just between 1996 and 2004. As the evidence and impacts of our changing climate are felt across the world, Alaska sits squarely at the crossroads of these issues. The impacts of climate change are amplified in colder regions such as Alaska and as the black gold courses through the pipeline, many Alaskans are starting to wonder what the true cost of this new wealth will be.

The Trans-Alaska Pipeline winds its way 800 miles across Interior Alaska. Over 50% of the pipeline is above ground.

Copper River

The newest addition to the Princess Lodge family has perhaps the most dramatic location. Sitting in the shadow of Mount Drum and the Wrangell St. Elias mountain range, the views from throughout the Copper River resort are breath-taking. Miles of taiga and boreal forest roll across the plains while snow capped mountains rise and rim the horizons in all directions. Add to this a truly remote location, floor to ceiling windows, some big leather chairs and a roaring fire, and you have the perfect "back-country lodge" setting.

While Mount St. Elias is the tallest mountain peak in the Wrangell St. Elias Mountains, it's the sheer extent of the mountain range that makes the panorama so spectacular. During the day you can hike trails that start straight from the lodge or take a shuttle up to the nearby park headquarters and begin your explorations there. Activities in the region run the full gamut from dog-sledding demonstrations to river-rafting and salmon fishing in the nearby Copper River. The river is one of the largest in the US; it has 13 tributaries, it's a mile wide, and currents can reach 7 miles per hour. Salmon migrate over 300 miles back up the river to their spawning sites; king and silver salmon also spawn in the river but it's the reds, or sock-eyes, for which the region is truly renowned. Locals will tell you that to make this migration the fish store extra energy supplies in the form of omega-3 fatty acids and that's why they taste so good. This may or may not be the explanation but Copper River Red salmon is undoubtedly some of the best salmon you'll find, even in by Alaskan standards.

Taking some time to explore this scenic area can provide a relaxing start or a gentle finale for your vacation. This is the perfect place to pause for a moment, to take deep breaths, reflect on your vacation and just enjoy the company of your family or traveling companions. As you look out from the lodge at the vast landscape and the majestically rising mountains, many profound literary quotes may spring to mind. Maybe the most fitting? To paraphrase my father-in–law, "Ain't life grand".

Princess Cruises' newest lodge at Copper River.

View from the lodge at Copper River

The rustling forest

In this region more than any other in Alaska, a mosaic of plant life covers the landscape. Variations in soil quality, aspect, elevation, and even insect distribution can be sufficient to stack the cards in favor of one tree species or another. White spruce are limited to deeper, well drained areas while black spruce occupy shallow, poorly drained soils. Poplar trees thrive in the river valleys, while stands of quaking aspen and paper birch line ridge tops, south facing slopes, and grow quickly in any newly opened areas or disturbed space. The broad leaves of the quaking aspen are known for their rainbow of fall colors. The tree's small, flattened leaf stems that lie perpendicular to the leaves give rise to the name quaking aspen: the leaves are in almost constant motion, even the gentlest of breezes sets them in motion, and their gentle rustle provides a soothing soundtrack across this most scenic region.

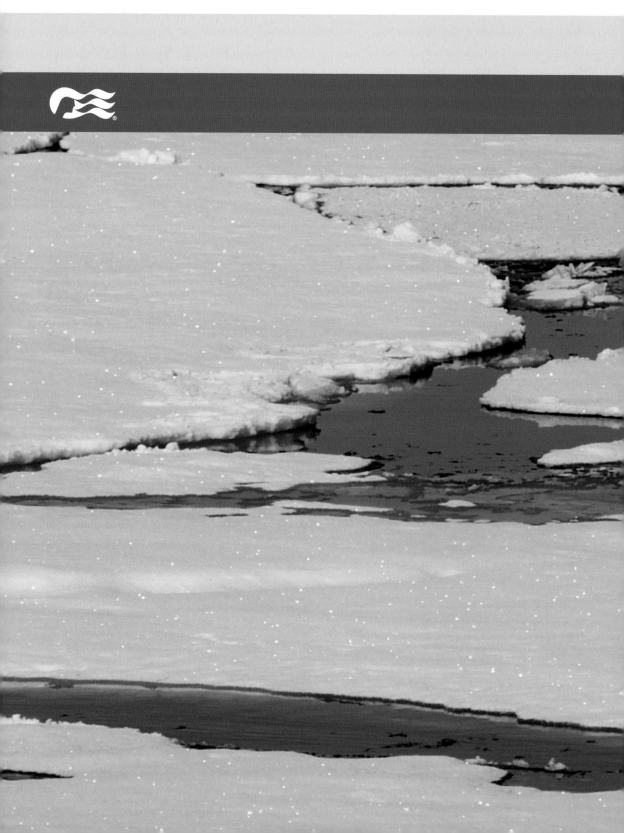

Chapter 8

The Road Ahead

The Bryn Mawr Glacier, College Fjord.

Photo taken during the Harriman Expedition, 1899

The Bryn Mawr Glacier, College Fjord.

Photo taken from Sky Princess, 1998

The Bryn Mawr Glacier, College Fjord.

Photo taken from Star Princess 2002

Times of Change in Alaska

Oh, the times they are a-changing.
Bob Dylan

Though it is a well-used analogy, Alaska really is the canary in the coal mine of climate change. A clear consensus on the issue of climate change today has now emerged and the scientific community finally has a single voice on this: increased levels of greenhouse gases, particularly carbon dioxide and methane, are accumulating in our atmosphere and causing a rise in the global mean temperature of the earth. Since the mid-1970's Alaska has warmed up three times faster than the rest of the lower 48 and like the ultra-sensitive canary, Alaska is especially impacted by the small, but consistent yearly up-tick in the mean global temperature.

Both the landscape and the lifestyle in the region show signs of the impact of a warming climate. The starting point for the world famous Iditarod race has been moved north to ensure they have sufficient snow for the dogs to run on, Portage, Exit and Mendenhall Glaciers are rapidly retreating out of sight of their respective visitor centers and in the Far North, eroding shorelines mean that remote villages such as Shishmaref are tumbling into a warmer, rising sea. Like an urgently worded postcard from the future, Alaska is showing us what a warmer world will look like.

Certainly, the temperature of the earth is not static, the earth swings between warmer and colder climates, between snowball earth and hothouse earth. Since the 1600's the earth has been in a warming phase and plants, animals and humans have adapted to slowly increasing temperatures. The problems arising now are due to the accelerated rate of the change. The pictures of the Bryn Mawr Glacier, to the left, illustrate this. The first photo was taken in 1899 by Edward Curtis, the photographer traveling with the Harriman expedition, the first expedition to document College Fjord in Prince William Sound. The second picture shows the same glacier 100 years later, in 1999. You can see that this glacier, like most glaciers in Alaska retreated somewhat over those 100 years. But now, take a look at the third picture, taken in 2002; dramatic differences can be seen just between 1999 and 2002. If your trip includes College Fjord, you'll pass by the Bryn Mawr Glacier and you'll see how far back the glacier has now retreated. The changes are striking and similar changes are taking place across Alaska.

Climate Change in a Nutshell

The greenhouse effect is a naturally occurring component of the earth's climate system. Heat travels to the earth from the sun as solar radiation and warms the surface of the earth. The earth in turn releases some of this heat back into the atmosphere as infra-red radiation. Greenhouse gases in the lower atmosphere trap this heat and reradiate it back to the earth; this adds to the warming of the earth and keeps the mean global temperature around 60˚F higher than it would otherwise be. This is the natural system, however in our newly changing system more greenhouse gases are accumulating in the atmosphere resulting in more heat radiated back to earth, causing temperatures to rise. This is where we are today, as concentrations of key greenhouse gases, namely carbon dioxide and methane, increase to record levels.

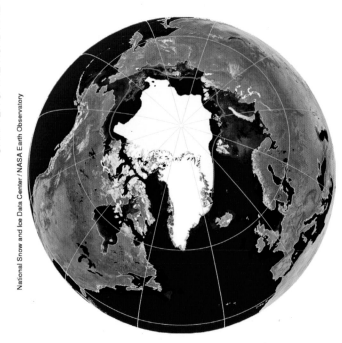

National Snow and Ice Data Center / NASA Earth Observatory

Monthly Sea Ice Extent for: Sep 2011

Sea Ice Stats

Data from the National Snow and Ice Data Center shows the changes in the extent of sea ice in the Arctic Ocean. The pink line indicates where the ice edge was in 1979, the white shows the ice front in September 2011. Overall, the amount of sea ice has been declining by 12% per decade since 1979.

US Global Change Research Program, National Assessment, 2001
"Sea ice has retreated by 14% since 1978 and thinned by 60% since the 1960s, with widespread effects on marine ecosystems, coastal climate, and human settlements."

National Snow and Ice Data Center, 2011
"The last five years have seen the five lowest extents of sea ice in the satellite record."

Changing Sea Ice

Sea ice forms when the surface of the ocean freezes. Temperatures need to drop to around -2°C (28°F) for the ice to form and most of the saltwater is forced out so sea ice is largely, but not entirely, freshwater. In a single year, a layer of ice between four and six feet thick may be laid down. The polar ice cap includes ice that is hundreds, if not thousands, of years old and over the course of the year, the extent of the sea ice naturally expands during the winter and then shrinks back slightly during the summer.

Sea ice is an integral component of the ecology of the Far North. Algae growing on the underside of the ice provide food for small plankton such as krill, and the abundant krill are the essential bottom layer in the food chain in these regions. Some animals, such as large whales, feed directly on the krill while other animals, such as seals and sea lions feed on big fish, which feed on small fish, which in turn feed on krill.

Topside, the ice is the arena of the polar bear. These are the largest of Alaska's bears and by all accounts the best hunters. Polar bears will attempt to catch small whales and walruses, but whales are too quick and walruses are too big and come well-equipped with very nasty looking tusks. In fact, seals are the favored food for polar bears. Ringed and harp seals are the preferred species and these seals are found out on the sea ice. So, the sea ice becomes the primary hunting platform for polar bears within this frozen realm.

As the sea ice contracts more and more each summer, the food supplies that are fueled by the algae growing on the ice move a little farther north. Animals follow the food and encounter new conditions and new competitors. Winners and losers have yet to be decided. For polar bears, the swim to the ice floes in search of food lengthens each year. For seals, the lack of predation by polar bears could lead to booms and crashes as their population goes un-regulated. For diving ducks, less ice is available on which to rest in between feeding dives. Even walruses are facing new challenges, retreating to the northern shorelines of Alaska and hauling out in previously unseen numbers as their favored ice-based feeding grounds shift ever further north.

The relocation of animals is impacting the lifestyles of the region's native people. Animals that they would normally hunt as part of a subsistence lifestyle are harder to find and further afield. The loss of sea ice is also impacting their towns and villages. Typically, the shelf of ice protects the shorelines from the worst winter weather. As the ice disappears, winter storms rush ashore unchecked and homes are inundated. Many villages are planning to relocate; six villages have already started packing and another 160 villages are considered threatened.

The rapid loss of sea ice may bring some benefits. Shipping routes across the Arctic Ocean, between the Pacific and Atlantic, continue to open up for a little longer each year and along with cargo ships, populations of bowhead whales are moving through these newly opened corridors to find new mates and feeding areas. Still, as winter storms wreck havoc in coastal villages and polar bears make the endangered species list, at this point the costs appear to be outweighing these potential benefits.

An uncertain future for polar bears

Current counts suggest between 20-25,000 polar bears survive in the wild today. They are split into the 19 groups that roam across the Arctic and seven of these groups are in decline.

Additionally, as polar bear spend more time in regions where they overlap with grizzles, hybrid bears called pizzlies are being reported. These hybrid bears lack many of the key adaptations of the polar bear. For example, true polar bears have hollowed out hair follicles that provide extra insulation in cold weather – a trait that is absent in "pizzly" hybrids.

A retreating glacier opens up a fjord in Glacier Bay.

Changing Scenery

Alaska's glaciers are the bellweather, the engine check-light of our glacial systems. While a small number of glaciers in Alaska are advancing, most of Alaska's glaciers have been in retreat for the last 300 years or more. In recent years, rates of retreat of glaciers across Alaska have been rapidly increasing. Many are now land-based and as they retreat whole new landscapes open up. This is how Glacier Bay, Yakutat Bay and Tracy Arm all came to be; these bays and inlets are all actually fjords, created by the advance and subsequent retreat of a glacier. It's estimated that by 2025, Glacier Bay will open up another 12 miles as the Grand Pacific Glacier continues its retreat.

As Alaska's glaciers melt, freshwater flows into the ocean making the water a little fresher and adding incrementally to the increasing level of the ocean. Such minor changes are not cause for concern; however the melting of other more extensive land-based glaciers could have far-reaching impacts. Melting of just 20% of the land-based Greenland Ice sheet could increase sea levels by up to 3 feet and many of the world's coastlines would be forever changed.

Warm Arctic – Cold Continents

"As climate change continues to impact the Arctic, what happens in Alaska may not stay in Alaska for much longer".
The Washington Post, November 2011.

This recent headline in The Washington Post was the lead-in for a story that reported on the recently released Arctic Report Card (2011). This report highlights the connections between a warmer Alaska and an increased frequency of severe weather events in the lower 48 states. Essentially, as the climate changes, the predominant directions of air flow in the Far North are changing. Atmospheric wind patterns have shifted so that colder Arctic air in the wintertime reaches down into North America and Europe, and warmer air is moving north. The record breaking cold spells of December 2009 and February 2010 have been attributed to this changing system. Meanwhile, warmer wintertime temperatures in the North are leading to melting of the permafrost, the permanently frozen ground that underlies vast swaths of the Alaskan landscape. And as permafrost melts, huge amounts of methane are released, further fueling the rate of climate change.

Caribou graze on the tundra.

The greening of the Tundra

The Arctic region continues to warm with less sea ice and greater green vegetation.
US National Oceanic and Atmospheric Administration, 2011

Tundra, that narrow strip of land between stunted taiga forest and barren, snow covered land, is a tough place to be a plant. Low winter temperatures and short summers require extensive adaptations. Fall comes quickly to these regions with a bright blast of color but once winter arrives, the land and the plants lie dormant for 6 to 8 months of the year.

So, warmer temperatures would be a good thing, right? Well, certainly, growing seasons are already lengthening but as they do, other plants which could not normally survive the brutal conditions of the tundra are on the move, shifting further up in altitude or latitude. Areas of tundra are blooming sooner each year and small shrubs and trees, plants that previously would not have been found in these challenging areas are moving in. As the plants move, animal distributions change too and that can cause problems for some species. Dall's sheep rely on both outstanding eye-sight to help spot predators, and amazing mountaineering skills to help scale bare rocks and reach safe ledges. As plant cover moves up, their predators now have hiding places and can follow them uphill. Clearly, one of the winners here could be the forests as this greening of the tundra would give them more room to expand. However, such expansion will include their pest species too. Spruce bark beetle infestations were previously very limited in Alaska because the beetles died off in the extreme winter weather. Now the beetles can expand their range, leading to widespread tree deaths. Spruce beetle is currently sweeping across the Kenai Peninsula, and leading to the largest loss of trees to insects ever recorded in North America; currently this stands at some 2.3 million acres since 1992. This also increases the risk of forest fires too.

Given the projection of continued global warming, it is very likely that major Arctic changes will continue in years to come, with increasing climatic, biological and social impacts."

Arctic Report Card 2011

So, what to do? Alaska is changing, landscapes are becoming greener, villages are relocating, and wildlife will have to adapt. But climate change need not play out to its most extreme scenario. With ingenuity and commitment, its pace can be slowed. The most recent report from the world-recognized IPCC - the Intergovernmental Panel on Climate Change - emphasizes that changes in lifestyle must be a part of the solutions package to address climate change.

We can all contribute to the effort to slow climate change. Here are a few websites you can check out to find out more about these issues. You can buy carbon credits to offset the impact of your trip and find out how you can reduce your contribution to greenhouse gas emissions.

Calculate your footprint at
http://www.earthday.org/footprint-calculator

Offset your trip at
http://www.terrapass.com

Audit your energy efficiency at home at
http://homeenergysaver.lbl.gov/consumer

We all make choices on how we spend our good fortune and live out our lives. Alaska, like no place on earth, reminds us that life is what we make of it. So, here's to your Alaskan moment, here's to these wild places and this wild life and most importantly, here's to Alaska's future, for in this great land is where we find ourselves.

"The sight of the bear stirred me like nothing else the country could contain. What mattered was not so much the bear himself as what the bear implied. He was the predominant thing in that country, and for him to be in it at all meant that there had to be more country like it in every direction and more of the same kind of country all around that. He implied a world. He was an affirmation to the rest of the earth that his kind of place was still here, still intact."

From Coming into the Country, John McPhee, 1977.

About the Author:

Author Rachel Cartwright has almost twenty years experience in Alaska. She worked as a seasonal naturalist with Princess Cruises while pursuing her doctoral degree in Conservation Biology. Today, she continues to run an active research program studying the behavior and development of humpback whale calves in both Alaskan and Hawaiian waters. She teaches biology at California State University Channel Islands and lives on the beach in Oxnard, California with her husband, Brian.

Contributors:

Photography:
Like many projects, this book could not have been completed without a great deal of assistance, especially with photography. While the author took most of the pictures of inanimate objects, like signs, buildings and the occasional scenic view, many of the spectacular wildlife shots were provided by other Alaskan Naturalists. Contributors include:

Terence Mangold – Terence Mangold is a boat charter captain and an avid naturalist. He spends his summers in Seward, Alaska, running wildlife tours and fishing trips and his winters in Hawaii running whale-watching tours.

Amy Venema – Amy Venema is also a charter boat captain. She too spends her summers in Alaska working as a naturalist and her winters in Hawaii, running whale-watching tours and supervising shore-side operations for America Safari Cruises.

Terence, Amy, the author (Rachel) and the graphic designer (Rob Hawes- see below) are also the founder members of the Keiki Kohola Project, a non-profit research group, based on Maui Hawaii. Keiki Kohola means baby whale in Hawaiian, and the research group is dedicated to the care and protection of the waters around Maui, Hawaii as a nursery for humpback whale calves. The whales that use Hawaiian waters are part of the same humpback whale population that is seen in Alaskan waters. For more on their work visit their website at www. caringforcalves.org. A portion of the profits from the royalties received through the sale of this book will go to support the work of the Keiki Kohola Project.

Additional photography was provided by Kevin Martin - Kevin works as a naturalist in Alaska and the Baja California. Julius Tallarico, a naturalist with Princess Cruises and Douglas Mac-Carter of Liberty wildlife rehabilitation, Arizona provided sea otter and bald eagle images. John and Dan Cesere, of C3 Submerged provided the underwater image on page 164. The Cesere Brothers work with the Keiki Kohola Project on Maui, Hawaii. Go to www.c3submerged.com for more of their stunning photography.

The field guide illustrations were provided by Yvette Hanson. Yvette is just beginning her career as an illustrator, and can be reached via email at yvettehanson@gmail.com. The marine art featured on pages 67 and 89 was provided by John Horton. John specializes in historically accurate illustrations such as those shown and you can see more of his work at www.johnhorton.ca. Cartography support was provided by Maps.com, in Santa Barbara, California. Street maps and the Denali map were provided by Rob Hawes, of Tradewinds Graphics, Kihei, Hawaii. Rob is also a founder member of the Keiki Kohola Project. More of his work, including links to his hand-made tiki mug collection can be found at www.tradewindgraphics. com. Up—to—date data on the current status of the Arctic Ice sheet, including the graphic on page 310, was provided by the National Snow and Ice Data Center.

Additional photo credits: Images of lighthouses along the Inside Passage were provided by Kraig Anderson. More information on these lighthouses can be found at www.lighthousefriends.com.

Images of Romeo the Glacier wolf were provided by Britteny Cioni-Haywood of Black Mutt photography (www.blackmuttphotography.com). Historical Images were used with permission from Alaska State Library, the Museum at Campbell River and University of Washington Special Collections. Image references and credits are provided alongside each image within the text. The image of John Muir, on page 38 is available within the public domain and was obtained at http://en.wikipedia.org/wiki/ File:John_Muir_Cane.JPG

Alaska Tourism Board photo credits are as follows: Page 196, ref 2996   Alaska Division of Tourism, Page 287 – ref 2866   Alaska Division of Tourism, Page 289 – ref 3241   Rick McIntyre, Alaska Division of Tourism, Page 283 – ref 6620 Ernst Schneider, Alaska Division of Tourism. Some images were obtained from Shutterstock.com and used under their copyright. Photo credit and images reference numbers in the Shutterstock catalogue are as follows: Page 16, Yu Ken; ref 15034681, page 22, MarkVanDykePhotography; ref 85035457, page 33 Gail Johnson; ref 85951114, page 40, ciapix; ref 16861270, page 41 Rigucci; ref 86593018, page 41 JPLDesigns; ref 85572433, page 44 Roseanne Smith; ref 15430717, page 52 Lijuan Guo; ref 13850080, page62 meunierd; ref 78471499 2009fotofriends, page 143 Centrill Media; ref 15691852, page 189 mikeledray; ref 83662237, page 180 Stew; ref 58514213, page 192 Lone Wolf Photos; ref 52540375, page 203 Murray Lundberg; ref 615668, page 248 Bonnie Fink; ref 83494900, page 253 Lee Prince; ref 61612195, page 272 karamysh; ref 62553034 2009; page 273 ref 49245205, page 274 Gail Johnson; ref 85951129, page 276 cecoffman; ref 87731359, page 277 MaxFX; ref 3448736, page 278 cecoffman; ref 81494545 page 279, Alan Bassett ; ref 17991238, page 280 Christopher Boswell; ref 79802815, page 295 Gail Johnson; ref 86692786, page 295, 299 Gail Johnson; ref 86621740, page 300 Roman Krochuk; ref 785923, page 304, Albert Pego; ref 99771647, Page 306 Yvonne Pijnenburg-Schonewille; ref 80533705, Page 311 Uryadnikov Sergey; ref 71791252. (30 images total).

Selected references and recommended reading:

A Reader's Companion to Alaska, edited by Alan Ryan. Published by Mariner Books
Coming into the Country, by John McPhee. Published by Farrar, Straus and Giroux (1977)
Cruising Alaska and British Columbia; from Skagway to Berkeley Sound, by Stephen Hilson. Published by Evergreen Pacific Cruising.
Gold Rush Women by Claire Rudolf Murphy and Jane G. Haigh. Published by Alaska Northwest Books
Guide to the Birds of Alaska, by Robert. H. Armstrong. Published by Alaska Northwest Books
Home Country, by Ernie Pyle. Published by Amereon Ltd
Salmon in the trees, by Amy Gulick. Published by Braided River
The Glacier Wolf; True Stories of Life in Southeast Alaska. By Nick Jans. Published by Arctic s.
The Milepost 2011: Alaska travel Planner. Edited by Kris Valenica. Published by Morris Communications.
The Nature of Southeast Alaska: A guide to Plants, Animals and Habitats by Robert H. Armstrong, Rita M. O'Clair and Richard Carstensen. Published by Alaska Northwest Books
Travels in Alaska, by John Muir. Published by Greenbook Publications.

INDEX